Unmasking White Preaching

Postcolonial and Decolonial Studies in Religion and Theology

Series Editor
Sheryl Kujawa-Holbrook, Claremont School of Theology

Series Editorial Board
Jon Berquist, Stephen Burns, Cláudio Carvalhaes, Jennifer Te Paa Daniel, Lynne St. Clair Darden, Christine J. Hong, Wonhee Anne Joh, HyeRan Kim-Cragg, Boyung Lee, Aprilfaye Tayag Manalang, Loida Yvette Martell, Stephanie Y. Mitchem, Jea Sophia Oh, Nicolas Esteban Panotto, Jeremy Punt, Patrick Reyes, Joerg Rieger, Fernando Segovia, Melinda McGarrah Sharp, Kay Higuera Smith, Jonathan Y. Tan, Mona West, and Amos Yong.

This series responds to the growing interest in postcolonial studies and re-examines the hegemonic, European-dominated religious systems of the old and new empires. It critically addresses the colonial biases of religions, the academy, and local faith communities, in an effort to make these institutions more polyvocal, receptive, and empowering to global cultures and epistemologies. The series will engage with a variety of hybrid, overlapping, and intersecting definitions of postcolonialism—as a critical discursive practice, as a political and ideological stance concerned with exposing patterns of dominance and hegemony, and as contexts shaped by ongoing colonization and decolonization. Books in the series will also explore the relationship between postcolonial values and religious practice, and the transformation of religious symbols and institutions in postcolonial contexts beyond the academy. The series aims to make high-quality and original research available to the scholarly community. The series welcomes monographs and edited volumes which forge new directions in contextual research across disciplines and explore key contemporary issues. Established scholars as well as new authors will be considered for publication, including scholars "on the margins" whose voices are under-represented in the academy and in religious discourse. Authors working in sub-disciplines of religious studies and/or theology are encouraged to submit proposals.

Titles in the Series
Unmasking White Preaching: Racial Hegemony, Resistance, and Possibilities in Homiletics, edited by Lis Valle-Ruiz and Andrew Wymer
Colonialism and the Bible: Contemporary Reflections from the Global South, edited by Tat-siong Benny Liew and Fernando F. Segovia
Ecologies of Participation: Agents, Shamans, Mystics, and Diviners, by Zayin Cabot
Feminist Praxis Against U.S. Militarism, edited by Nami Kim and Wonhee Anne Joh
Postcolonial Preaching: Creating a Ripple Effect, by HyeRan Kim-Cragg
Decolonial Futures: Intercultural and Interreligious Intelligence for Theological Education, by Christine Hong

Unmasking White Preaching

Racial Hegemony, Resistance, and Possibilities in Homiletics

Edited by
Lis Valle-Ruiz and Andrew Wymer

LEXINGTON BOOKS
Lanham • Boulder • New York • London

Published by Lexington Books
An imprint of The Rowman & Littlefield Publishing Group, Inc.
4501 Forbes Boulevard, Suite 200, Lanham, Maryland 20706
www.rowman.com

86-90 Paul Street, London EC2A 4NE

Copyright © 2022 by The Rowman & Littlefield Publishing Group, Inc.

All rights reserved. No part of this book may be reproduced in any form or by any electronic or mechanical means, including information storage and retrieval systems, without written permission from the publisher, except by a reviewer who may quote passages in a review.

British Library Cataloguing in Publication Information Available

Library of Congress Cataloging-in-Publication Data

Names: Valle-Ruiz, Lis, 1973- editor. | Wymer, Andrew, 1982- editor.
Title: Unmasking white preaching : racial hegemony, resistance, and possibilities in homiletics / edited by Lis Valle-Ruiz and Andrew Wymer.
Description: Lanham : Lexington Books, [2022] | Series: Postcolonial and decolonial studies in religion and theology | Includes bibliographical references and index.
Identifiers: LCCN 2022001802 (print) | LCCN 2022001803 (ebook) | ISBN 9781793652997 (cloth) | ISBN 9781793653017 (paperback) | ISBN 9781793653000 (epub)
Subjects: LCSH: Preaching. | Racism—Religious aspects—Christianity.
Classification: LCC BV4211.3 .U56 2022 (print) | LCC BV4211.3 (ebook) | DDC 251—dc23/eng/20220216
LC record available at https://lccn.loc.gov/2022001802
LC ebook record available at https://lccn.loc.gov/2022001803

Contents

Beginnings   1
Lis Valle-Ruiz and Andrew Wymer

RACIAL HEGEMONY IN HOMILETICS   17

1. The Missionary Connection: White Preaching in the British Colonies of the Caribbean   19
   Gennifer Benjamin Brooks

2. Unmasking the Homiletical Whiteness of Jerry Falwell Sr. and the Moral Majority   29
   Debra J. Mumford

3. The Towering Sermon: Duke Chapel as Monument to White Supremacy   45
   Peace Pyunghwa Lee and David Stark

4. Theorizing about the Whiteness of Asian American Homiletics   55
   Gerald C. Liu

5. White Mainline Protestant Preachers Addressing Racial Issues: 2017 vs. 2021   69
   Leah D. Schade

6. Civility and the "Purple Church": An Insufficient Response to White Supremacy   85
   Andrew Thompson Scales

7. Resisting White Fragility: Preaching toward Indigenous-Settler Reconciliation in Canada   97
   Sarah Travis

8   Through a Glass Dimly: White Preaching and
    Epistemological Ignorance   111
    Christopher M. Baker

RESISTANCE AND POSSIBILITIES IN HOMILETICS   **125**

9   Multitasking Preaching: The Liberating Power of Unmasking
    Whiteness from the Pulpit   127
    HyeRan Kim-Cragg

10 Wrestling with Whiteness in Homiletic Pedagogy:
    A Reflection on Teaching "Proclaiming Justice
    in the Church and Public Square"   141
    Richard W. Voelz

11 Of Handmaids, Mediatrixes, and Mothers: The Idealized
    Feminine and Rhetorics of Whiteness   155
    Jerusha Matsen Neal

12 Betraying White Preaching: Homiletical Domination,
    Racial Treason, and the Pursuit of Abolition   171
    Andrew Wymer

13 Who Are You? White Identity Formation and Re-formation
    in Homiletics   185
    Suzanne Wenonah Duchesne

14 Non-Preaching? Unmasking (White) Preaching
    through Negation   205
    Lis Valle-Ruiz

15 An Icon of Exclusion: Deconstructing the Pulpit
    through the Homiletical Practice of Black Women   221
    Chelsea Brooke Yarborough

(In)conclusion   231
Lis Valle-Ruiz and Andrew Wymer

Index   233

About the Contributors   237

Beginnings
Lis Valle-Ruiz and Andrew Wymer

First and foremost, resistance to and disruption of white colonialism remains a matter of life and death. The brutal violence of colonialism is partially visible in the violence of white-dominant systems of racialization, and the murderous actions of settler colonial states continue to unfold today, increasingly shaping conversation in the church and broader society. This brutal violence is also evident in the "epistemicide" of colonialism, which erases minoritized and non-dominant knowledge and practice.

The European-dominant homiletical canon, the long-standing bias of white-dominant homiletical guilds, and the normative European preaching methods in communities of faith are implicated in white colonial violence. The dominant homiletical guilds in mainline Protestant and conservative, Evangelical Christianity are, respectively, the Academy of Homiletics (AOH) and the Evangelical Homiletics Society (EHS), and both of these guilds have long reflected and continue to recreate racially dominant space that is inhospitable—even violent—to racially minoritized scholars. Through these guilds, racially minoritized scholarship and non-dominant knowledge continue to be subjugated, marginalized, and erased.[1]

However, at this present moment, there is an expanding awareness of the need to address the interwovenness of dominant preaching with white colonial systems of race. While the impact of race on homiletics can be traced implicitly or explicitly through racially minoritized scholarship that emerged even prior to the mid-twentieth century founding of the dominant guilds of today, only recently has race emerged as a significant concern of the AOH—the 2019 annual gathering was dedicated to the theme, "unmasking white preaching." After only one year of limited critical attention to whiteness at the annual meeting, we, the AOH, abruptly pivoted in 2020 to discourse on decentering whiteness. The change in focus was allegedly intended to center the voices of homileticians of color so that white homiletics would no longer be at the center of the conversation. The effect, however, was to leave white preaching and its dominance in the guild practically unexamined and unchanged.

It is out of concern that we are attempting to decenter that which we have not yet critically engaged that this volume emerges. As such, this volume seeks to grow this increasing interest in race and homiletics in a manner that both grounds subsequent discourse in a sustained critique of whiteness and amplifies subjugated and racially minoritized practice, pedagogy, and theory.

These nascent efforts in the dominant guild provide an opportunity to expand critical engagement of race to encompass the unfolding history of white colonial domination in the Americas and around the globe. This volume emerges out of concern that recent engagements of preaching and systems of white racial dominance may render homiletical discourse on race as disconnected from a broader, global critique of the origins of race in colonialism and the role that homiletics has played and continues to play in the fluid development of racisms in order to consolidate the power of settler colonial states. This volume also emerges from concern that recent attempts to decenter whiteness have not been grounded in a sustained and careful critique of the sinister depth of whiteness' impact on homiletics, potentially glossing over it. While postcolonial or decolonial theories have begun to impact the broader field of liturgical studies—in which homiletics can be nestled—postcolonial or decolonial theories have only just begun to substantively impact the theory and practice of Western homiletics.

After the AOH annual meeting in 2018, Andrew and Lis coincidentally attended a dinner that the Wabash Center sponsored for early career scholars. While we waited for the program to begin, we informally debriefed our experience at the AOH. We found out that we were equally disgruntled and disappointed with the ways in which the AOH operates, talking against racism but conducting business as usual with procedures where whiteness is deeply embedded. We shared how we were both ready to disengage, to leave the guild. Then Andrew shared Gennifer Brook's advice and challenge. She had asked him, "Why leave the Academy? Why not stay and change it from within?" Knowing that there was at least one more person who perceived things the same way, we decided that it was worth a try. That was the first sparkle of life for this project. Granted, several members of the academy, past and present, share in our desire to change the racist ways of the academy and have stayed to operate that change, Brooks being one of them. What Brooks did was to join a long tradition of resistance within the academy and then invite us to join this shared labor as well. That the labor has been shared is evident in part in non-dominant efforts within the academy, for example, the academy's Black Caucus, and more broadly within the study of homiletics that have nurtured the production of scholarship about non-white homiletics for decades, as the chapters from Andrew Wymer and Gerald Liu will expose and examine. One further example of this is that the theme of the 2017 annual meeting of the AOH, "preaching taboo," offered an opportunity for some members of the academy to examine homiletical practices of preaching about racism.

To address our main concern of the dissonance between the saying and the doing in the AOH regarding racial matters, we decided to organize a workgroup. The theme of the 2019 Annual Meeting, "unmasking white preaching," corresponded with our interest, and we applied to create an eponymous workgroup. Over the next three annual meetings of the AOH (2019–2021), the Unmasking White Preaching Workgroup investigated the meaning and evolution of white preaching, its nature, its function, and its impact. This workgroup attempted to foster a sustained and focused conversation about intersections between homiletics and invisible and uninterrogated whiteness, which manifest at least partially in assumptions of Western thought and white-dominant culture. Each one of those years, a third of the chapters of this collection were presented for feedback from peers attending the annual meeting. Additionally, as this work coalesced into a published collection, each contributor received feedback from two reviews, one from the co-editors of the volume and one from another contributor. Through these processes, the authors had the chance to revise and strengthen their arguments, and this created an opportunity for ongoing development of anti-racist and postcolonial thought.

In the summer of 2020 and in response to the increase of racist public and communal behaviors that were exacerbated by the global pandemic of COVID-19, the AOH conducted a series of "Decentering Whiteness" conversations, which mostly white colleagues organized and ran with POC colleagues functioning as guests or panelists. In the fall of 2020, we, the AOH, held a town hall meeting to continue the work that the decentering whiteness conversations had "started." The town hall meeting generated several ideas to "continue" to decenter whiteness in the AOH. In order to execute the ideas, the Executive Committee of the AOH created a Decentering Whiteness Taskforce to follow up on the recommendations emanating from the 2020 AOH "Decentering Whiteness" conversations and town halls. The taskforce has been meeting since April 2021, and at the time of writing this introduction it was in the process of gathering data such as themes, keynotes, and sermons of the last twenty annual meetings and the demographics of the authors publishing in the Homiletic journal. All these efforts have yet to generate structural change in the AOH. These efforts have yet to generate an ethos of sustained racial justice where whiteness no longer dictates the AOH's ways of being. These efforts have yet to generate an ethos where white preaching is no longer the norm, the center, or the invisible force that permeates all spaces, forcing preaching of other colors to situate themselves in reference to and distinct from white preaching.

As counterpoint to all this "progress" that we, the AOH, have made, we offer two examples from the AOH's behavior that depart from and may even hurt the aforementioned efforts. First, in June 2021, the academy announced a "summer conversation series," in an email referencing the "Decentering Whiteness" conversations of the previous summer. However, out of five guests, only one was a racially minoritized scholar. What was presented as a "Decentering Whiteness" conversation never actually materialized a decentralization. Perhaps this was because it was conceived of as primarily a time for white homileticians to grapple with their whiteness in a manner that did not burden scholars of color. No matter what the case may be, decentralization of whiteness was given much lip service without tangible results.

Second, the theme of the 2021 annual meeting of the AOH, "Dreaming of a Preaching Renaissance," takes us back to Europe. We, the AOH, are again centering European culture and Western worldviews and ways of being. The utilization of dreaming is also particularly frustrating, because this is a significant example of the ways in which colonial frames have restricted our homiletical imaginations in harmful ways. Our awareness of the messiness and complexity of the work of overcoming racist and colonial ways of being that have been deeply enmeshed in systems built upon the foundation of white supremacy and colonial empire are heightened by the role that racially minoritized leadership played in selecting this theme. Here we recognize the need to expansively decenter, not just in ways that promote racially minoritized visibility in the AOH but that also lead all of us to grapple with the internal and external scars and, in the language of Gerald Liu, the continuing "traumatization" of whiteness. These two examples point out the complexities of the anti-racist work that we are trying to do.

After three years, we are forced to realize how monumental the work ahead of us is and how modest our contribution is through this collected volume. This collection is but a drop on oceanic waters. We can only hope that this drop will generate a "ripple effect," to use the leading imagery in Kim-Cragg's *Postcolonial Preaching: Creating a Ripple Effect*. The hope is that the concentric circles that expand out of this contribution that now joins a decades-long conversation will constitute long-term effects along with all the other efforts the AOH is engaged in right now to correct our ways and become a more hospitable and just environment for diverse ways of preaching.

We also believe that unmasking whiteness and dismantling colonialism in homiletics requires the centering of those racially minoritized homiletical scholars whose work already implicitly or explicitly unmasked white preaching, yet whose voices have long been ignored or silenced. We are grateful to these racially minoritized scholars from whom this work draws so much wisdom and to whom this work attempts to be responsible. The specter of a host of named and unnamed faithful who preached and engaged preaching amid the brutal experience of the violence of whiteness and white preaching pierces through the mask of white homiletical history and the white-dominant homiletical canon, inviting the white-dominant homiletical guild to sobriety about why it has taken this long to take even these cursory initial steps to deeply listen.

THE YEARNINGS OF THE VOLUME

The European-dominant homiletical canon, the long-standing bias of white-dominant homiletical guilds, the normative European preaching methods in communities of faith, and the corresponding marginalization or erasure of racially minoritized theory and practice suggest that the Christian pulpit—in both a literal and metaphorical sense—remains a ritual site of contestation of the still-unfolding impact of settler colonialism and accompanying structures of race. This edited volume interrogates the white colonial bias of European homiletical practice, pedagogy, and theory with particular attention to the intersection of preaching and racialization. In particular, this work seeks both to unmask and destabilize white colonial hegemony that continues to shape the field of homiletics today and to explore alternative, non-dominant homiletical pathways toward a more just future for the church and the world.

We believe that decentering whiteness and dismantling colonialism in homiletics requires diverse perspectives from both racially minoritized scholars and white scholars. This volume ensures its heterogeneous contribution to this discourse through its curation of diverse perspectives from emerging and established homiletical scholars. As such, this anthology represents polyvocal efforts to identify and decenter the homogenizing impact of white racialization in homiletics and to subsequently contribute diverse critical homiletical approaches emerging in conversation with racially minoritized scholarship and racially subjugated knowledge and practice.

Attempting to avoid the limitations of ethno-specific publications that may unintentionally re-center white-dominant discourse, this volume contributes to homiletical discourse contesting race and colonialism in a manner that a single author monograph could not. This volume forges new directions in the field through curating a sustained, heterogenous engagement of the impact of white racial hegemony on homiletics and through building upon and centering a rich stream of racially minoritized scholarship and subjugated knowledge that has been too frequently neglected or disregarded by the white hegemonic field.

This volume represents collective efforts of its contributors to disrupt the still-unfolding global impact of settler colonialism and the hegemony of whiteness in homiletical guilds, homiletical scholarship, homiletical pedagogy, and the practice of preaching in communities of faith. This volume identifies the boundaries of white, European homiletics, transgressing those boundaries in order to identify alternative homiletical possibilities. As an edited collection of chapters from emerging and established homiletical scholars from a variety of geographical and social locations and with varied racialized identities and formations, this work brings diverse voices to bear on the present unfolding of white colonial homiletics.

To date, a number of monographs have been published that indirectly or implicitly critique white colonialism and its impact on homiletics. These include (1) a broad array of monographs by scholars constructing explicitly racially informed homiletics, homiletical histories, and practical methodologies and (2) limited monographs—in English—constructing explicitly postcolonial or decolonial homiletics.

There are a number of recent monographs—published in the last five years—by scholars constructing explicitly racially informed homiletics, homiletical histories, and practical methodologies. Examples of explicitly racially informed homiletical histories include Kenyatta Gilbert in *A Pursued Justice: Black Preaching from the Great Migration to Civil Rights* (Baker, 2018) and Wayne Croft in *The Motif of Hope in African American Preaching During Slavery and the Post-Civil War Era* (Lexington Books, 2017). Examples of explicitly racially informed homiletics and practical methodologies include Lisa Thompson's *Ingenuity: Preaching as an Outsider* (Abingdon Press, 2018); Carolyn Helsel's *Preaching About Racism* (Westminster John Knox, 2018); Kimberly Johnson's *The Womanist Preacher: Proclaiming Womanist Rhetoric from the Pulpit* (Lexington Books, 2017); Will Willimon's *Who Lynched Willie Earle? Preaching to Confront Racism* (Abingdon Press, 2017); and Marvin McMickle's *Be My Witness: The Great Commission for Preachers* (Judson Press, 2016). While these works engage issues of race, they do not engage in a sustained critique and examination of the formation and perpetuation of homiletical whiteness. This work seeks to expand upon these works by deeply interrogating the theoretical and practical impact of white racialization and to situate that racialization against the brutally expansive backdrop of colonial systems of violence.

Explicitly postcolonial or decolonial monographs in English focused on homiletics have been more limited. Two examples come to mind. The first example is a volume that shows promise for addressing issues of Eurocentrism in preaching, that is, Luiz C. Nascimento and Cleophus J. LaRue's *The Future Shape of Christian Proclamation: What the Global South Can Teach Us About Preaching* (Cascade, 2020). The second example is *Exodus*

Preaching: Crafting Sermons About Justice and Hope (Abingdon Press, 2018), in which Kenyatta Gilbert engages the term "colonial imagination," but does so superficially and with an intense practical focus on helping readers construct sermons that press against systems of whiteness.

Monographs proposing postcolonial preaching exist in the work of Sarah Travis and HyeRan Kim-Cragg. Travis's *Decolonizing Preaching: The Pulpit as Postcolonial Space* (Wipf and Stock, 2014) develops a postcolonial homiletic, but does not significantly engage the emergence and function of race in colonial systems, rendering race a secondary theme. Kim-Cragg's *Postcolonial Preaching: Creating a Ripple Effect* (Lexington, 2021) develops a different kind of postcolonial homiletic, one that draws on postcolonial insights to generate six preaching principles for preaching that creates a ripple effect, for preaching that is not colonial. This volume expands upon these works by drawing explicit and sustained connections between issues of race today and the sustained brutality of colonialism from a wide range of perspectives.

We can already perceive that a major critique to this volume has been or could be that defining the contours of white preaching is re-centering it rather than decentering it. While we concede that there is an inherent risk of centering white preaching by talking about it, we argue that the risk of not talking about white preaching requires taking an even bigger and more harmful risk. In fact, not naming the existence of white preaching generates the need for this collection. Not naming white preaching is what we have always done until now. The effects of such silence about the "*white* elephant in the room" include making white preaching ubiquitous to the point that is normalized as "preaching" (without an adjective), thus becoming the measuring rod for or the original point of the development of any other kind of preaching. In other words, right now, white preaching covers everything, not only the center. In order to decenter white preaching, it is necessary to name it and constrain it so it does not occupy as much space as it does now. Only when we reach the point of containing it will we be able to decenter it.

This volume does not present a single narrative nor build toward a single argument. Instead, this book features a wide range of perspectives on the topic of white preaching, with some authors defining the phrase, others applying the concept in case studies, others resisting the use of the phrase or the existence of the practice, others confronting and critiquing white preaching, and some imagining other futures. In that sense, the volume represents the diversity already present within the AOH and also lives into the polyvocality that, according to Kim-Cragg in her *Postcolonial Preaching*, is a distinctive feature of postcolonial preaching. Embracing such a variety of perspectives results in some chapters contradicting one another. This is the truth of our complex and difficult conversation.

The polyvocality that exists in the guild is also evident in writing styles in this collection. The reader will notice that some of the chapters display what would be considered "incorrect" written language. Using colloquial language and contractions, beginning sentences with conjunctions, abstaining from capitalizing words that "should" be capitalized, and writing from an "I" perspective are some ways in which authors embody their concept of decoloniality. By resisting the impositions of "correct language" as expected in academia, these authors make a decolonial move that goes beyond talking about decoloniality and into performing decoloniality.

We are aware that the contestation of settler colonialism and whiteness within homiletics is even recognizable within this volume itself, and this manifests in the work of white contributors to this volume. There are varying degrees to which the white contributors to this volume listened to non-white voices, unmasked systems of whiteness, and decentered themselves. We also note the varying degrees to which these chapters framed racism in ways that implicitly or explicitly attend to the broader context of settler colonialism. This is both a hopeful sign to us and one that indicates how deeply entrenched whiteness is within mainline Protestant homiletics. We find hope in the collaborative process of contributing to and editing this volume, which included countless opportunities for dialogue and to mutually push ourselves and our colleagues further along in this task. However, we also recognize the ways in which graduate training in homiletics at mainline Protestant seminaries has not consistently prepared us to participate in this task, thus further stabilizing whiteness in homiletics.

LEARNINGS FROM OUR JOURNEY

Reflecting on working together as co-editors who find themselves in two different social locations, we have come to understand that working together is both beautiful and messy. While we have some shared social locations, we also have two very distinct ones. On the one hand, we are both early career scholars in the field of homiletics who hold jobs with multiple roles (teaching preaching and worship, being part of the faculty and administration of a doctoral program, and/or overseeing communal worship life). On the other hand, identity and cultural upbringing are very different. Andrew is a white cis straight man who grew up in Washington State, USA, and is currently married with young children. Lis is a "Hispanic/Latina" cis straight woman who grew up in Puerto Rico, is currently divorced, and has two adult sons. Since we hold different identities and come from different social and cultural contexts, the experience of getting a PhD in the United States and of belonging to the AOH is dissimilar. While we can both reflect critically and feel emotions regarding white supremacy within the AOH and the field of homiletics, the conversations and work needed do not affect us in the same way.

The work we are doing as co-editors is beautiful in that we both paid attention to our social locations throughout the process. We started with earnestness and good faith, which we tried to keep throughout the process. One of the ways in which we upheld our good faith was through making decisions together, especially the important ones. Another way was Andrew's intentionality in taking on service tasks such as writing emails and keeping track of the documents we were receiving from the contributors. Aware of the status in school as early career scholars, super busy, overworked, we tried to distribute labor fairly. But what really is "fair" when the same circumstances weigh heavier on one in contrast to the other?

Lis wanted the labor distribution to be equal, but we are not equal. Lis noticed that Andrew was volunteering a lot for the "menial" tasks and accepted the unequal distribution of labor as a gift but without knowing Andrew's rationale. Lis did not realize how taxing for her whole being this work would be. This is not just any academic project from which she can effectively and affectively detach herself. Racism and white supremacy rips her apart daily, and writing and reading about it is emotionally and psychologically exhausting. Consciously and unconsciously her being postpones it, resists it, wants to quit and run away, which takes us to the challenges of working together, the messy side of this project.

The work we are doing as co-editors is messy in seeking a fair distribution of labor and in the clash of perspectives due to different identities. Seeking a fair distribution of labor seemed like an impossibility, because we are still living within systems that are not fair. With her whole being avoiding the pain that produces this kind of work, Lis showed up to too many meetings with her homework partially done or not done at all. Andrew always assumed a position of solidarity and understanding, and many conversations turned into exchanges of strategies to manage the multiple roles that we were both playing as early career scholars in a tenure track. The apparent asymmetry in labor distribution helped balance out the inequalities embedded in the bigger systems of labor in which both of us move. We did not know this, however, because as much as we both remained aware of our different social locations, reflected critically on those, and acted according to what each of us would consider just or fair or corrections of unfair systems of oppression, we did that separately. We did not have these conversations. We did not practice communal reflexivity until we had edited all the chapters and were getting ready for submission of the manuscript.

Working together is messy also in the clash of perspectives that may arise due to different identities. There were times when Lis thought, "this is where Andrew is showing his white male identity," mostly when editing all the chapters, especially Lis's chapter or when Andrew was asking Lis the same questions that she typically gets from white men whenever she shares her scholarship. Andrew "redeemed" himself by responding to Lis's answers very unlike other white and/or male homileticians. Consonant with his stance of solidarity, Andrew would repeatedly encourage Lis to bend or break the rules of academic writing and/or production of knowledge so that her chapter would perform its content or at least the message would agree with the method. Another example of the clash of perspectives had to do with our roles as editors when we disagreed with the argument that an individual author was making. We found ourselves pushing back and then having to critically assess our feedback.

At the end of the process, we realize that we could have embraced the messiness more intentionally and that messy interaction generates beauty for the betterment of this world. In your hands you hold a volume full of contradictions, of pain, of cluelessness, of trials and errors, of frustrations and celebrations. It is messy and beautiful!

THE FLOW OF THE VOLUME

In this anthology, we engage topics that are immediately relevant both to the work of the academy and to the practice of ministry. While this work is primarily focused on contributing to homiletical discourse, homiletics is a field within practical theology, and this work correspondingly has a distinctively accessible and practical nature with many of the chapters providing suggestions for practical ministry. We hope that this work has value for various constituencies who may have interests in the field of homiletics, racialization, and postcolonial or decolonial thought. It is also our hope that this will be a valuable source for graduate students engaging the aforementioned topics. Due to expanding interest in issues of race across the Christian church and our society, this volume may also generate interest on the part of clergy and all practitioners of preaching.

The three central themes of this book (racial hegemony, resistance, and possibilities) are interwoven to varied degrees and in a number of methods throughout each chapter; however, this book is organized into two primary sections. The first section examines manifestations of racial hegemony in homiletics. The second section examines resistance and possibilities in homiletics. Each of the two sections is begun by the chapter(s) of our elders, those senior scholars (Brooks, Mumford, and Kim-Cragg) whose generous presence and thought has broken ground for this collection and whose scholarship provides important frames for our task in this collection. In addition, we have structured this collection to center the voices of racially minoritized scholars. In this overview of the flow of the projects, we have utilized edited language from the authors' descriptions of their own work, in order to allow for as much self-description as possible.

The first section is composed of chapters that examine manifestations of racial hegemony in preaching, and it begins with a chapter written by our elder and motivator, Gennifer Brooks, "The Missionary Connection: White Preaching in the British Colonies of the Caribbean." Brooks examines how the era of British Protestant foreign missions to colonies of the British Empire of the West Indies during the heyday of British foreign missions in the period from 1700 to 1886 resulted in a missionary presence that had great negative impact on the culture of African slaves who were the subject of their evangelistic fervor. She explores how white preaching reflects and is undergirded by a white supremacist racist agenda that denies the full humanity of Indigenous persons and people of color, specifically the African slaves and their descendants. Brooks's work invites us to examine how white preaching was and continues to be deeply "connected" to racial and cultural hegemony that has a long legacy of violence, and she calls preachers to share "good news" in ways that respect and honor diverse cultures.

In the second chapter, "Unmasking the Homiletical Whiteness of Jerry Falwell Sr. and the Moral Majority," Debra Mumford analyzes Jerry Falwell's sermons through which she unmasks the whiteness at work in the principles of the Moral Majority, which, even though disbanded in 1989, continues to influence politics and policies of the U.S. government. Mumford's work sheds light on the current political landscape in the United States and the nature of the preaching of a good many white evangelicals today.

Continuing in the pattern of the first two chapters crucially situating white preaching in the unfolding of our present moments amid the ongoing legacies of settler colonialism and its accompanying racial hierarchies, Peace Lee and David Stark examine a concrete (and stone) case study of how the legacy of white supremacy has been literally built and maintained in the life of a white-dominant institution. The third chapter, "The Towering Sermon: Duke Chapel as Monument to White Supremacy," examines the history of Duke University's Chapel and its legacy of white supremacy. Their chapter invites a broad engagement of white preaching that encompasses but also moves beyond the words of white preaching, to examining how racial hierarchies are embedded in and proclaimed through a building, aesthetics, and art. Lee and Stark help us to imagine a dismantling of white supremacy that leads to the literal crumbling of this cathedral of whiteness, and their work allows us to glimpse the contestation of this white homiletical space over the course of its history. While very particular in focus, the third chapter models an interrogation of a particular space that may cue our own awareness of the all too common nature of monuments to whiteness, even those that may be in our own cities or owned by our religious communities.

In a pattern that will repeat itself throughout the volume, the movement from chapter 3 to chapter 4 involves a shift from a concrete case study to a more theoretical engagement of homiletical scholarship, in this case a critical survey of homiletical literature. Doing so honors the inductive ways of reasoning of many communities of people of color around the world, as opposed to the deductive and abstract logic of academia. The fourth chapter, "Theorizing about the Whiteness of Asian American Homiletics," by Gerald Liu asks the question, "Is Asian American homiletics indelibly traumatized by whiteness?" Liu explores how white expectations surface in a number of prominent Asian American homiletical works, and he poses questions regarding how entrenched whiteness is at the root of the American preaching. Liu's chapter also draws our attention to a horizon for Asian American homiletics where it must also begin to address the black-and-white paradigm that governs American homiletic scholarship.

The fifth chapter, "White Mainline Protestant Preachers Addressing Racial Issues: 2017 vs. 2021," by Leah Schade compares the results of two surveys of mainline Protestant clergy in the United States conducted in 2017 and 2021 on the issues of race, immigration, and white privilege. Using both quantitative and qualitative methods, Schade assesses how preachers are approaching their sermons during this divisive time in our nation's history, and her work reveals some of the complexities and challenges of preaching about controversial social issues such as race. Schade provides us with a glimpse into the self-perceptions of white preachers in mainline Protestantism through which we can glimpse some present dynamics present in white preaching about race.

Chapter 6, "Civility and the 'Purple Church': An Insufficient Response to White Supremacy," by Andrew Scales continues in this theme of present realities shaping preaching in white mainline Protestant churches by contesting notions of "purple church" through which white churches communicate their desire to embrace a broad spectrum of convictions. Scales argues that despite shared values of civility and deliberative progress, the denial of racism and the pervasive influence of white supremacy in American society call for explicitly anti-racist preaching and actions.

Expanding beyond the context of the United States, Sarah Travis's work attends to the defensive responses of white and settler fragility to preaching about race with particular reference to the relationship among white settler Canadians and aboriginal peoples in Canada. Drawing upon these insights, she discusses barriers to preaching about racial reconciliation. Travis's work resources literature addressing how white fragility must be confronted with persistence and sensitivity in order to unmask racial assumptions and lead to an environment in which reconciliation can occur.

The eighth chapter, which is the final chapter of the first section, is "Through a Glass Dimly: White Preaching and Epistemological Ignorance" by Christopher Baker. In this chapter, Baker explores why so much white liberal mainline Protestant preaching today fails to join in the ongoing struggle against white supremacy. His work uses resources from Philosophy of Race to construct an account of the epistemological ignorance of whiteness and how that shapes the theological approaches to race that then make their way into white pulpits. Key to this is understanding of "whiteness" as an epistemological formation, is an "epistemology of ignorance" that shapes the contours of knowing; the bounds of the known, the mis-known, and the intentionally un-known.

The second section of this collection examines resistance and possibilities in homiletics as inextricably linked topics. Chapter 9, "Multitasking Preaching: The Liberating Power of Unmasking Whiteness from the Pulpit," by our elder, HyeRan Kim-Cragg, whose generous insight helped guide this volume in significant ways, unmasks whiteness in preaching as it examines significant issues of preaching the lectionary, biblical exegesis for preaching, and the use of language in preaching. Kim-Cragg models for us the ways in which postcolonial preaching must simultaneously attend to a number of issues. She does so through a postcolonial, contrapuntal, anti-racist exegesis of Vashti in the Book of Esther, followed by an examination of the power of language in preaching. Her work shows how the multi-tasking that exposes the thick and complex mask of whiteness is hard but liberating work, because it aims to dismantle the tangled oppression of racism in order to recognize the agency and the dignity of all people regardless of race.

Following Kim-Cragg's rich engagement of multi-tasking preaching, Richard Voelz recounts and critically examines the complexity of anti-racist course at Union Presbyterian Seminary entitled "Proclaiming Justice in the Church and Public Square." In this tenth chapter, "Wrestling with Whiteness in Homiletic Pedagogy: A Reflection on Teaching 'Proclaiming Justice in the Church and Public Square,'" Voelz provides us with glances into the design and implementation of a course intended not only to help equip and empower students for the work of proclaiming justice but also to explore just ways of learning in community. He reflects on that experience as an act of "Unmasking White Preaching" through anti-racist pedagogy. Through Voelz's work, we gain further insight into critical self-reflection and the pedagogical complexity of addressing issues of race in a white-dominant institution.

Chapter 11, "Of Handmaids, Mediatrixes, and Mothers: The Idealized Feminine and Rhetorics of Whiteness," Jerusha Matsen Neal examines how the long-standing trope of "proper rhetoric" as the "proper woman" supports the agenda of whiteness particularly in the pulpit performance of white women. Matsen Neal notes how rhetorical training has worked to control, objectify, and perpetuate cultural lineage through pulpit speech. Like the previous chapter, Matsen Neal turns toward the contemporary homiletic classroom, asking if rhetorical training can subvert agendas of patriarchal racism or if the two are inextricably linked. As Matsen Neal notes, the question is particularly potent for white female preachers called to "proper" proclamation. She calls white female preachers to resist the temptation of Western rhetoric's "proper woman" and her complicity with whiteness.

Expanding on the possibility of Matsen Neal's engagement of resistance, chapter 12, "Betraying White Preaching: Homiletical Domination, Racial Treason, and the Pursuit of Abolition," by Andrew Wymer, explores the possibility of preachers betraying, if only ever temporary and conditionally, their white racial formation. He surveys homiletical discourse on the nature of black preaching as one example of the long-standing unmasking of white preaching done by some racially minoritized homiletical scholars working at the intersection of race and preaching. Drawing from these discourse observations about the identification of white preaching as a distinct racial and homiletical category, this chapter explores a pathway that might lead preachers—particularly those who are claimed by whiteness—toward decentering, deconstructing, and destabilizing white preaching, reimagining neo-abolitionist discourse on racial treason through the lens of contemporary abolition movements.

In chapter 13, "Who Are You? White Identity Formation and Re-formation in Homiletics," Suzanne Duchesne continues the theme of exploring alternative possibilities for white preachers through sharing her journey of identity formation and re-formation. Duchesne explores the influence of identity formation and re-formation, particularly white identity formation with its concomitant manifestations of white fragility, on the preacher's voice. She offers reflexive attention to identity as a means of unmasking whiteness in the pulpit. This journey of reflexive attention calls for internal confrontation of identity assumptions and encourages preachers to take the time necessary to identify themselves, take responsibility for their ancestral sins, acknowledge the resultant trauma, and seek to know their own identity more fully.

Chapter 14, "Non-Preaching? Unmasking [White] Preaching through Negation," by Lis Valle-Ruiz presents to us the burlesque-esque proclamation of Sophia Divinatrix, who, without words, vividly exorcises white supremacy and proclaims the good news of an alternative future. Valle-Ruiz explores how burlesque-esque preaching exposes the social norms established by a Western and Euro-descendant gaze upon Christian preaching. This restrictive perspective on preaching binds it to a pulpit inside a church building within the context of a worship service, and it leaves out other preaching practices within Christian traditions and their Jewish precedents, including prophetic preaching on the streets and the tradition of the Holy Fools. Valle critically expands the possibilities emerging from these traditions in a manner that increases our awareness of what might constitute prophetic preaching.

Building upon this theme of the need to expand what constitutes preaching, chapter 15, "An Icon of Exclusion: Deconstructing the Pulpit through the Homiletical Practice of Black Women," by Chelsea Yarborough names the preaching pulpit as a place of power, prestige, and exclusion. Yarborough argues that even though powerful and important preaching has stemmed from the pulpit, centering and maintaining the pulpit as the primary space and place preaching occurs is a by-product of whiteness that requires the one (preacher) to be over the many (congregants). Utilizing womanist preaching as a tool to move beyond this stagnant understanding of preaching, she reimagines the spatial demarcation of preaching, considering the necessary ways in which we must move beyond this idea of where preaching happens and therefore, what preaching can be. Tracing the history of the pulpit, and the ways in which its exclusionary nature has reinforced white ideologies, Yarborough aims to liberate preaching and open the ears to the possibilities of the diversity of preaching spaces and places.

We encourage you to embrace the messiness of the volume as you read through these chapters. Doing so might provide you a path to grow your decolonial work for yourself, your classrooms, your institutions, and the numerous communities to which you belong. As you face your own contradictions, pain, cluelessness, trials and errors, frustrations, and celebrations, you will hopefully encounter glimpses of a different, more beautiful world.

NOTE

1. While this work emerges out of our participation in and awareness of the AOH, the underlying whiteness which we address in relationship to the AOH is a pronounced feature of the EHS.

RACIAL HEGEMONY
IN HOMILETICS

Chapter 1

The Missionary Connection
White Preaching in the British Colonies of the Caribbean

Gennifer Benjamin Brooks

The subject of foreign missions and white missionaries being sent to countries inhabited by people of color has always caused great angst in my inner being. The source of that deep discomfort eluded me for a long time even after my theological horizons broadened during the study of significant theological theories and ecclesial movements. But eventually I traced the origin of my angst to the realization that the missionary movement was the purveyor of a theology of whiteness that reflected a belief in white supremacy.[1] This aberrant theology inflicted further injury on the lives of persons who were already suffering the hegemony of slavery in places far from their native shores and made a distinct connection between missionary outreach and whiteness in part through the proclamation of the gospel.

White missionaries sent by their denominations, or compelled by their inner voice to go and preach Christ to the natives, did so supposedly out of a conviction of a divine call or the sense of the need to spread the gospel of Jesus Christ to the world. If asked, most might well say that they were responding to Christ's command and commissioning as recorded in Matthew 28:19–20, "Go therefore and make disciples of all nations, baptizing them in the name of the Father and of the Son and of the Holy Spirit, and teaching them to obey everything that I have commanded you." Unfortunately, the reality was the invasion by and the infusion of a white patriarchal system that brought a condemning God, a selective redeemer, given to partiality that favored the cause of whiteness or white supremacy and a condescending Holy Spirit that offered grace according to a caste system where native thriving and dignity ranked low, if not last on the list of divine favor. According to this system, human sin engaged by native peoples was magnified based on a value system that stemmed from a belief in white supremacy, which in turn placed missionaries second, only to if not in line with the person of Jesus Christ. This value system originated from and was sustained by a hierarchical, anthropological structure of their own making and disseminated to the people upon whom they unleashed their missional zeal.

This chapter addresses the missionary connection in the advancement of the hegemonic culture of white supremacy among enslaved African people in the Caribbean. The historical context for this work is the British Protestant foreign missions, and particularly the cultural impact of the missionary presence and their evangelistic preaching in the British colonies of the West Indies during the heyday of British foreign missions in the period from 1700 to 1886. It identifies the content of the preaching of the white missionaries of the period as white preaching, which I define loosely as preaching that reflects and is undergirded by a white supremacist racist agenda. Such an underpinning of homiletical engagement denies the full humanity of natives and people of color, and specifically in this context, African slaves and their descendants.

In the period immediately following the beginning of the slave trade by Portuguese traders, and the subsequent enslavement and degradation of African people, as slavery spread to the many nations on the African continent and was adopted as a legitimate commercial enterprise. This highly profitable venture served to expand European empires and people of goodwill (or so they thought), both Catholic and Protestant, individuals and churches set out with Christian zeal into what they considered to be fertile fields of mission among the unknown people, considered heathen, and to whom they determined to preach the Christian gospel. History, written as it mainly has been by proponents of empire, tends to absolve the missionary movement from direct collusion with the goal of expansion of the British Empire. However, as Max Warren notes, it is relatively easy "to show how, during this period (1785–1859) and even more in the nineteenth century, Christianity was closely interwoven with both Commerce and Imperialism, infusing into both an element never easily digested."[2] For this writing, that element is the impact of white (supremacist) preaching that continues to extend its tentacles into the preaching of the established Protestant churches in the West Indies in the twenty-first century. The reality of the mission enterprise and the structure that systematized the work of the missionaries, although not fully recognized by the churches involved, owed its identity and ultimately much of its success to the empire within which the missionary societies existed and operated. As Andrew Porter notes:

> The growth and adaption of Christian missions and the processes of empire-building or dissolution have often coincided in both period and place. Periodically intertwined as they have been, the relevance of the one to the other

in particular settings overseas has been much discussed. Nevertheless, even for the period 1790–1914, when the modern missionary movement got into its stride and enthusiasm for imperial expansion reached its peak not only in Britain but throughout Western Europe and the Atlantic world, there has been no general recognition or study of the problem as a whole. . . . Occasionally it was acknowledged that missionary activity contributed to imperial expansion, but the manner in which it did so remained undefined. There was a tendency for religious questions to be treated in the context simply of growing secularization of European society, and for histories of Europe to ignore the significance of overseas agents such as missionaries for the continent's own domestic transformation.[3]

In much the same way, the white supremacist behavior of the missionaries and its impact on and transformation of the countries, nations, societies, and cultures of the peoples to whom they spread their Christian witness were also ignored. The white (supremacist) agenda of their privileged status was so ingrained in these missionaries and made such inroads into the lives of the native peoples, that despite the subordinate and dismissive treatment the people suffered at the hands of their white "superiors," they were made to believe and became convinced for the most part that it was an honor and privilege to serve their white missionary family, even when it meant neglecting their own families.[4] This system of belief was the basis from which white missionaries preached to the people.

Preaching is the proclamation of the gospel. That is and ever will be my mantra for the homiletical task to which I believe I have been called. And the gospel that Christian preachers are called to proclaim is the salvation of Jesus Christ offered freely as the epitome of divine grace to all people equally. In the case of white missionaries, that gospel became subverted, infected by, inculcated with a white supremacist agenda that made of the Christian proclamation something much less than the freedom which Christ has offered to all people. Christianity and the church became an institution, a place where empire, human empire, and in the case of my reality as a native of the Caribbean, the British Empire had ascendency over the idea of the beloved community, under the sovereignty of Jesus Christ. As a new territory caught in the web of ongoing exploration and expansion, the hierarchy wherein the subject nation was ruled by a distant monarchy was perpetuated in the structure and content of worship and preaching.

As a Methodist, Max Warren's analysis of this period as "A Time of Exploration" and the role of Methodism's founder in it are of particular importance for me and for this writing. Warren states, "The century which was to see John Wesley and many others exploring the world of religious experience and mapping in a new way the highlands of Christian perfection was a century which can be described as an age of curiosity."⁵ Perhaps that curiosity extended to the peoples, especially those of color encountered by white missionaries. If that held sway in their encounter with native peoples, it seemed to be of the type that viewed any but those who resembled them in all aspects, especially with respect to racial identity, as something less than and therefore worthy of the same exploitation as that suffered by the lands "discovered" during exploration on behalf of the empire.

It bears noting that the reality of empire as a system is based on a hierarchical structure that strives to maintain a mode of dominance over its subjects. That was the reality that prevailed in the mission churches. The culture of empire that white missionaries impressed upon native peoples resulted not simply in a devaluation of their culture, but did widespread damage to the prevailing society, even as the missionaries strove to replace native culture with their own. In the case of African slaves in the Caribbean, having been torn from Mother Africa and the myriad cultures and religions represented in the melting pot of tribes forced together as a result of their enslavement, the yet unformed community was not only vulnerable to, but unable to withstand the pressure of a fully formed, operational system of white supremacy represented by the British Empire and her missionary subjects.

It is certain that the British missionaries dismissed immediately any thought that the slaves had a recognizable culture or any formal system of belief. Dale Bisnauth, writing on the *History of Religions in the Caribbean*, notes that "the general view of English planters that the African slaves did not hold to a system of beliefs that could be described as a religion. At best—so the planters felt—their beliefs amounted to nothing more than heathenish superstition."⁶ That belief was erroneous, as the Africans were generally a religious people. That may even have worked to the favor of the missionaries and the African religious history may have been the preparatory foundation to their indoctrination by the missionaries. However, that was not the understanding of either the missionaries or even of those who later documented the mission activities. In fact, in a chapter entitled "To Preach Deliverance to the Captive," F. Deaville Walker, writing on missionary activity in the West Indies, notes:

> The task Methodism undertook in the West Indies was no light one; but it was one for which she was singularly well-fitted and prepared by God. Had her first missionary effort been to the subtle-minded Brahmins of India the results would have been less satisfactory. But to preach salvation through Christ to the lowly and sinful that was her own peculiar work. Long experience of evangelism in England and Ireland had trained her messengers in just such methods as would succeed in the West Indies.

> Dark and helpless was the condition of the slaves who formed the bulk of the population in those beautiful islands. . . . They were mere cattle in the eyes of the law. . . . In most of the islands legal marriage was forbidden, and the slaves herded together like cattle. Can we wonder that their few opportunities for pleasure led them too often to drunkenness, dancing and immorality? Their revelries were often carried far into the night, fires were lighted, and drunken songs were accompanied by such wide musical instruments as could be obtained. It would be difficult to paint the picture too dark, but there were gleams of light. The marvelous cheerfulness of the African race; the love of music, song, and dance; the love for their children; their friendliness and sense of comradeship among themselves; their kindness and generosity, and above all their tendency to look for brighter days—all these traits made their wrongs and sufferings easier to bear. It was quite a thing for slaves to show the utmost devotion, gratitude, and love to kind masters and mistresses; and many, in times of peril, have cheerfully given their lives to save masters and children from harm.[7]

Walker's description of the people is indicative of the erroneous analysis of African people that exists to the detriment of their personhood, their mores and culture(s), which were (and are) derided, devalued, and dismissed as primitive, heathen, ungodly, highly sinful, and even unnatural (where white ways are seen as normal, acceptable, and natural, if not perfect).

Given that both slave owners and missionaries were white, the reality of their way of being was that it more closely resembled and fit quite easily into the practices of white slave owners. Certainly, the missionaries considered themselves a cut above cruel slave owners, but despite their so-called Christian message of freedom in Christ, their preaching did not extend into territories that may have encouraged slaves to seek freedom from daily oppression. Their focus in preaching was "to teach the slaves about the Love of God and to implant within their hearts the Christian hope."[8] However, the missionaries, like their slave exploiting counterparts, did not see these African peoples as equal to whites, believing that "it was less easy to teach them to live a Christian life."[9] In fact, they may have even missed the reality that the slaves were full persons imprinted with the *imago Dei* in the same way as both the missionaries and the slave owners were. They were unable to see beyond their white supremacist prejudice against people of color.

Walker names his own prejudices even as he describes the preaching task of the missionaries. His belief in the enormity of the preaching challenge of the white missionaries continues in his description of their mission context. Speaking of the slaves, he says:

> Most of them were little removed from the heathenism of West Africa, and many had been made worse by contact with white men, whose vices they had

learned. There were many failures among the converts. It could scarcely have been otherwise. Often it was necessary for the missionaries to exercise discipline; sometimes members had to be suspended or even expelled.[10]

What does it say about Christ's church that those who declare their Christian identity and are initiated into the body of Christ can be expelled? Are we all not repeating sinners continuously justified and redeemed by Christ? With the foundation of whiteness (or white supremacy) found in both the mission church and in their society, for their preaching, it seemed almost a natural progression that the missionaries would follow a trajectory in both their proclamation and their lives that would locate them in the hierarchy that existed in the mission field, at the highest rung, perhaps even in the place of God, although it is certain they would have denied any such accusation.

As such, the slaves, previously a religious people in their own way but converts to the missionaries' teaching of Christ would be placed in the role of the rejected sinner, needing to be saved by being brought into line by their missionary saviors. And based on their actions that stemmed from their belief in their superiority over the converts, it enabled the empire to continue to use the missionaries to their gain by using the converted status of the slaves as the erstwhile whip to keep them in line. The work of missionaries and particularly the substance of their preaching so impressed the governing bodies that as Walker records, in one case on the island of Tortola: "The Governor sent for missionary Turner and requested him to organize a force of slaves for the defense of the island—feeling able to trust them with arms if under the leadership of the missionary."[11] That the missionary in question did so with success speaks directly to the impact of the preached message on the native people.[12] It was an indoctrination, the like of which changed the nature of African peoples with respect to their worship practices, from that of open and exuberant joy, to somber, sedate, repressed, and even silent worship.

An example of such indoctrination into the white supremacist culture of missionary preachers of which I have actual experience is the requirement that worship services be somber and worshippers maintain silence except when required to join in communal prayer or song. In my own time, not only was any type of outburst or verbal or emotive expressions forbidden, or perhaps not even considered, but if one attended a concert within the church premises, no outward sign of appreciation for a good performance could be shown, except the waving of the program—no clapping, no noise. Additionally, in some denominations, despite the extremely hot temperatures in the Caribbean, women were required to cover themselves completely—long sleeves, high necked, ankle length dresses, somber colors with no adornment on either their person or their clothing such as makeup or jewelry. Such items or modes of apparel that were contrary to these dictates were considered heathen and those who wore or used them were denounced in preached sermons or even read out of the church. Additionally, musical instruments, especially those connected with African culture, such as drums, were condemned as instruments of the devil and the subject of vituperative sermons. White was the preferred color for garments worn in worship and was absolutely required for participation in Holy Communion. One might consider if this requirement was a way of reinforcing the superiority of the whiteness of people over persons of color. White was perfect and every other shade was a discoloration of perfection and those who wore such colors in worship represented a lower rung on the hierarchy of people.

In my estimation, the hegemony of slavery that made real and popular the devaluation of individuals was a disease that infected the preaching of the gospel and made suspect the efficacy of mission work in spreading the gospel of Jesus Christ to all nations. Even beyond the abolition of slavery by Britain, the gospel that was proclaimed to the people found its base in those biblical texts that highlighted best the sinful state of human beings, and necessitated a strident call to the hearers to repent and to abase themselves to the preacher (in the place of God) in order to attain divine favor. It called for hard and diligent work, a sacrifice of both dignity and self-worth in order to be heard by God and ultimately receive the blessing of God. And that blessing was doled out reluctantly, minuscule drop by minuscule drop by the preacher, who in the mission of Christ dispensed the largesse found in the cup of salvation.

Brian Stanley provides some important words of summation on the issue of white missionary preaching, which I submit had more to do with the expansion of empire than the spread of the reign of God. Stanley writing on the relationship of British missions to political or economic imperialism notes:

> The contribution of the missionary movements as a whole to cultural imperialism (substitute white supremacist preaching) . . . is overwhelming . . . missionaries have been guilty of foisting their own cultural values on their converts. They have upset the stability of indigenous social systems, and saddled the younger churches of the Third World with a thoroughly "foreign" Christianity . . . one of the highest priorities for the Third World churches today is to unwrap the gospel from its alien cultural packaging and develop expressions of the Christian faith which are genuinely indigenous to their particular cultured contents. . . . There can be little dispute that, for most of the nineteenth century, British Christians believed that the missionary was called to propagate the imagined benefits of Western civilization alongside the Christian message. It was assumed that the poor, benighted "heathen" were in a condition of massive cultural deprivation, which the gospel alone could remedy.[13]

Stanley's analysis fits directly the tenet of white supremacy that plagued the missions undertaken by the church and continues to plague church and society alike. That one group should presume to substitute its culture and norms for another on the basis of believing that theirs is the best and should take precedence over any other is the foundation of whiteness and white preaching.

What makes this study relevant for the present is that a new model of missionary zeal has overtaken many Caribbean countries and even places in South America such as Brazil, that once again brings to light the missionary connection to the spread of the destructive structures of whiteness and white supremacy among communities of color. Like the missionaries of the earlier period, the current evangelicals have brought with them a zeal for evangelizing the natives that impinges on current culture in much the same way that British missionaries did. The white preaching of present-day missionaries, often denominationally Pentecostal (although many consider themselves non-denominational), is also directed to the prevailing cultures and whether the preachers are racially white (and many are) or African American, their zeal for Christ seems less about proclaiming the inclusive gospel of Jesus Christ and more about creating a structure centered on exclusivity. Much of their preaching is predicated on spreading a message that attacks cultural activities that they consider primitive and which they believe have a negative impact on one's soul. This includes participation in native festivals and gatherings that they consider heathen and ungodly.[14] It is missionary preaching at its worst in my estimation, since the good news of God's love gets lost in the vituperative rhetoric used to name sin in the people. To my way of thinking, it is white missionary preaching at its worst, that makes clear the missionary connection with whiteness. In most, if not all cases, this white preaching is foisted on people of color who are considered less than or other in the eyes of the preacher, despite their claim that all are one in Christ.

As preachers, we are called to disseminate one gospel equally to all people. That gospel is the proclamation of free divine grace, salvation for all equally, without cost or price. To offer anything else is to defame the message of Christ and it is to circumvent the mandate of Christ that sends each and all of us into the mode of proclamation. To follow that mandate by engaging in missionary preaching is commendable only when the proclamatory message is given in a way that respects and honors the context of the people's culture. To deny the full worth of the people by defaming who they are and not making every effort to engage their culture is to change the message we are called to preach. As messengers of the gospel of Jesus Christ, our mission must be to proclaim the love of God made manifest in the sacrifice of Jesus Christ. As such, our connection must be to Christ and through Christ to one another. To modify the substance of preaching in any way that makes real any other connection is a hegemony that must be rooted out and avoided at all costs in order to make one's preaching truly the gospel (good news) of Jesus Christ and make real the mission of "making disciples of Jesus Christ for the transformation of the world."[15]

NOTES

1. Here I am referring specifically to British Protestant Missions as described by Andrew Porter in *Religion Versus Empire: British Protestant Missionaries and Overseas Expansion, 1700–1914* (Manchester: Manchester University Press, 2004.)
2. Max Warren, *The Missionary Movement from Britain in Modern History* (London: SCM Press Ltd., 1965), 18.
3. Porter, *Religion Versus Empire*, 2.
4. "Native" here refers to the Africans and their descendants, slaves, who inhabited the islands. The original native peoples, the Arawaks and the Caribs, had been virtually killed off by Europeans.
5. Warren, *The Missionary Movement from Britain in Modern History*.
6. Dale Bisnauth, *History of Religions in the Caribbean* (Trenton, NJ: Africa World Press, 1996), 82.
7. F. Deaville Walker, *The Call of the West Indies: The Romance of Methodist Work and Opportunity in the West Indies and Adjacent Regions* (London: The Cargate Press), 49–51.
8. Walker, *The Call*, 56.
9. Ibid.
10. Ibid.
11. Ibid, 57.
12. The slaves of these islands during this period were no longer African born, but descendants of erstwhile African slaves, born in the Caribbean.
13. Brian Stanley, *The Bible and the Flag: Protestant Missions and British Imperialism in the Nineteenth and Twentieth Centuries* (Leicester, England: Apollos 1990), 157.
14. In Brazil, the Pentecostal missionaries have condemned the religion of Candomblé, which is considered to be of African origin. There have been serious and concerted attempts to stop the practice of this venerable and venerated way of worship.
15. This is the stated mission of the United Methodist Church.

BIBLIOGRAPHY

Benitez-Rojo, Antonio. *The Repeating Island: The Caribbean and the Postmodern Perspective*, 2nd ed., Translated by James E. Maraniss. Durham, NC: Duke University Press, 1996.

Bisnauth, Dale. *History of Religious in the Caribbean*. Trenton, NJ: Africa World Press, Inc., 1996.

Le Grys, Alan. *Preaching to the Nations: The Origins of Mission in the Early Church.* London: SPCK, 1998.

Lewis, Kingsley. *The Moravian Mission in Barbados 1816–1886.* New York: Verlag Peter Lang, 1985.

Porter, Andrew. *Religion Versus Empire: British Protestant Missionaries and Overseas Expansion, 1700–1914.* Manchester: Manchester University Press, 2004.

Porter, Andrew, ed. *The Imperial Horizon of British Protestant Missions, 1880–1914.* Grand Rapids, MI: William B. Eerdmans Publishing Company, 2003.

Stanley, Brian. *The Bible and the Flag: Protestant Missions and British Imperialism in the Nineteenth and Twentieth Centuries.* Leicester, England: Apollos, 1990.

Walker, F. Deaville. *The Call of the West Indies: The Romance of Methodist Work and Opportunity in the West Indies and Adjacent Regions.* London: The Cargate Press.

Warren, Max. *The Missionary Movement from Britain in Modern History.* London: SCM Press Ltd., 1965.

Chapter 2

Unmasking the Homiletical Whiteness of Jerry Falwell Sr. and the Moral Majority

Debra J. Mumford

Whiteness is a social construction that has created a racial hierarchy that has shaped all the social, cultural, educational, political, and economic institutions of society. Whiteness is linked to domination and is a form of race privilege invisible to white people who are not conscious of its power.[1]

The power of Whiteness, however, is manifested by the ways in which racialized Whiteness becomes transformed into social, political, economic, and cultural behaviour. White culture, norms, and values in all these areas become normative natural. They become the standard against which all other cultures, groups, and individuals are measured and usually found to be inferior.[2]

From this definition of whiteness, it follows that homiletical whiteness is the art of preaching racial hierarchy that shapes the social, cultural, educational, political, and economic institutions of our society. However, to allow homiletical whiteness to focus solely on race is to negate what Christine Smith calls a "web of oppressions" of which white racism is part.[3] White racism cannot be separated from sexism, heterosexism, ageism, classism, and handicappism because of their primary source in the United States—elite white men. Therefore, unmasking homiletical whiteness entails not only identifying racism, but other oppressions that disempower all of those who do not fit the straight, white, able-bodied, youthful, financially independent male mold. So a more comprehensive definition of homiletical whiteness is *the art of preaching racial, social, political and economic hierarchy that seeks to persuade the social, cultural, educational, political, and economic institutions of our society to support the mythology of white supremacy*. For the duration of this chapter, whiteness will be inclusive of the aforementioned web of oppressions.

Once preached, homiletical whiteness is transformed into social, political, economic, and cultural behavior. Homiletical whiteness is a type of hegemony in which the values of powerful white (primarily male) constituencies are held to be superior to and aspirational for all others. Through the imposition of whiteness in every segment of society, all people are forced to adopt the norms, culture, and values of powerful whites in order to fully integrate into dominant society. For example, in order to earn a PhD in homiletics from my predominantly white institution and be prepared to teach homiletics in a predominantly white seminary, I had to achieve a mastery of white homiletical traditions and contemporary practices. For most predominantly white institutions, white scholarship forms the baseline of knowledge upon which curriculums are based. Therefore, white scholarship must be mastered by all who hope to teach in or earn degrees from those institutions.

Homiletical whiteness is most insidious when it not only claims widely accepted societal norms, cultures, and values as its basis for legitimacy, but it also professes God to be the originator and ultimate enforcer of its claims. By claiming that their agendas are God's agenda, whites, who are able to pair their religious claims with other dominant social, economic, and political powers to force their agenda onto others, are able to wield tremendous social, economic, and political influence.

Understanding and locating homiletical whiteness, like locating whiteness in other manifestations, is challenging because its theology, approaches to biblical interpretation, and cultural assumptions have been widely taught to be the norm, the standard by which all homiletical approaches are judged. Therefore, analyzing sermons for whiteness can only be done thoroughly by first understanding the worldviews and social and cultural locations of the preachers who deliver them.

I will analyze for whiteness a particular sermon preached by Rev. Dr. Jerry Laymon Falwell Sr. for homiletical whiteness and will reference other sermons he preached as well. I chose Falwell's preaching for several reasons. First of all, Falwell, a Southern white male, was the founder of the Moral Majority movement. The Moral Majority was a coalition of evangelical Christians organized to influence public policy. Their stated goal was to help America regain her former greatness.[4] Second, the Moral Majority's legacy of mobilizing conservative Christians for political engagement is alive and well in the work of numerous conservative Christian organizations. By understanding Falwell and the Moral Majority, we may be able to better understand how and why Christian conservatives were able to so steadfastly support Donald Trump and his policies. Third, Falwell Sr. founded Liberty University, a private, liberal arts college which has educated hundreds of thousands of people since its founding in 1971. Through the university, the values of the Moral Majority are being instilled in current and future generations. One of the primary missions of Liberty University is

> encourage a commitment to the Christian life, one of personal integrity, sensitivity to the needs of others, social responsibility and active communication of the Christian faith, and, as it is lived out, a life that leads people to Jesus Christ as the Lord of the universe and their own personal Savior.[5]

Falwell Sr. was born on August 11, 1933, in Lynchburg, Virginia, to a father who was an atheist and a mother who was a devout Christian. At the age of eighteen in 1952, Falwell accepted Jesus Christ as his personal savior. He graduated from the Baptist Bible College in Springfield, Missouri, and founded the Thomas Road Baptist Church in his hometown of Lynchburg in 1956.[6] In 1967, he founded the Lynchburg Christian Academy.[7]

Two years before he founded the academy, the Supreme Court ruled in *Brown v. Board of Education of Topeka* that segregation of children in public schools was unconstitutional. After this ruling, private white Christian schools began to spring up all around the country as a protest against Brown. Lynchburg Christian Academy was one such school. Private schools were not required to follow the Brown decision. Falwell Sr. was a segregationist. In a sermon he preached in 1965, nine years after the Supreme Court ruling, he defended racial segregation. He used the story of the encounter between Jesus and the Samaritan woman at the well in John 5:6–12 to make his point. He claimed that when the woman said to Jesus, "How is it that you, a Jew, ask a drink of me, a woman of Samaria?" she was trying to draw Jesus into a discussion about segregation by highlighting the reality that Jews discriminated against Samaritans. But instead of being drawn into that discussion, Jesus ignored her prompting and instead focused on her spiritual well-being. Jesus told her all about her sinful life and her need for salvation. She received the gift of salvation that Jesus offered and through her testimony her hometown was also saved.[8]

For Falwell, Jesus's interaction with the woman was instructive for those who claimed to be Christians in his day. Christians, he argued, were not called to reform external conditions. Christians should only be focused on saving souls. He made this statement long before he decided to found the Moral Majority. In a sermon he preached at Thomas Road after the *Brown v. Board* ruling, he preached about his objection to the ruling:

> If Chief Justice Warren and his associates had known God's word and had desired to do the Lord's will, I am quite confident that the 1954 decision would never have been made. . . . The facilities should be separate. When God has drawn a line of distinction, we should not attempt to cross that line.[9]

Falwell believed that the Bible clearly prohibited racial integration. He felt God wanted the races to live separately. In the same sermon he went on to say, "The true Negro does not want integration. . . . He realizes his potential is far better among his own race."[10] So, in keeping with his own biblical interpretation and racist beliefs, he founded the Lynchburg Christian Academy to keep white children from being forced to attend school with African American children.

However, his efforts and the efforts of other white Christian segregationists were thwarted by a decision of the United States District Court for the District of Columbia, *Green v. Connally*. The decision declared that even private schools cannot discriminate based on race.[11] Soon after this ruling in 1971, Christian schools such as Lynchburg Christian Academy began receiving letters from the Internal Revenue Service inquiring about their admissions policies as it relates to race. This ruling and subsequent requirements to submit to government intervention of their private school admissions policies had many white Christian evangelicals looking for a way to reverse this government policy. They looked for a presidential candidate who would support their agenda.

Evangelicals believed they had found their candidate in fellow evangelical Christian, Jimmy Carter. However, rather than helping to further their cause of segregation, Carter's IRS commissioner proposed that schools that were founded or expanded during the period of desegregation of public schools should also meet a quota for minority students.[12] In addition, Carter supported the Equal Rights Amendment, gay rights, and abortion rights. So evangelicals, completely frustrated with Carter, looked for someone who would support their agenda for the 1980 presidential election.[13]

Evangelicals chose to support Ronald Reagan, a divorced, remarried former actor who became governor of California and signed a bill into law legalizing abortion during his governorship. Choosing Reagan indicates that abortion was not a central issue for conservatives until the 1980s. During the presidential campaign, Reagan shared his belief that the federal government had been overreaching for years. He contended that power needed to be returned to states and local communities. He supported the teaching of creationism[14] in public schools, was a virulent anticommunist, denounced the decline of the traditional family, and criticized the promiscuity of the 1960s generation.[15] He made no promises related to abortion.[16]

Falwell's views on race can be understood not only by his commitment to segregation but also through his views of the Civil Rights Movement in general and Martin Luther King Jr. in particular. During the 1960s as Lyndon Johnson introduced civil rights legislation, Falwell conspired with J. Edgar Hoover to distribute propaganda created by the FBI against Martin Luther

King Jr. to discredit him and the entire Civil Rights Movement.[17] In a sermon entitled "Ministers and Marchers," Falwell expressed his disapproval of the Civil Rights Movement:

> While the church leaders are so obsessed with the alleged discrimination against Negroes in the South, very little is said about the same situation in the North. . . . If as much effort could be put into winning people to Jesus Christ across the land as is being exerted in the present civil rights movement, America would be turned upside down for God. Hate and prejudice would certainly be in a great measure overcome. Churches would be filled with sincere souls seeking God.[18]

In a *Crossfire* interview with Pat Buchanan in 1983, Falwell objected to the establishment of a Martin Luther King Jr. holiday supposedly because King's FBI records were under seal. Since the records were under seal, Falwell contended there was no way of attesting to King's true character. "He could be as clean as Billy Graham," Falwell said.[19] But there was no way of knowing without having access to his FBI records.

Falwell's commitment to racial segregation was not only exemplified in his opposition to integration of schools; he also supported segregation on an international scale through his support of the Botha regime in South Africa. While many public officials and clergy throughout the world and in the United States called for economic sanctions against the Botha regime to help bring an end to Apartheid, Falwell opposed sanctions. He publicly denounced Bishop Desmond Tutu as a phony and began a campaign to stop the imposition of sanctions against South Africa.[20]

Having established Falwell's history of racism, we can now move to analysis of one of his sermons for the ways his preaching supports the hierarchies that have shaped the social, cultural, educational, political, and economic institutions of the United States. We will also examine his preaching for ways white culture is portrayed as being the norm against which all other cultures, groups, and individuals are measured and often found wanting.

In March 1982, Falwell spoke at the Cleveland City Club. Though the setting was secular, Falwell contended during the question-and-answer period at the end that the words he had spoken are ones he spoke often from his own pulpit at the Thomas Road Baptist Church. Therefore, we will consider this speech a sermon. The purpose of the sermon was to convey to the listeners the principles of the Moral Majority. In the sermon, Falwell highlighted several principles that facilitated America's ascendency to greatness in the past and if embraced once more, would allow America to experience greatness again. I will summarize the introduction and key principles before providing an analysis of each.

INTRODUCTION

"Living by God's principles promotes a nation to greatness. Violating Godly principles brings a nation to shame." With this statement Falwell communicates one of the central tenants of the Moral Majority. It is also foundational for the subsequent arguments he makes in the sermon. He shares his belief that after World War II America began to forget the principles that made the nation great.

Analysis

The whiteness that needs to be unmasked here lies in the contention that the United States was a moral nation before World War II. In order to focus on the post–World War II era as the period of the United States' moral demise, he had to ignore obvious immoralities such as Native American genocide, African American slavery, discriminatory immigration policies (such as the Chinese Exclusion Act of the late 1800s), and Japanese internment during World War II, just to name a few. Whiteness often does not perceive atrocities perpetrated against people of color to be immoral. In homiletical whiteness, wrong exists when laws, traditions, and practices negatively impact white people. When white people are benefitting from immoral behavior against people of color who are the minority, the immoral behavior is deemed necessary or inconsequential for the well-being of the majority.

After World War II, social unrest began to be the norm in American society. The Civil Rights Movement of the 1950s and 1960s, the gay rights movement of the 1960s and 1970s, and the fight to pass the Equal Rights Amendment in the 1970s and early 1980s were all affronts to the values of the Moral Majority. The web of oppressions that supported whiteness was beginning to unravel. The Moral Majority was a way for those committed to whiteness to fight back.

PRINCIPLE ONE: THE PRINCIPLE OF THE DIGNITY OF HUMAN LIFE

Falwell argued that if people looked back through the history of this nation, they would find that the United States had always stood up for the dignity of human life. He then rationalizes Reagan's policies in El Salvador that led to the deaths of hundreds of people. He shares that he supported Reagan's policies in El Salvador because it was a rational thing to do. Reagan's policies were intended to stop the spread of communism before it made its way to the United States. *Roe v. Wade* was a great violation of this principle of the dignity of human life. With the deaths of 10–12 million people (since abortions were made legal), he claimed that more died by abortion than by all the wars that have ever been fought. God is displeased with this nation for participating in this "biological holocaust."

Analysis

Whiteness can justify the use of military force against people of color when it is in support of policies they feel advance the preservation of their culture and beliefs. Reagan was a virulent anticommunist. When the leftist Sandinista revolutionaries in El Salvador overthrew the corrupt government and began to redistribute wealth and expropriate large estates, Reagan began funding the overthrow of the Sandinistas to the tune of 3 billion dollars. While Reagan's policies claimed to be stopping the spread of communism, the policies of the Sandinistas were socialist. Reagan effectively stopped the spread of socialism in Central America.[21] Hundreds of innocent men, women, and children were massacred by Reagan administration-backed forces.[22]

Whiteness often does not apply the principle of the dignity of human life to people of color. Whiteness, in this case, prioritized the lives of the unborn over the lives of already born people of color because powerful social conservatives discovered that white Christian conservatives would vote if abortion was on the ballot.[23] Once white Christian conservatives showed up to the polls, they would support other policies the Moral Majority wanted them to.

PRINCIPLE TWO: PRINCIPLE OF THE TRADITIONAL MONOGAMIST FAMILY

Falwell insisted that marriage is for one man and one woman for a lifetime. He claimed that since World War II, with the assistance of Hollywood, the television industry, and social engineers, the nation had forgotten that the family is the basic unit of society. Falwell contended that there was little emphasis on family besides *Little House on the Prairie* and *The Waltons*. Television should reflect the reality that 93% of all Americans believe the husband and wife relationship is the ideal. Falwell stated that he did believe in civil rights and housing accommodations for homosexuals. However, society should not condone homosexuality as an acceptable lifestyle (legally or otherwise).

Analysis

Whiteness is threatened by abortion. The fertility rates of whites have been decreasing for several decades while the fertility rates of African Americans and Hispanic Americans have been increasing. If white women in particular are given access to abortion, the cultural dominance of the white race is in peril.[24] In addition, if women have access to abortion they can achieve social independence and no longer need men to take care of them. The roles of women in society would change because they would no longer be confined to the home and be full-time nurturers of children.[25] Whiteness requires iconic portrayals of "traditional" white families to uphold its cultural ideals. Note the ideal television families Falwell cited were white where the males are head of the households, women stayed at home to raise the children, and the children were obedient to the parents.

Whiteness is also threatened by homosexuality. The stated objection to homosexuality is that it is in contradiction with Scripture. One actual objection is that homosexuality is outside of the white, straight male norm that is taught, socialized, and politicized. The inability of two males to naturally procreate is also a concern for those concerned about the diminishing rates of fertility among white people. In addition, sexism, male domination, and heterosexism are completely dependent on men having unrestricted access to women and women relating exclusively to men.[26] To make their public case against gay rights, adherents of whiteness likened homosexuals to criminals such as pedophiles, rapists, and murderers.[27]

PRINCIPLE THREE: PRINCIPLE OF THE WORK ETHIC

Falwell contended that the government should help those who cannot help themselves. Instead, this country raised up two or three generations that believe they are owed a living because they belong to the human family. He believed that we should teach young people, even those who do not have to work, to learn how to make a living, learn how to live and become self-sufficient. Instead, he argued, this country has become lazy. A doctor in Boston was criticizing Reagan because of cutbacks in entitlements and claiming that the aged are being hurt while at the same time Reagan is spending on warheads, building a $50,000 dollar dining room at the White House where senior staff could eat and meet at the same time. Falwell defended Reagan by arguing that Reagan did not create the problems. Problems are not going to be corrected next week or next year. It is going to take a long time. Falwell also contended that redistribution of wealth is problematic.

Analysis

Whiteness rears its head in this principle through its unwavering commitment to the quintessential individualistic, pull-yourself-up-by-your-bootstraps

American mentality. While Falwell acknowledged that cutbacks on entitlements may be hurting seniors, he was still staunchly opposed to the redistribution of wealth even if it meant that the elderly had to suffer. This unqualified commitment to support Reagan and his policies revealed that though he said he believed the country should help those who could not help themselves, he was willing to sacrifice this belief to publicly support a president he hoped would pass legislation that would promote the Moral Majority's agenda.

Implicit in this principle is the Moral Majority's support of Welfare Reform which was built on the racist trope of the black "Welfare Queen." The Welfare Queen was a narrative produced for white culture to denigrate the image of a single black woman who is head of her household. She works full time and has several children whom she cannot properly supervise because she is away from home for large periods of time working to support them. She is single because of her attitude and aggressiveness that her male friends and husbands find emasculating. Her black children fail in school and in life because of her failure to embody good moral values that would translate into better social status and conditions were they fully embraced. From a white, male, epistemological worldview, white upper- and middle-class children succeed because of the care and nurture they receive at home. Black children could succeed as well if they received similar attention.[28] The mythology of the Welfare Queen fails to acknowledge the reality of racial systemic injustice.

PRINCIPLE FOUR: THE ABRAHAMIC COVENANT

For this principle, Falwell proclaimed that God deals with nations based on how they relate to the Jews, even though God loves all the races. The Moral Majority opposes any peace accords with the Jordanians. Falwell insisted that many nations that surround Israel are committed to its extinction, but that God is dealing with America favorably because of our treatment of the state of Israel. He asserted that there can be no doubt that legally, beginning in 1948, the land belongs to the Jews. He based this belief on the Abrahamic Covenant in Genesis 12:1–3 which says, "I will bless those who bless you."

Analysis

In this principle, whiteness is upheld by the presumption that the fate of the United States is dependent on the Moral Majority's interpretation of Genesis 12:1–3, also known as the Abrahamic Covenant. The Moral Majority maintains that it relies on a literal interpretation of Scripture, which they claim as the source of their moral authority as arbiter of national and international events. As such, their steadfast support of Israel and its policies is buttressed by their literalist interpretation of the Bible that they believe should result in the United States supporting Israel. This, in turn, will result in God blessing the United States. But if we waver in our support in any way, we will be cursed by God.

Their biblical interpretation prevents them from acknowledging Israel's human rights abuses. Whiteness, in this case, does not object to the suffering and death of people they deem to be living outside of the will of God. They are collateral damage.

PRINCIPLE FIVE: PRINCIPLE OF GOD-CENTERED EDUCATION

Falwell and the Moral Majority believe in God-centered but not Christ-centered education. He was educated in public schools which were his only contact with the Bible or hymn or prayer. He shared with his listeners that his father never attended church in his life. He (Falwell) was studying mechanical engineering in a college at the age of eighteen when he heard Dr. Charles E. Fuller's radio broadcast, the old-fashioned revival hour. He accepted Christ as his savior and bought his first Bible in January 1952. He enrolled in Baptist Bible College in Springfield, Missouri. He then clarified that the Moral Majority is not in favor of (prescribed) mandated prayers or Bible readings. They are for the recognition of God in schools. He argued that Madalyn (O'Hair)[29] had the right to be an atheist with all the rights and privileges and that she did not build this country nor her vintage. Rather, he contended, the nation was built by God-fearing people and has become great because of it. He believed that voluntary silent prayer would not be a violation of the separation of church and state.

Analysis

The term "God-centered education" is code for educating children into the ways, beliefs, traditions, and values of white conservative evangelical Fundamentalist Christianity. The principle of God-centered education is a means of ensuring the future of whiteness by teaching future generations to live by its core tenants. Whiteness is at the center of this principle because its impetus derives from white conservatives striving for racial segregation.

Beginning with the *Green v. Connally* decision which required private schools to admit students of all races, conservatives have been in pursuit of policies that would enable them to receive tax exempt status for their private Christian schools without any mandate for racial integration. The Moral

Majority had hoped that Reagan would be the one to facilitate this. However, Reagan did not advocate policies that supported private Christian schools.

PRINCIPLE SIX: PRINCIPLE OF DIVINELY ORDAINED INSTITUTIONS

According to Falwell, there are only three institutions ordained by God: home, state or civil government, and religious institutions (the tabernacle, temple, synagogue, church). In order for any nation to be on solid footing, the three legs of this tripod must be equal and sturdy. Falwell contended that the Moral Majority worked for the rebuilding of the traditional family, healthy government and free government. They do not believe in violating the separation of church and state. He argued that nobody ever yelled at Dr. King for violating the separation of church and state. However, when conservative men stand up, everybody has a hernia and there are more of us. Falwell insisted that he has the right to speak as long as he doesn't violate the rights and privileges of others. He asserted that there was a president in the White House who believed in the sanctity of life and was taking a stand on these issues. He further espoused Reagan's agenda by stating that the president believed in the free enterprise system and was trying to reverse the terrible trend toward socialism and was committed to rebuilding the military defenses of this country. He ended this part of the sermon by insisting that Reagan hates war.

Analysis

Falwell packed this part of the sermon with a jumble of thoughts and ideas that he believed supported the beliefs of the Moral Majority. The whiteness underlying this particular principle can be unmasked by highlighting Falwell's wholehearted endorsement of the free enterprise system while denouncing the evils of socialism. Falwell and the Moral Majority perpetuate the American Dream mythology that specifically excludes those who are not white. They repeat the false belief that in this country anyone who "works hard and plays by the rules" can attain the American Dream while ignoring the fact that whites enjoy significant economic advantages not afforded to people of color who start from a deficit before even entering the marketplace. Nevertheless, free market capitalism is at the heart of their oft-told myth of the American Dream.

The whiteness of the Moral Majority also relies upon the hierarchy of biblical texts to further its economic agenda. Texts such as Romans 13 instruct the members of the early Christian community to subject themselves to governing authorities because governing authorities have been appointed by God. Texts such as the household codes in Colossians 3 and Ephesians 5 provide details of a divinely ordered household. Texts such as Matthew 16 declare that the founding of the church was God's will. However, biblical scholars have critiqued these texts as being written to maintain power and influence of particular factions in the church. For example, Elisabeth Schussler Fiorenza critiques the household codes. Fiorenza believes that, like Paul, the authors of Colossians, Ephesians, 1 Timothy, Titus, and 1 Peter were motivated to prescribe patriarchal hierarchy by their desire for the Christian community to meet the Aristotelian-inspired patriarchal standards of the larger Greco-Roman society. The household codes directed wealthy women not to serve as leaders of churches. The codes made it possible for male and female slaves to be exploited, even in the Christian community.[30] Highlighting divine ordination as principle provides the Moral Majority with biblical justification for many elements of its agenda such as female subordination, LGBTQIA+ oppression, and racial discrimination and marginalization. As a result, they reject academic biblical scholarship and its critique of the Bible for fear that this would threaten their hold on patriarchal power inside and outside of the church.

CONCLUSION

Homiletical whiteness is the art of preaching racial, social, political and economic hierarchy that seeks to persuade social, cultural, educational, political, and economic institutions of our society to support the mythology of white supremacy. Jerry Falwell Sr.'s sermon provided a vision of a world dominated by the principles of the Moral Majority. In that world, women are dominated by men; LGBTQIA have few, if any, civil rights; and black and brown people throughout the nation and around the world suffer from collateral damage from the military and economic dictates of a would-be theocracy thought to be divinely ordained by God. Just as we interrogated Falwell Sr.'s sermon, all preachers need to interrogate our own sermons for elements of whiteness that serve to empower some while disenfranchising, marginalizing, and oppressing others. Guiding our interrogation must be our belief that racial hierarchies, as well as all other hierarchies, are anathema for the kin-dom of God.[31] We must continually strive for a world in which all people are able to live the lives they were created by God to live and the principles of the Moral Majority are supplanted by the more Godly principles of equity, justice, and peace for all.

NOTES

1. Carol Tator and Frances Henry, *Racial Profiling in Canada: Challenging the Myth of "a Few Bad Apples"* (Toronto, ON and Buffalo, NY: University of Toronto Press, 2006), 353.

2. Ibid, 46–47.

3. Christine Smith, *Preaching as Weeping, Confession, and Resistance: Radical Responses to Radical Evil* (Louisville, KY: Westminster John Knox Press, 1992), 3.

4. Doug Banwart, "Jerry Falwell, the Rise of the Moral Majority, and the 1980 Election," *Western Illinois Historical Review* V, no. Spring (2013): 133.

5. "Mission Statement," *LU Online* (2019), http://www.liberty.edu/index.cfm?PID=6899 (accessed on October 14, 2019).

6. The Editors of Encyclopedia Britannica, "Jerry Falwell American Minister," *Encyclopedia Britannica* (2019), https://www.britannica.com/topic/Moral-Majority (accessed on September 13, 2019).

7. "Founder," *Liberty University Online* (2019), http://www.liberty.edu/aboutliberty/index.cfm?PID=6921 (accessed on September 13, 2019).

8. Matthew Avery Sutton, *Jerry Falwell and the Rise of the Religious Right: A Brief History with Documents*. The Bedford Series in History and Culture (Boston, MA: Bedford/St. Martin's, 2013), Kindle Edition. Chapter 2.8.

9. Max Blumenthal, "Agent of Intolerance," *The Nation* (2007), https://www.thenation.com/article/agent-intolerance/ (accessed on September 13, 2019).

10. Blumenthal, "Agent."

11. A. Section 501(c) (3) of the Internal Revenue Code of 1954 does not provide a tax exemption for, and Section 170(a)–(c) of the Code does not provide a deduction for a contribution to, any organization that is operated for educational purposes unless the school or other educational institution involved has a racially nondiscriminatory policy as to students. B. As used in this Order, the term "racially nondiscriminatory policy as to students" means that the school or other educational institution admits the students of any race to all the rights, privileges, programs, and activities generally accorded or made available to students at that school, and which includes, specifically but not exclusively, a policy of making no discrimination on the basis of race in administration of educational policies, applications for admission, of scholarship and loan programs, and athletic and extra-curricular programs. See "Green V. Connally, 330 F. Supp. 1150 (D.D.C. 1971)," *Justia US Law* (1971), https://law.justia.com/cases/federal/district-courts/FSupp/330/1150/2126265/ (accessed on September 27, 2019).

12. Randall Herbert Balmer, *Evangelicalism in America* (Waco, TX: Baylor University Press, 2016), 112–13.

13. Sutton, Part One, Kindle Edition.

14. Creationism, in this case, refers to the belief that the actual history of the origins of the universe and all life (human, animal, plant, etc.) lived on it can be found in the early chapters of the book of Genesis. See *The Stanford Encyclopedia of Philosophy*, s.v. "Creationism," https://plato.stanford.edu/cgi-bin/encyclopedia/archinfo.cgi?entry=creationism (accessed July 6, 2021). Also see "Creation," *Answers in Genesis* (2021), https://answersingenesis.org/creation/ (accessed on July 6, 2021).

15. Sutton, Part One.

16. In the years leading up to the 1973 *Roe v. Wade* Supreme Court decision, the Southern Baptist Convention passed a resolution to work for legislation that would

allow for the possibility of abortion under conditions such as rape, incest, severe fetal deformity, and evidence of damage to the emotional, mental, and physical health of the mother. The Southern Baptists reaffirmed that position on abortion in 1974 and in 1976. W. A. Criswell who had been president of the Southern Baptist Convention stated when *Roe v. Wade* was handed down, "I have always felt that it was only after a child was born and had a life separate from its mother that it became an individual person." He further stated, "and it has always, therefore, seemed to me that what is best for the mother and for the future should be allowed." Some Baptists even applauded the decision. W. Barry Garrett of Baptist Press wrote, "Religious liberty, human equality and justice are advanced by the Supreme Court abortion decision." Even the evangelicals who disagreed with the decision were not motivated to mobilize against the ruling. Floyd Robertson of the National Association of Evangelicals did not believe the decision would warrant legal action by evangelical. Rather, he contended that the decision was an indication of how different the moral standards of the state were from the higher standards of evangelicals, "The church and state must be separate. The actions and conduct of Christians transcend the secular community for which the state is responsible."

17. "Jerry Falwell Sr., Laying Racist Foundations," *The Rogue Fundagelical: Going AWOL from the Culture Wars and Loving Humanity* (2019), https://rcwilkinson.com/2019/05/09/jerry-falwell-sr-laying-racist-foundations/ (accessed on September 13, 2019),

18. Sutton, Kindle Edition, Chapter 2.8.

19. Jerry Falwell and Pat Buchanan, "Falwell Opposes MLK Day in 1983," recorded 1983, *CNN*, Atlanta, GA, https://www.youtube.com/watch?v=lcQbzZM-W2Vo (accessed on September 13, 2019).

20. Robert Pear, "Falwell Denounces Tutu as a Phony," *The New York Times*, August 21, 1985, https://www.nytimes.com/1985/08/21/world/falwell-denounces-tutu-as-a-phony.html?login=email&auth=login-email (accessed on September 15, 2019).

21. "Reagan and the 'Iran-Contra' Affair," *BBC News* (2004), http://news.bbc.co.uk/2/hi/americas/269619.stm (accessed on September 9, 2019).

22. Raymond Bonner, "Time for a UA Apology to El Salvador," *The Nation* (2016), https://www.thenation.com/article/time-for-a-us-apology-to-el-salvador/ (accessed on September 28, 2019).

23. "Jerry Falwell Sr., Laying Racist Foundations."

24. Manuel Garcia Jr., "Abortion: White Panic over Demographic Dilution?" (2019), https://www.counterpunch.org/2019/05/20/abortion-white-panic-over-demographic-dilution/ (accessed on June 30, 2021).

25. Banwart, *Jerry Falwell*, 139.

26. Christine M. Smith, *Preaching Justice: Ethnic and Cultural Perspectives* (Cleveland, OH: United Church Press, 1998), 87–109.

27. Banwart, *Jerry Falwell*, 146.

28. Debra J. Mumford, *Envisioning the Reign of God: Preaching for Tomorrow*, 1st ed. (Valley Forge: Judson Press, 2019), 135–36.

29. Madalyn Murray O'Hair sued Baltimore Public Schools in 1960 for requiring students to read from the bible and recite the Lord's Prayer in school. The case went

all the way to the Supreme Court and resulted in a decision to end the requirements of read from the bible and recite prayers. PBS, "People & Ideas: Madalyn Murray O'Hair," *God in America* (2010), https://www.pbs.org/wgbh/pages/frontline/godinamerica/people/madalyn-murray-ohair.html (accessed on September 25, 2021).

30. Elisabeth Schüssler Fiorenza, *In Memory of Her: A Feminist Theological Reconstruction of Christian Origins*, 10th anniversary ed. (New York: Crossroad, 1994), 291.

31. The "kin-dom" of God is a term coined by Ada Maria Isasi Diaz for a new world order in which abuse and exploitation are a thing of the past. See Debra J. Mumford, *Envisioning the Reign of God: Preaching for Tomorrow*, 1st ed. (Valley Forge: Judson Press, 2019), 146.

BIBLIOGRAPHY

Balmer, Randall Herbert. *Evangelicalism in America*. Waco, TX: Baylor University Press, 2016.

Banwart, Doug. "Jerry Falwell, the Rise of the Moral Majority, and the 1980 Election." *Western Illinois Historical Review* V, no. Spring (2013), 133–157.

Blumenthal, Max. "Agent of Intolerance." *The Nation* (2007), https://www.thenation.com/article/agent-intolerance/ (accessed on September 13, 2019).

Bonner, Raymond. "Time for a Us Apology to El Salvador." *The Nation* (2016), https://www.thenation.com/article/time-for-a-us-apology-to-el-salvador/ (accessed on September 28, 2019).

Britanica, The Editors of Encyclopedia. "Jerry Falwell American Minister." *Encyclopedia Britanica* (2019), https://www.britannica.com/topic/Moral-Majority (accessed on September 13, 2019).

"Creation." *Answers in Genesis* (2021), https://answersingenesis.org/creation/ (accessed on July 6, 2021).

Falwell, Jerry and Pat Buchanan. *Falwell Opposes MLK Day in 1983*. Atlanta, GA: CNN, 1983.

"Founder." *Liberty University Online* (2019), http://www.liberty.edu/aboutliberty/index.cfm?PID=6921 (accessed on September 13, 2019).

Garcia, Manuel, Jr. "Abortion: White Panic over Demographic Dilution?" (2019), https://www.counterpunch.org/2019/05/20/abortion-white-panic-over-demographic-dilution/ (accessed on June 30, 2021).

"Green V. Connally, 330 F. Supp. 1150 (D.D.C. 1971)." *Justia US Law* (1971), https://law.justia.com/cases/federal/district-courts/FSupp/330/1150/2126265/ (accessed on September 27, 2019).

"Jerry Falwell Sr., Laying Racist Foundations." *The Rogue Fundagelical: Going AWOL from the Culture Wars and Loving Humanity* (2019), https://rcwilkinson.com/2019/05/09/jerry-falwell-sr-laying-racist-foundations/ (accessed on September 13, 2019).

"Mission Statement." *LU Online* (2019), http://www.liberty.edu/index.cfm?PID=6899 (accessed on October 14, 2019).

Mumford, Debra J. *Envisioning the Reign of God: Preaching for Tomorrow*, 1st ed. Valley Forge: Judson Press, 2019.

PBS. "People & Ideas: Madalyn Murray O'Hair." *God in America* (2010), https://www.pbs.org/wgbh/pages/frontline/godinamerica/people/madalyn-murray-ohair.html (accessed on September 13, 2019).

Pear, Robert. "Falwell Denounces Tutu as a Phony." *The New York Times*, August 21, 1985, https://www.nytimes.com/1985/08/21/world/falwell-denounces-tutu-as-a-phony.html?login=email&auth=login-email (accessed on September 15, 2019).

"Reagan and the 'Iran-Contra' Affair." *BBC News* (2004), http://news.bbc.co.uk/2/hi/americas/269619.stm (accessed on September 9, 2019).

Ruse, Michael. *The Stanford Encyclopedia of Philosophy*, 2021.

Schüssler Fiorenza, Elisabeth. *In Memory of Her: A Feminist Theological Reconstruction of Christian Origins*, 10th anniversary ed. New York: Crossroad, 1994.

Smith, Christine M. *Preaching Justice: Ethnic and Cultural Perspectives*. Cleveland, OH: United Church Press, 1998.

Sutton, Matthew Avery. *Jerry Falwell and the Rise of the Religious Right: A Brief History with Documents*. The Bedford Series in History and Culture. Boston: Bedford/St. Martin's, 2013.

Tator, Carol and Frances Henry. *Racial Profiling in Canada: Challenging the Myth of "a Few Bad Apples."* Toronto, ON; Buffalo, NY: University of Toronto Press, 2006.

Chapter 3

The Towering Sermon

Duke Chapel as Monument to White Supremacy

Peace Pyunghwa Lee and David Stark

This is the memorial chapel, the little side chapel inside Duke Chapel. And, it's a memorial chapel, because it's here that we remember the Duke family. In particular, three Dukes are laid to rest: Washington Duke, James B. Duke, and Benjamin Duke. And, this chapel—side chapel and also Duke Chapel—really stand in their honor because Duke Chapel represents their legacy.[1]

I, Peace, want to start by naming the violence and psychological and emotional labor of having to spell out what is obvious to my body and write what I know in my bones to be true. Given that this writing is included in a larger collective project to the goal of "Unmasking homiletical whiteness," I also want to write in a way that is comfortable for me and resists the academic norms and conventions that in themselves perpetuate whiteness.

I, Peace, am a member of the AAPI community, more specifically I am a Korean immigrant who was born in Korea and lived there and the Philippines before immigrating to the United States against my will and under duress at the age of eleven. I mostly identify as a member of the Korean diaspora and my writing stems from my body that is marked by the larger history of imperial colonialism, war, Christian missionizing, and ongoing U.S. military occupation of my motherland. My life in the Amerikkkan empire can be summed as a series of "bad days" ever since I landed on this part of Amerikkka as its project is global and worldwide.[2] I want to name that I am attempting to write this chapter in the cruel month of April 2021 in Amerikkka that is still in the throes of a COVID-19 pandemic that has needlessly cost the lives of millions across the world. I want to name that even as I grew up experiencing precarity when it comes to health care access, I was more terrified of the virus that is white supremacy and white racial terrorism as it continues to metastasize and seeks to annihilate people of color in all sorts of insidious ways. I write with anguish about the ongoing state-sanctioned murder of black and brown and Indigenous and yellow and disabled bodies. But I also want to name that I am especially grieving the victims of March 16 Atlanta spa shooting and April 15 Indianapolis FedEx shooting which were clearly racially motivated. I am ultimately writing this from a place of 恨/한/ "han" as I mourn and grieve the ceaselessly piling bodies of color who are sacrificed at the altar of white supremacy.[3]

I, David, write as someone seeking to confront whiteness in the academy, in the church, and in my own thinking.[4] I am a white man. I am a Methodist whose seminary and doctoral work was at Duke University. I have been connected to this institution for over twenty years—long enough to have imbibed most of their stories and wrestled with many of their poisoning aftertastes. Currently, I teach at an Episcopal University whose original aim was to be *the* institution that best supported and promoted an enslaving white supremacist society. Even today, the campus of the University of the South has been described by its own historian as "a Confederate memorial."[5] This same historian, Woody Register, is leading a group of scholars, supported by the University regents and the vice chancellor, who seek to confront and dismantle these memorials and the white supremacist ideology they perpetuate.[6] This is work to which I am committed personally and professionally.

We seek to write this chapter centering our own experiences as well as what we have come to uncover and learn about Duke Chapel during our years of living in Durham and working on various projects at Duke University that centered the preaching in Duke Chapel. Our aim in this chapter is more than to communicate that Duke Chapel is a monument to white supremacy. We are not interested in simply scapegoating Duke Chapel when it is just like any other white Amerikkkan church whose physical structure cannot be separated or disentangled from the larger Amerikkkan history of racially gendered settler colonialism.[7] As a member of the Korean diaspora, Peace cannot help but think of Christian churches in Korea that were built and established by Western missionaries in Western architectural tradition with white Jesus to boot. So, monuments to white Christian supremacy are found beyond the borders of this country. That said, it is interesting to think about Duke Chapel given that it is situated in the formerly Confederate South and used to be a segregated institution that has now emerged as a world-class institution due to the obscene amount of wealth generated by slave laborers for the Duke family. Studying the history and architecture of this chapel helps uncover ways that homiletical space in Amerikkkan churches continues to be shaped by and for white supremacy. Further, we believe that unmasking the towering sermon that is Duke Chapel can offer insights for confronting and dismantling white supremacist homiletical space in other contexts.[8]

PLANNING A MONUMENT TO WHITE SUPREMACY

The university's own self-mythologizing of the founding of Duke Chapel is of deep interest. In "A Brief History" under "History & Architecture" of Duke Chapel on its website, it reads that James "Buck" Duke while walking through a forest with his friend to find a suitable site for a new university "paused at the highest point" and said, "Here's where it ought to be."[9] Note here that Buck was born to wealthy industrialist Washington Duke, who owned a tobacco plantation and company. Buck took over the business and under his ruthless leadership and robber baron business tactics he amassed a fortune. Buck's American Tobacco Company had a stranglehold on the market.[10] Buck's avaricious and ruthless business practices directly contributed to the Black Patch Tobacco Wars.[11] He was also repeatedly sued by his business partners and shareholders, so one can imagine what kind of a plantation owner he might have been.

So, it is this Buck and his insatiable greed because of whom so much blood and sweat and tears have been shed that Duke Chapel was first conceived. Buck simply decides where to plot the chapel, settling on "the highest point" without consulting anyone. There is no acknowledgment, much less care, that the area he claims and plans to deforest is part of the ancestral lands of the Shakori, Eno, and Tuscarora people.[12] Perhaps Buck, a white supremacist, was thinking of the verse, "You are the light of the world. A city built on a hill cannot be hidden" (Mt. 5:14), when he decided the new campus church "ought" to be on this high point. Whatever the case, it seems clear that Buck was more influenced by supremacy than the gospel,[13] for by his own account the chapel was intended to be "a great towering church which will *dominate*" and "have a profound influence on the spiritual life of the young men and women who come here."[14]

The building of Duke Chapel's domination was designed specifically to extend into anti-black domination and to influence white supremacist spirituality. While at Duke Chapel and West Campus in 1939, Louis Austin reflected:

> If white people have labored in the factories of the American tobacco industry for less than enough on which to live, they have had the satisfaction of knowing that their children may reap the benefits in a school that provides the very best training. If Negroes have done the same thing, it must pierce their hearts to know that Duke University has been built for every other race under the sun but

theirs. Chinese, Japanese, Germans, Russians or any other foreign race may be admitted to the school; but the American Negro stands alone as the one human being on earth, too loathsome in the eyes of the American white man to share the benefits of Duke University. Is this the price of humbleness? Is this the price of faithfulness? Where is justice? Where is right? Where is God?[15]

It took minutes for Austin, who was a journalist and editor of the *Carolina Times*, the preeminent black newspaper in North Carolina, to understand that the chapel and its surrounding campus were designed to use truth, justice, and divinity to perpetuate white male dominance, especially over black human beings.

Duke Chapel was the first building that was planned for the new campus and the last to be completed. This drawn-out process gave ample opportunity for practicing domination. It is noteworthy that in the early 1930s, as the first stones were laid of this monument, "students often gathered near the huts of the stone carvers that occupied the land directly behind the construction site; they enjoyed watching the Chapel rise higher and higher."[16] This seemingly benign statement is quite sinister when we consider that the students watching this white supremacist man's dream tower rise higher and higher were privileged white men and perhaps women who were literally overseeing a monument to white supremacy built by black laborers as well as poor or skilled white laborers.

There has been some attempt to tell the stories of who built Duke Chapel. Most notably, in the summer of 2018, a handful of undergraduate students of Duke University in partnership with Franklin Humanities Institute and Duke Chapel, under the leadership of the current dean, Luke Powery, examined building and genealogical records. Their research uncovered hundreds of names of laborers and craftsmen who worked to build the chapel and the campus.[17] The desire to interrogate who actually built the Duke Chapel was itself prompted by the removal of the Robert E. Lee statue after it was defaced following the Charlottesville race riot. Removing Lee from the portico created a gap in the chapel's monument to white supremacy. While there was some debate about what or who should fill the niche, ultimately Duke University decided to leave it empty.[18]

About this gap, Luke Powery commented: "That open space is also an opening toward the possibility of healing and hope in the future."[19] Perhaps there is indeed an opening for change now. Yet, stepping into this gap will require more than the removal of one offending statue. For instance, it is surprising that the university did not also remove the statue next to Robert E. Lee, a depiction of Sidney Lanier who is known as the "poet of the confederacy."[20] And, beyond memorials to Confederate, white men, the chapel still has many other monuments that preach white supremacy.

THE TOWERING SERMON TODAY

Monuments are designed to claim space and shape memory in ways that have ongoing impact on the surrounding community. In his recent book, *Cut in Stone: Confederate Monuments and Theological Disruption*, Ryan Newson observes:

> Confederate monuments unquestionably conjure forces and attitudes that cry out for theological analysis: questions about where a society should be headed, the nature of remembrance, and constant evocations of the language of sacrifice. . . . Undermining Confederate monuments at their most fundamental level must include undermining the theology that they assume and reinforce for future generations; anything less is to ignore a huge part of their performative power.[21]

Implicit to Newson's assessment is that Christian proclamation in and beyond the pulpit needs to reflect more and to communicate better about the role monuments play in shaping our theological worldviews. It is not simply the Lee and Lanier statues that are a problem at the Duke Chapel. It is the white supremacist theology etched in stone and cut into glass that lies at the heart of this preaching monument.

When I, Peace, first visited Duke Divinity School in March 2016 to discern matriculation after I was offered an acceptance, I was unable to visit its famed chapel because it was under renovation that lasted several months. Growing up charismatic and "low church," I remember thinking even then how buildings like Duke Chapel required tremendous cost and care for its upkeep. It was only in writing this chapter that I uncovered that "Duke University invested $19.2 million in a significant restoration of the Chapel."[22] When I finally did visit for the first time, accompanied by mostly white colleagues of mine, I remember being absolutely scandalized. My body went into shock registering the sheer whiteness and blasphemousness of the space in terms of its representations of divinity and disciples in the stained glass.

Most troubling is the central stained glass window above the chancel that depicts fifteen white figures, including a Jesus at the center who is slightly differentiated with a deeper shade of blue. Above this depiction is a floating head of an angry white man. I, Peace, remember scoffing and being filled with rage at this image. I have heard chapel tour guides express an agnosticism about what this window actually depicts. Perhaps this is some misguided attempt to minimize the white supremacist theology etched in glass and presiding over the chancel. However, the online exhibit about Duke Chapel from Duke University Libraries leaves little room for doubt. "An Iconic Identity: Stories and Voices of Duke University Chapel," makes it very clear that this disembodied head of an old, angry white man is indeed the "Face of God."[23]

Here is the God of white supremacy staring down on the people *he* seeks to form in *his* image.

In *The Gendered Pulpit: Preaching in American Protestant Spaces*, Roxanne Mountford shows that the material spaces of preaching—"architecture, pulpits, and church communities—anticipate and reinforce" the status quo. She writes that church buildings "have a history written in stone and the social imagination that reminds even a casual passerby of the . . . authorities who dwell within."[24] Mountford's research tells us that it is not enough for the Duke Chapel (or any church) to remove a particularly offending statue or two. It is not enough to preach in more diverse and inclusive ways from the pulpit therein. It is not enough to invite more diverse preachers or to hire a more diverse dean. How can it be enough when even a casual passerby can see the towering sermon of white supremacy preached every day in the architecture and artwork? Ignoring the gods and goals of white supremacy etched in glass and stone is as foolish and as deadly as ignoring the corpse at a funeral. With a white Jesus, white disciples, and a wild-eyed, angry, white, male God staring down on the congregation, how could anyone expect to leave the chapel without some sermonic lyric of white supremacy etched in their consciousness? What is a preacher or a chapel to do?

A BUILDING THAT GLORIES IN THE CRUMBLING

In his book, *After Whiteness*, Willie Jennings describes what theological education can be. We think he also names what the church can be: "We are an overturning that facilitates a building up . . . a building up that glories in the crumbling."[25] Among other things in this book, Jennings speaks about uncovering and peeling back histories of colonial harm, overturning systemic racism, undoing patriarchal domination, and dismantling imprisoning individualism—not because Christianity is free from these harmful ways of teaching but because Christians are confronted regularly with a gospel and a God who challenge these teachings in us. While we do not disagree, we fear the history of the church does. Or, maybe to be fairer to God, the history of the church shows that we can be quite effective in resisting a liberating gospel and a loving God. The Duke Chapel is but a recent generation of this long family line.

That takes us back to our initial quote of Jennings. "We are an overturning that facilitates a building up . . . a building up that glories in the crumbling." What if we thought of removal and remodeling as gospel proclamation? To be clear, not all remodeling can be gospel. We fail to see how Duke University's $19.2 million spent to *maintain* Buck's monument is in any way a gospel overturning or building up. But that empty niche where Robert E.

Lee once stood—that might be. A preacher, or even a casual passerby, might say, "that's not just a gap in the portico; that's gospel." We like to imagine this is good news that glories in the crumbling.

Further, even at the Duke Chapel there is a gospel building up through the witness of preachers who crumble the monument of white supremacy. We pay homage to Samuel Proctor, the first black man to preach at Duke University Chapel, "a chapel where a former president once vowed 'colored' would preach at the church 'over my dead body.'"[26] And we are grateful for the witness of James Forbes's at Duke Chapel. Though rejected from Duke Divinity School on the basis of his race, nevertheless Forbes returned a decade later on Duke University's Founder's Day to preach a gospel word on forgiveness and to call people and institutions not to cover up sin.[27] We honor Frank A. Thomas, whose sermon on the Sunday immediately following the Charlottesville riot was an unforgettable word drawing on the resurrection power of black prophetic preaching and witnessing to God's love and hope. We also honor William C. Turner Jr., a beloved professor who has taught preaching at Duke Divinity School for many years. We grieve that COVID-19 disrupted an opportunity to interview the emeritus professor regarding his experiences of navigating Duke and telling his story here. Turner was part of the first wave of black students to be integrated at Duke. His very presence is a testimony to the power of the Spirit building in the crumbling of white supremacy. Finally, we want to share our utmost respect and gratitude for our mentor and friend Luke Powery for embodying gospel, hope, and resurrection every day; his presence itself is a "visual for justice" in the words of womanist homiletician Teresa L. Fry Brown.[28]

In fact, what the preaching of Luke Powery and other minoritized bodies shows is the potential of doxological proclamation that glories in the crumbling of monuments to white supremacy in ways that can help build up a different community. And while I, Peace, hope for nothing less than a literal crumbling, a dismantling of this chapel in my own lifetime, and while I, David, long for the removal of Duke's supremacists and their theological symbols from the chapel, we both find hope in the choir of black and minoritized preachers who witness to the power of resurrection and hope by their sheer presence in this place.

NOTES

1. Luke Powery, "A Tour of Duke University Chapel," YouTube Video, 4:38, January 23, 2017, https://youtu.be/nF8kOUjHyz8 (accessed on September 16, 2021).

2. In thinking through this lens of intersectionality, I, Peace, pull from Patricia Hill Collins and Sirma Bilge. They write, "Intersectionality is a way of understanding

and analyzing the complexity in the world, in people and in human experiences. . . . When it comes to social inequality, people's lives and the organization of power in a given society are better understood as being shaped not by a single axis of social division, be it race or gender or class, but by many axes that work together and influence each other." Patricia Hill Collins and Sirma Bilge, *Intersectionality* (Cambridge: Polity Press, 2016), 2.

3. For expositions on the Korean cultural concept/meaning of Han, refer to Wonhee Anne Joh, Tara Hyun Kyung Chung, Andrew Sung Park, and others.

4. I, David, am thankful for the works of James Cone, Henri Mitchell, Willie Jennings, Kenyatta Gilbert, and Cleo LaRue that have helped me recognize and confront the overt and subtle ways whiteness has worked in and around me as a seminarian and doctoral student at Duke University. And, I am especially grateful for the anti-racist, BIPOC embracing, principalities-confronting (re)formation I received from Charles Campbell, Gennifer Brooks, and Luke Powery.

5. Lawrence Rogers, "Dr. Woody Register to Lead Slavery Project," *The Sewanee Purple*, August 13, 2017, https://thesewaneepurple.org/2017/04/13/dr-woody-register-to-lead-slavery-project/ (accessed on September 16, 2021).

6. For a recent example of this commitment, see "A Statement by the Board of Regents of the University of the South," September 8, 2020, https://new.sewanee.edu/news/university-takes-next-step-toward-equality-and-diversity/statement-by-the-board-of-regents/ (accessed on September 16, 2021).

7. Peace Lee uses the phrase "racially gendered settler colonialism" drawing on the work of Sylvia Wynter. See Sylvia Wynter, "Unsettling the Coloniality of Being/Power/Truth/Freedom: Towards the Human, After Man, Its Overrepresentation—An Argument," *CR: The New Centennial Review* 3, no. 3 (2003): 257–337.

8. According to estimates from the Southern Poverty Law Center, there are more than 1,700 Confederate Monuments in public places throughout the United States. They are commonly located in cemeteries, on courthouse grounds, and in capitol buildings (Ralph Widener, *Confederate Monuments: Enduring Symbols of the South and the War Between the States* (Washington, DC: Andromeda Associates, 1982)). This count does not include public monuments to specific figures of the Civil War or of white supremacist ideas. Neither does it include memorials on parish grounds or in worship spaces.

9. "History and Architecture: A Brief History," Duke University Chapel, https://chapel.duke.edu/about-chapel/history-architecture (accessed on May 20, 2021).

10. See Robert F. Durden, *Bold Entrepreneur: A Life of James B. Duke* (Durham, NC: Carolina Academic Press, 2003). As the Duke Homestead Corporation notes, "In 1890, James B. Duke controlled the largest tobacco industry in the world, and the combined firms continued to grow in the next two decades" ("The Dukes of Durham," Duke Homestead Education and History Corporation, https://dukehomestead.org/history.php) (accessed on August 17, 2021).

11. See Tracy Campbell, *The Politics of Despair: Power and Resistance in the Tobacco Wars* (Lexington, KY: University Press of Kentucky, 2005).

12. See "Native Land Digital," https://native-land.ca (accessed on August 23, 2021).

13. A brief report on Washington Duke and James Buchanan Duke shows that Washington "hired slaves from other plantations" and "owned one slave girl who worked as the housemaid." James Buchanan grew up within this culture of white supremacy. While the report speculates that James Buchanan may have had different racial views, it also notes that he inherited the tobacco empire and "continued the legacy of his father." See "Slavery and Segregation," Duke Human Rights Center, https://humanrights.fhi.duke.edu/who-we-are/history-of-human-rights-at-duke/slavery-and-segregation/ (accessed on August 17, 2021).

14. "I want the central building to be a great towering church which will dominate all of the surrounding buildings, because such an edifice would be bound to have a profound influence on the spiritual life of the young men and women who come here" (James Buchanan Duke). See "History and Architecture: A Brief History," Duke University Chapel, https://chapel.duke.edu/about-chapel/history-architecture (accessed on May 20, 2021).

15. Louis E. Austin, editorial, *Carolina Times*, May 6, 1939. Dedication in Theodore D. Segal, *Point of Reckoning: The Fight for Racial Justice at Duke University* (Durham, NC: Duke University Press, 2021).

16. "History and Architecture: A Brief History," Duke University Chapel, https://chapel.duke.edu/about-chapel/history-architecture (accessed on May 20, 2021).

17. See https://stonebystone.wixsite.com/duke/worker-info (accessed on September 16, 2021).

18. A recent virtual tour of the chapel explains the reasoning: "Between the two statues is a pedestal where a statue of Robert E. Lee used to be. The University removed the statue in 2017 as an expression of the deep and abiding values of the University, and is leaving the space empty as a symbol of a hole that is in the heart of the United States of America, and perhaps in our own human hearts—that hole is from the sin of racism and hatred of any kind" ("Duke Chapel Virtual Tour," YouTube Video, 12:28, August 28, 2020, https://youtu.be/hhlhJzE_FuA) (accessed on September 16, 2021).

19. Susan Svrulga, "Where a Statue of Robert E. Lee Once Stood, Duke's Chapel Will Have an Empty Space," *Washington Post*, August 17, 2018, https://www.washingtonpost.com/news/grade-point/wp/2018/08/17/where-a-statue-of-robert-e-lee-once-stood-dukes-chapel-will-have-an-empty-space/ (accessed on September 16, 2021).

20. See Don Noble, "Review of Brother Sid: A Novel of Sidney Lanier," *Alabama Public Radio*, May 5, 2014, https://www.apr.org/post/brother-sid-novel-sidney-lanier#stream/0 (accessed on September 16, 2021). The third statue in the portico is of Thomas Jefferson whose own enslaving legacy stands alongside his writings and accomplishments.

21. Ryan Newson, *Cut in Stone: Confederate Monuments and Theological Disruption* (Waco, TX: Baylor University Press, 2020), 8–9.

22. "History and Architecture: A Brief History," Duke University Chapel, https://chapel.duke.edu/about-chapel/history-architecture (accessed May 20, 2021).

23. See "Stained Glass Windows" in "An Iconic Identity: Stories and Voices of Duke University Chapel," Duke University Libraries Exhibits, https://exhibits.library.duke.edu/exhibits/show/chapel2016/stain (accessed on September 16, 2021).

24. Roxanne Mountford, *The Gendered Pulpit: Preaching in American Protestant Spaces*. Studies in Rhetorics and Feminisms Series (Carbondale, IL: Southern Illinois University Press, 2003), 3.

25. Willie Jennings, *After Whiteness: An Education in Belonging* (Grand Rapids, MI: Eerdmans, 2020), 124.

26. Jim Stratton, "Cracking the Code of Intolerance, NN Gathering Looks at Life in Black and White: Final Edition," *Daily Press* (Newport News, VA: Final Ed., 1993).

27. James Forbes, "Let's Forgive Our Fathers," *Duke Chapel*, June 19, 1977, https://idn.duke.edu/ark:/87924/r4cv4c677 (accessed on September 16, 2021). See also Luke Powery's interview with James Forbes, https://chapel.duke.edu/bridging-pulpit-and-practice-james-forbes (accessed on September 16, 2021).

28. Teresa Fry Brown, "An African American Woman's Perspective: Renovating Sorrow's Kitchen," in *Preaching Justice: Ethnic and Cultural Perspectives*, Reissue Edition, edited by Christine Marie Smith, 43–61 (Eugene, OR: Wipf & Stock, 2008), 55.

BIBLIOGRAPHY

Brown, Teresa Fry. "An African American Woman's Perspective: Renovating Sorrow's Kitchen." In *Preaching Justice: Ethnic and Cultural Perspectives*, Reissue ed., edited by Christine Marie Smith, 43–61. Eugene, OR: Wipf & Stock, 2008.

Campbell, Tracy. *The Politics of Despair: Power and Resistance in the Tobacco Wars*. Lexington, KY: University Press of Kentucky, 2005.

Collins, Patricia Hill and Sirma Bilge. *Intersectionality*. Cambridge: Polity Press, 2016.

Durden, Robert F. *Bold Entrepreneur: A Life of James B. Duke*. Durham, NC: Carolina Academic Press, 2003.

Jennings, Willie. *After Whiteness: An Education in Belonging*. Grand Rapids, MI: Eerdmans, 2020.

Mountford, Roxane. *The Gendered Pulpit: Preaching in American Protestant Spaces*. Studies in Rhetorics and Feminisms Series. Carbondale, IL: Southern Illinois University Press, 2003.

Newson, Ryan. *Cut in Stone: Confederate Monuments and Theological Disruption*. Waco, TX: Baylor University Press, 2020.

Segal, Theodore D. *Point of Reckoning: The Fight for Racial Justice at Duke University*. Durham, NC: Duke University Press, 2021.

Widener, Ralph. *Confederate Monuments: Enduring Symbols of the South and the War Between the States*. Washington, DC: Andromeda Associates, 1982.

Wynter, Sylvia. "Unsettling the Coloniality of Being/Power/Truth/Freedom: Towards the Human, After Man, Its Overrepresentation—An Argument." *CR: The New Centennial Review* 3, no. 3 (2003): 257–337.

Chapter 4

Theorizing about the Whiteness of Asian American Homiletics

Gerald C. Liu

A TRAUMA FROM WHITE PREACHING

Asian American preaching is traumatized by white preaching. By traumatized, I mean that even when homiletic literature intends to carve out a space for idiomatic Asian American preaching methodology and practice, indelible impressions of white Christian influences and white Christian movements and institutions still define how Asian American preaching voices itself. By white preaching, I mean proclamations of the Christian message (gospel) declared by preachers racially identifiable as white, and by whiteness here and going forward, I mean an inescapable and dominating historical lens that has set precedents and current standards for what constitutes genuine and faithful Christian preaching, especially as it pertains to American democratic ideals and interrelated geopolitical agendas. Ironically, naming and pushing against deeply embedded whiteness within Asian American preaching discourse can still end up holding in place the white grip upon Asian American homiletic innovation.

A DEFICIENCY OF ASIAN AMERICAN CONSIDERATIONS

American Christianity in general has a deficient political, psychological, and social understanding of Asian American identity, Asian American Christianity, and Asian American preaching, due in large part to uncritical reflection upon the success of Christian mission and evangelization with Asian Americans. A white lens blurs particular Asian American identities as representative of an imaginary Asian American Christianity whole. For example, in theological study of preaching, a Korean aperture determines a lot of what constitutes Asian American homiletics. A prevailing Korean viewpoint is traceable to a genealogy of white American Christianity that in effect exported Korean Christianity to the United States and helped to develop it nationwide as the United States became a global superpower. Though Korean American Christianity and preaching firmly stand on their own today and far exceed the growth of any form of Christianity or Christian preaching that might be considered white, the legacy of the original benefacting white American Christianity that introduced Korean Christians to the United States still shapes how Asian American homiletics is understood and undertaken. Broadening the range of Asian American homiletics to include more voices remains latent or nascent. Narrow understandings of Asian American Christian identity and preaching from the white majority complicate such innovation. So does the multiplicity of Asian American identity, which if taken seriously, might require an entirely new approach to consensus identity-based homiletic discourse, one that departs not only from a white homiletic paradigm, but a black one as well.

THE KOREANNESS OF ASIAN AMERICAN PREACHING

The Koreanness of Asian American homiletics in large part grows out of the formidable legacy of American Methodist and Presbyterian missionaries such as Henry Appenzeller (Methodist), Horace N. Allen (Presbyterian), Horace G. Underwood (Presbyterian), William B. Scranton (Methodist), and Mary F. Scranton (Methodist) who served as missionaries in Korea from 1884 to 1902. Appenzeller first translated the New Testament into Korean. Allen became a court physician to Emperor Gojong during the Joseon dynasty. William B. Scranton went to Korea to assist Allen at a Royal hospital but ended up establishing a separate Methodist hospital. Mary F. Scranton, mother of William, began Ewha Girls School or the Pear Blossom Academy which would become Ewha Womans University, the first university founded in Korea and the world's largest female educational institute. Underwood, a colleague of Appenzeller and Allen, also helped to translate the Bible into Korean, established the Seoul YMCA with James Scarth Gale, and served as president of Pyeongtaek University and Joseon Christian College, which would later become Yonsei University. Allen's relationship with the Korean emperor laid the groundwork for what is now the Yonsei University Health System. In 1890, Allen served as secretary to the American legation in Korea. In 1897, he was promoted to U.S. minister and General Consul. Allen's political rise enabled him to help shape U.S. missionary and state interests in Korea for the next decade and initiate Korean immigration to Hawai'i in 1903. It is not a stretch to say that South Korea's educational, health care, and political systems have their beginnings in U.S. Protestant missionary activity.[1]

The formidable influence of Korean American homileticians makes sense given the mission history and success of American Protestant Christian mission in Korea. Christianity has established itself in Korea more than any other country within continental Asia.[2] Today, one in every three Koreans is Christian. In China, Christians comprise only approximately 3–5% of the population. In Japan, Christians are approximately 1% of the population. In India, Christians number approximately 3% of the population. Missionaries also found success in Singapore. There, 20% of the population claim the Christian faith. The Philippines is 86% Christian. Yet most of the Christians there are not Protestant, but Roman Catholic. With regard to Asian American religiosity in general, three-quarters of Asian Americans claim a religious belief. One-quarter of Asian Americans are religiously unaffiliated. Of the three-quarters who are religious, two-thirds of religious Asian Americans are Christians.[3]

Crucially, just as the Appenzeller, Underwood, and Scranton families were in the final years of their missionary activity in Korea, the United States annexed Hawai'i in 1898. At the close of that year, following victory in the Spanish-American War, the United States took control of Puerto Rico, Guam, and the Philippines. The Philippines were not seen as an especially valuable territory for U.S. interests and were unlikely to enter statehood as Hawai'i eventually would. Torn with what to do with the new territory and unconvinced by guidance from Democrats and Republicans, President William McKinley, a Methodist, told the *Christian Advocate*, a Methodist publication and at the time one of the largest circulating weeklies in the United States, that he "went down on his knees and prayed to Almighty God for light and guidance."[4] From that prayer, McKinley decided that Christianizing the Philippines was the way forward. The United States purchased and protected Filipino lands with Vatican interest in a way that provided the U.S. discretion to replace Spanish priests with Filipino ones. The United States also negotiated with the Muslim Moro population and sultan in the southern Philippine islands to relinquish political power and end the practice of slavery in exchange for maintaining religious leadership of the region. In short, the exportation of religious freedom as a democratic ideal driven by American Mainline Protestant belief enabled the United States to practice becoming a geopolitical superpower without explicitly practicing colonialism.

The rise of U.S. global power coincided with Koreans first arriving as laborers on sugar cane plantations in the territory of Hawai'i in 1903. U.S. Protestant missionaries brought many of them.[5] In fact, there were so many Korean Christian immigrant workers that 64% of all Methodists in Hawai'i were Korean by the time the first session of the Hawaiian Mission was held.[6] American Protestantism provides the cultural foundation for Korean Christianity and Korean American identity is at its root Christian. Asian American Christianity is in large part a Korean story even though the ethnically Chinese, for example, have historically been the largest Asian immigrant group in the United States.

While the historical portrait I have recounted provides only an introductory glimpse of the complicated history that informs Asian American Christianity, it does retrieve select, critical historical moments to show how whiteness began and continues to shape Asian American Christianity and especially Asian American preaching. Principally white transmission of the gospel at the inception of Korean and Korean American Christianity complicates attempts to envision a distinctly Asian American homiletic. Ghosts from a white past still manage to conjure up white expectations even within explicitly Asian American homiletic writing.

A BROADER CONUNDRUM OF ASIAN AMERICAN HOMILETICS

Transposing a line of argumentation from Courtney Goto in "On Being Caught Enacting White Normativity" to clarify the challenge of distinguishing Asian American homiletics from whiteness, she helps us consider how attempts to unmask whiteness in Asian American homiletic discourse risk participating in subnarratives of contradictory fiction where authors play the role of one who resists white normativity while being relentlessly entrenched in it. Goto writes:

> [For scholars of color] [t]o focus solely on whites becoming woke is a misguided interpretation of the problem of white normativity. I would welcome the opportunity to explore with other people of color how we have internalized white normativity and how it affects what we enact. People of color could learn from one another by comparing their varied experiences of racism and their internalization of it. Whites would also benefit from understanding more fully the subtle differences between how diverse people of color experience and are themselves at times implicated in white normativity.[7]

The internalization of white normativity that Goto diagnoses captures what I see as a haunting of whiteness that still traumatizes efforts at constructing an Asian American homiletic.

Across mainline and evangelical homiletic guilds, there are not many texts that focus upon Asian American preaching. Three perhaps come to the fore:

(1) Eunjoo Mary Kim's *Preaching the Presence of God: A Homiletic from an Asian American Perspective*, (2) Matthew D. Kim and Daniel L. Wong's *Finding Our Voice: A Vision for Asian North American Preaching*, and (3) Sunggu Yang's *Evangelical Pilgrims from the East: Faith Fundamentals of Korean American Protestant Diasporas*.[8]

Sunggu Yang's *Evangelical Pilgrims from the East: Faith Fundamentals of Korean American Protestant Diasporas* (2016) presents what is arguably the most nuanced and interdisciplinary treatment of Asian American preaching. Though he draws from an array of Asian American thinkers, and he admits the complexity of describing Asian American identity, especially as a starting point for developing an Asian American homiletic, he looks especially to Korean American Christian identity as a pentagonal locus for Korean American Christian preaching.[9] His argument details how a set of five "codes" or social and cultural frameworks provide the foundation to identity formation, meaning making, and religious practices that construct Christian faith within Korean American evangelical Christianity: two socio-ecclesial codes—the Wilderness Pilgrimage code and Diasporic Mission code, two interreligious historical codes—the Confucian Egalitarian code and Buddhist Shamanistic code, and fifthly—the Pentecostal Liberation code. For Yang, preaching is at the center of Korean American worship and preaching is where the significance, interplay, and fruit of the five codes become most apparent.

Preaching the Presence of God (1999), a groundbreaking but underexamined precedent, responds to the continued struggle of Asian Americans "to define their distinctive ethnic roots and cultural identity as a minority group in Eurocentric American society."[10] The text does not attempt to provide a comprehensive statement regarding Asian American homiletics. Rather, it is a conversation starter.[11] It presents a model for Asian American preaching that draws upon understandings of Chinese, Japanese, and Korean Confucian, Buddhist, and shamanistic hermeneutics, combined with an eschatological pneumatology that together spirals around the Bible, Asian American Christian community (especially within Asian American congregations), and God's self-revelation in order to equip Asian American preaching with a holistic pathway for proclaiming the presence of God. At the time of its publication, it was the only book about Asian American preaching written by an Asian American trained in homiletics. *Korean Preaching: An Interpretation* was authored by Jung Young Lee, a professor of systematic theology at Drew Theological School.[12]

Finding Our Voice (2020) is an evangelical Asian North American homiletic that attempts to balance what the authors of the book position as core evangelical beliefs regarding scripture, such as infallibility and inerrancy, and Christian exclusivism, that "Christianity is an exclusivist religion regardless of one's race, ethnicity, culture, gender, or any other distinction," with probing self-examinations of what it means to be Asian North American and recommendations for how Asian North American identity can resource rather than threaten evangelical preaching intent on forming disciples for the sake of building the kingdom of God.[13] What is critical to notice in their use of the identifier "Asian North American or ANA" is a doubling down upon Asian American identity as it pertains to those of Asian heritage living in the United States and Canada.[14] Matthew Kim writes from an Asian United States perspective. Daniel Wong writes from an Asian Canadian perspective. The term ANA is used interchangeably throughout the text to refer to both regional identifiers.

In order to prevent confusion for readers that may arise from distinguishing between authors sharing the same last name—Eunjoo Mary Kim and Matthew D. Kim—as well as further entanglement that might arise by giving proper acknowledgment to the co-authorship of *Finding Our Voice*, I will refer to each text by title instead of by author last name in the following pages.

Finding Our Voice is a co-authored piece written by Matthew D. Kim, who is of Korean heritage, and Wong, who is of Chinese heritage. Yet all three titles, *Evangelical Pilgrims from the East*, *Preaching the Presence of God*, and *Finding Our Voice* are productions of Korean American authors. All three also provide illuminating snapshots that exemplify the pervasion of whiteness in Asian American homiletic discourse. A generation separates the publication dates of *Preaching the Presence of God* on the one side and *Evangelical Pilgrims from the East* and *Finding Our Voice* on the other. In a way, each text represents different generational starting points for how Asians understand themselves as American. *Preaching the Presence of God* and *Evangelical Pilgrims from the East* represent what some might describe as a "first-generation" approach to the question of Asian American homiletics as the authors were born in Korea and then later emigrated to the United States. *Finding Our Voice* emphasizes that their focus is "English-speaking, second- and multi-generational, US- and Canadian-born Asian north Americans."[15] Yet what they hold in common over a twenty-plus year span is wrestling with whiteness that is both commendable but also revealing in terms of how entrenched Asian American homiletics is in white ways of thinking about preaching.

AN INESCAPABILITY OF NORMATIVE WHITENESS

In its opening, *Preaching the Presence of God* takes care to displace the work of Western missionaries, which can be seen as a move to displace normative whiteness. The book states that the Trinitarian God was present among Asian and Asian American communities long before missionaries visited them.[16] Furthermore, the task of constructing an Asian American homiletic is a shared one that "should be a continuing process because the Asian American community of faith must be, like every faith community in the church universal, *ecclesia reformata reformanda*."[17] *Preaching the Presence of God* not only sees developing an Asian American homiletic as a shared endeavor, but it also sees potential for wide application as the book attempts to offer a vision for Asian American preaching that "extends and enriches all homiletical studies."[18] Indeed, *Preaching the Presence of God* sparked what is now a growing body of Asian American homiletic literature with the potential to enter into preaching classrooms focused upon questions of Asian American preaching, intercultural preaching, or just American preaching more broadly conceived.

Nevertheless, even though *Preaching the Presence of God* begins with a necessary correction to locating the origins of Korean American Christianity in God, rather than the missionaries who delivered the good news, couching the theological task of developing an Asian American homiletic as *ecclesia reformata reformanda*, while perhaps a tongue-in-cheek nod to theological minds who lean more toward European ways of thinking, also exhibits a need to address white expectation at the outset. To be fair, *Preaching the Presence of God* also does not disavow the goods of European and American white theologies. It engages them and departs from them with Asian considerations of eschatological pneumatology, holistic community, and multiple registers of using language and more that are developed in detail that exceeds what space allows here. Yet the opening of the book is still significant to examine as a departure point for thinking about the pervasion and hiddenness of whiteness in Asian American homiletics. Even if the Latin idiom *ecclesia reformata reformanda* is a crafty way to win the appeal of non-Asian readers at the outset, the European American Christian majority so to speak, it nevertheless indicates the lingering power of whiteness to legitimate homiletic discourse that seeks to break out of it. What is further destabilizing is that the idiom is itself a white theological fiction. Church historian R. Scott Clark sees no historical evidence for the phrase, ostensibly a shortening of *ecclesia reformata semper reformanda secunda verbum Dei* [the church reformed, always reforming according to the Word of God]. Instead, Scott locates the origins of the longer source phrase in the postwar writings of Karl Barth and Princeton Seminary professor Edward Dowey (1918–2003).[19]

If *Preaching the Presence of God* was a conversation starter for Asian American preaching broadly concerned, *Finding our Voice* shifts the dialogue to specific geographical spaces—the United States and Canada—and anchors the articulation of Asian North American preaching in the English language. The authors of *Finding Our Voice* write:

The focus of our book, however, is on the second category of ANAs: English-speaking, second- and multi-generational, US- and Canadian-born Asian North Americans. Further because of our own experience in these contexts, we will primarily address those from East Asian backgrounds like our own, namely ethnic Korean and Chinese. However, we hope that other ANAs will find we are describing their experiences as well.[20]

Two aims guide the entirety of *Finding Our Voice:* (1) to clarify what Asian North American means and (2) to identify the distinct characteristics and promise of Asian North American preaching.

Moreover, *Finding Our Voice* admits that ANA preachers sound "white," whether conscious or not. The authors locate the reasons for the whiteness of ANA preaching to the homiletic education from "European American preaching professors" in Bible colleges and seminaries.[21] Western modes of homiletical training do not translate into the specific needs of Asian American preachers preaching in Asian American contexts. Here, *Finding Our Voice* identifies a similar white adversary as seen in *Preaching the Presence of God*. Written as both an academic and practical guide for practitioners and students who identify as ANA, have interest in ANA preaching, guest preach in ANA contexts, or want another resource to deepen multicultural understandings of Christian worship and preaching, *Finding Our Voice* attempts to provide a homiletic outlook that discovers and describes ANA preaching in order to help articulate ANA preaching vision and shape a distinctly ANA preaching voice.

The insistence of *Finding Our Voice* that ANA preaching align itself with doctrines such as biblical inerrancy, however, undercuts the shift in homiletic perspective that the book attempts to make. Charles Hodge laid the intellectual groundwork for biblical inerrancy and infallibility when he wrote in his *Systematic Theology*, "With Protestants, the Bible is the only infallible source of knowledge of divine things."[22] Doctrines of infallibility have been key for shielding scripture from ethical interpretations that might expose white transgressions against human dignity, such as the proliferation of slavery, as no verse in the Bible condemns slavery. Inerrancy and infallibility calcify holy text into literal abstraction that risks proof texting racialized oppression and violence. Hodge himself spoke vehemently against abolition and owned slaves.[23] Furthermore, the authors point to Asian Americans such as Michael Oh becoming the global executive director/CEO of the Lausanne Movement, Tom Lin as president of InterVarsity Christian Fellowship, and Sharon Koh, who is now the executive director and CEO of International Ministries or the American Baptist Foreign Mission Society, as examples of how ANAs are shaping the evangelical world through remarkable positions of leadership by suggesting that traditionally white ministries are becoming more Asian.[24] This may be partly true. Yet the embrace of ANAs in evangelical leadership also represents another kind of alignment to whiteness by showing how adept whiteness is at masking itself as ANA. What does it mean that Asians would even aspire to lead those predominantly white institutions? Are they agents of change or tokens of white supremacy or both? I want to suggest that their rise paradoxically represents conformity to whiteness as much as it does transformation toward distinguishing the place of ANA leadership within the upper echelons of American evangelicalism.

As stated earlier, *Evangelical Pilgrims from the East* excels in its explication of how the marginal status of Asian Americans and Asian American preaching is both biblical (Jesus of Nazareth lived at the margins) and positive (Jesus made the marginalized his own people). It builds upon the Chinese, Japanese, and Korean Confucian, Buddhist, and shamanistic hermeneutics and apocalyptic framework introduced by *Preaching the Presence of God*. It also captures the evangelical dedication of *Finding Our Voice* without adopting similar hardline doctrinal stances. Instead it opts for a Pentecostal Liberation code where the Korean American preacher becomes "spiritual midwife" invoking and receiving the Holy Spirit to enunciate and explore new dimensionalities of preaching for what is signature to Asian American church communities and also necessary in order to achieve social justice within and in concert with Asian American people and remain open to the capricious yet capacious grace of God. Yet the entire thrust of *Evangelical Pilgrims from the East* rests upon a white homiletic methodology—John McClure's Four Codes.[25] Modeled after European structuralist philosophy that seeks to classify and organize thought into particular modes and categories, one can see the risk of how such thinking can quickly lead to exclusion of ideas, experiences, or embodiments that do not neatly fit into such typologies and that collide with each other to spark new ways of thinking. Here, I am not suggesting that McClure is a white supremacist but rather that the *Four Codes* is an example of a white homiletic.

The Wilderness Pilgrimage code, Diasporic Mission code, the Confucian Egalitarian code, the Buddhist Shamanistic code, and the Pentecostal Liberation code of *Evangelical Pilgrims from the East* permutate the Scriptural, Semantic, Theosymbolic, and Cultural codes of McClure almost beyond recognition. Nevertheless, McClure is there in *Evangelical Pilgrims from the East*, providing not so much a trauma that wounds, but something more like an impression or permanent indentation that makes possible the entire homiletic apparatus of the book run.

TWO HORIZONS FOR DEFINING ASIAN AMERICAN HOMILETICS

Of course it would be too simple to assert that appeal to white authors destabilizes attempts to establish idiomatic Asian American approaches to homiletics. To a certain extent, using white authors is inevitable and understandable. Resourcing the thoughts of white authors also does not make a text suffer from whiteness necessarily. But the persistent deference to historical and contemporary modes of white theological and homiletic thought does present itself as a sign of white trauma, I want to suggest. Respect is good of course. I only want it to flow both ways. There is an Asian American neglect that is causing a woeful imbalance. It is not due to lack of interest or lack of Asian American homiletics personnel, but rather results from historical omission and continuing lack of opportunity and bias. What I am trying to point out in my all-too-quick survey of slits of whiteness within prominent Asian American preaching titles is how thoroughgoing and varied whiteness embeds itself in Asian American homiletics, from the mention of what seems minuscule in introductory pages to core theological commitments to the frame enabling an argument to take shape. Even I, as a United Methodist homiletician formerly employed by the alma mater of Appenzeller and who has taught at a PC(USA) campus where Hodge was once president, am one who masks whiteness. At the same time, as a convert to Christianity and a native of Mississippi, the three texts I have examined share quite different understandings of Asian American identity as I have experienced it.

The challenge remains for Asian American preaching not only to wrestle with what cannot be left behind—whiteness—and wring away from it something distinct and idiomatic. Asian American homiletics must also look deeper within its own history and mine American history further, remembering, for example, that the first Bible in the New World was a translation in the Algonquian Native American language (New Testament, 1661; Full Canon, 1663), and that the Indigenous peoples were already making sense of the Christian God with oral, pictorial, and hieroglyphic language long before John Eliot wrote the Algonquian Bible or *Mamusse Wunneetupanatamwe Up Biblum God*.[26] Whiteness is deep but also not as deep as some expressions of American faithfulness. We Asian American homileticians would also do well to recognize that mother Asian languages and English are only two linguistic origin points for Asian American preaching. Many historians locate the earliest Asians in North America to a group known as los Chinos, who landed in Acapulco in the 1580s. Erika Lee cites historian Edward Slack Jr., who asserts that Asians could be found all over colonial Mexico from Loreto in Baja, California to Mérida in Yucatan.[27]

In the contemporary era, we Asian Americans need to orient our writing to the wideness of Asian American religiosity, that on the whole, Asians are less likely to believe in God and less likely to pray more than any other racial or ethnic group in the United States.[28] How do facts like those inform evangelical Asian American preaching? We need also to take seriously the overwhelmingly conservative leanings of Asian American churches and their adherents. There is a stark political divide between Asian Americans who consider themselves Christian within congregations and halls of theological education. The fourteen endorsements of enthusiasm around *Finding Our Voices* show just how prevalent conservative Asian American Christian preaching is. This also becomes apparent in the gender imbalance of Asian American preaching leadership. Across the wide variety of American Christian churches, only approximately 6.2% are led by women. Only approximately 3.5% are led by Asian Americans. While Asian Americans may be three-quarters religious and mostly Christian, Asian American Christian preachers remain an anomaly with regard to American Christianity as a whole and a big correction needs to be made with regard to gender.

Considerations like these and many more will keep Asian American homileticians busy for years to come. As I mentioned above but cannot explore at the moment, it will require homiletic writing that studies, expands, and disrupts not only whiteness, but also directly engages the prevailing black-and-white paradigm of homiletic scholarship too.

NOTES

1. A similar thoroughgoing shaping of public life from U.S. protestant missionary activity can also be seen in a country like Singapore.

2. For more on the history of Christianity in Korea, see Sebastian C. H. Kim and Kirsteen Kim, *A History of Korean Christianity* (Cambridge, UK: Cambridge UP, 2015), Sung-Deuk Oak, *The Making of Korean Christianity: Protestant Encounters with Korean Religions* (Waco, TX: Baylor University Press, 2013), and K. Kale Yu, *Understanding Korean Christianity: Grassroot Perspectives on Causes, Culture, and Responses* (Eugene, OR: Pickwick, 2019).

3. Tony Carnes, "Asian American Religions," *Oxford Research Encyclopedia of Religion* (New York: Oxford University Press, 2017). https://oxfordre.com/religion/view/10.1093/acrefore/9780199340378.001.0001/acrefore-9780199340378-e-502 (accessed on October 10, 2020).

4. James Rusling, "Interview with President William McKinley," *Christian Advocate,* January 22, 1903, 17.

5. For more on the history of Korean American Christianity, see David Yoo, *Contentious Spirits: Religion in Korean American History, 1903–1945* (Palo Alto, CA: Stanford University Press, 2010).

6. "History of Korean United Methodists," https://www.umc.org/en/content/history-of-korean-united-methodists (accessed on October 10, 2020).

7. Courtney T. Goto, "On Being Caught Enacting White Normativity," *Religious Education* 114, no. 3 (May 2019): 359.

8. See Eunjoo Mary Kim, *Preaching the Presence of God: A Homiletic from an Asian American Perspective* (Valley Forge, PA, 1999); Matthew D. Kim and Daniel L. Wong, *Finding Our Voice: A Vision for Asian North American Preaching* (Bellingham, WA: Lexham Press, 2020; and Sunggu Yang, *Evangelical Pilgrims from the East: Faith Fundamentals of Korean American Protestant Diasporas* (Cham, Switzerland: Palgrave, 2016).

9. Sunggu Yang, *Evangelical Pilgrims from the East: Faith Fundamentals of Korean American Protestant Diasporas* (Cham, Switzerland: Palgrave, 2016).

10. Kim, *Preaching the Presence of God*, 3.

11. Ibid, 4.

12. Jung Young Lee, *Korean Preaching: An Interpretation* (Nashville, TN: Abingdon, 1997).

13. Kim and Wong, *Finding Our Voice*, 81.

14. Ibid, 13.

15. Ibid, 14.

16. Kim, *Preaching the Presence of God*, 5.

17. Ibid.

18. Ibid.

19. R. Scott Clark, "Always Abusing Semper Reformanda," https://www.ligonier.org/learn/articles/always-abusing-semper-reformanda/ (accessed on October 7, 2020).

20. Kim and Wong, *Finding Our Voice*, 14.

21. Ibid.

22. Charles Hodge, *Systematic Theology* 1:33.

23. Joseph Yannielli, "Princeton and Abolition," Princeton Theological Seminary, https://slavery.princeton.edu/stories/princeton-and-abolition (accessed on June 2, 2021). For more on infallibility and its relationship with white supremacy, see Joanna Brooks, "Originalism, Infallibility, and the Institutionalization of White Supremacy: 1880s–1940s," in *Mormonism and White Supremacy: American Religion and the Problem of Racial Innocence* (New York: Oxford UP, 2020), Oxford Scholarship Online, 2020. doi: 10.1093/oso/9780190081768.003.0003 (accessed on October 10, 2020).

24. Kim and Wong, *Finding Our Voice*, 15.

25. John S. McClure, *The Four Codes of Preaching: Rhetorical Strategies* (Louisville, KY: WJK (Westminster John Knox), 2003).

26. Linford D. Fischer, "The Bible and Indigenous Language Translations in the Americas," *The Oxford Handbook of the Bible in America*, edited by Paul C. Gutjahr (New York: Oxford University Press, 2018).

27. Erika Lee, *The Making of Asian America: A History* (New York: Simon & Schuster, 2016), 24.

28. National Congregational Study: Wave 3 Tables, Table 1: "Continuity and Change in American Congregations: Attendees' Perspective," 33, https://sites.duke.edu/ncsweb/files/2019/03/NCSIII_report_final_tables.pdf (accessed on September 26, 2021).

BIBLIOGRAPHY

Brooks, Joanna. "Originalism, Infallibility, and the Institutionalization of White Supremacy: 1880s–1940s." In *Mormonism and White Supremacy: American Religion and the Problem of Racial Innocence*. New York: Oxford University Press, 2020, Oxford Scholarship Online, 2020. doi: 10.1093/oso/9780190081768.003.0003 (accessed on September 25, 2021).

Carnes, Tony. "Asian American Religions." In *Oxford Research Encyclopedia of Religion*. New York: Oxford University Press, 2017, https://oxfordre.com/religion/view/10.1093/acrefore/9780199340378.001.0001/acrefore-9780199340378-e-502 (accessed on October 10, 2020).

Clark, R. Scott. "Always Abusing Semper Reformanda." https://www.ligonier.org/learn/articles/always-abusing-semper-reformanda/ (accessed on October 7, 2020).

Fischer, Linford D. "The Bible and Indigenous Language Translations in the Americas." In *The Oxford Handbook of the Bible in America*, edited by Paul C. Gutjahr, 39–59. New York: Oxford University Press, 2018.

Goto, Courtney T. "On Being Caught Enacting White Normativity," *Religious Education* 114, no. 3 (May 2019): 39–59.

Hodge, Charles. *Systematic Theology* 1:33, New York: Scribner, 1872–1873.

Kim, Eunjoo Mary. *Preaching the Presence of God: A Homiletic from an Asian American Perspective*. Valley Forge, PA, 1999.

Kim, Matthew D. and Daniel L. Wong. *Finding Our Voice: A Vision for Asian North American Preaching*. Bellingham, WA: Lexham Press, 2020.

Kim, Sebastian C. H. and Kirsteen Kim. *A History of Korean Christianity*. Cambridge: Cambridge University Press, 2015.

Korean United Methodist Church. "History of Korean United Methodists." https://www.umc.org/en/content/history-of-korean-united-methodists (accessed on October 10, 2020).

Lee, Erika. *The Making of Asian America: A History*. New York: Simon & Schuster, 2016.

McClure, John S. *The Four Codes of Preaching: Rhetorical Strategies*. Louisville, KY, 2003. National Congregational Study: Wave 3 Tables, Table 1: "Continuity and Change in American Congregations: Attendees' Perspective," 33, https://sites.duke.edu/ncsweb/files/2019/03/NCSIII_report_final_tables.pdf (accessed on September 26, 2021.

Oak, Sung-Deuk. *The Making of Korean Christianity: Protestant Encounters with Korean Religions*. Waco, TX: Baylor University Press, 2013.

Yang, Sunggu. *Evangelical Pilgrims from the East: Faith Fundamentals of Korean American Protestant Diasporas*. Cham, Switzerland: Palgrave, 2016.

Yoo, David. *Contentious Spirits: Religion in Korean American History, 1903–1945*. Palo Alto, CA: Stanford University Press, 2010.

Yu, K. Kale. *Understanding Korean Christianity: Grassroot Perspectives on Causes, Culture, and Responses*. Eugene, OR: Pickwick, 2019.

Chapter 5

White Mainline Protestant Preachers Addressing Racial Issues

2017 vs. 2021

Leah D. Schade

INTRODUCTION

Race, whiteness, white privilege, and white supremacy are among the most volatile topics for many clergy to address in the U.S. mainline Protestant churches in the current political climate. Especially in predominantly white congregations, pastors who address race in the pulpit are vulnerable to accusations of "preaching politics." Many preachers field angry emails and some even receive threats to remove them from their positions. These efforts may be motivated by the desire to silence the pastor's prophetic voice or simply avoid discomfort. Regardless, the end result is that congregations and clergy tend to avoid confronting the sins of racism.

For the purposes of this chapter, I am defining racism as a system of oppression that confers unfair advantages for white or lighter-skinned people while disadvantaging black, Indigenous, Asian, Latinx, or other persons of color. The word *system* is key in this definition, in that racism is more than just individual behaviors; it is structured into society and culture and reinforced by systems of power and privilege. Examples of systemic racism include gerrymandered voting districts designed to ensure the election of white candidates, under-funded infrastructure in communities of color, and media portrayals of black persons that play on negative stereotypes. Systemic racism is also built into our denominations and congregations due to the fact that U.S. Christianity is embedded within—and helped to create—the racist structures of the society in which it exists.

The ways in which systemic racism manifests within churches are myriad, but here is an example that illustrates the challenge this poses to preachers.

At the invitation of the Illinois-Wisconsin Region of the Christian Church (Disciples of Christ), Rev. Soniyyah "Sonna" B. Key, an African American pastor and cross-cultural trained leader, and I co-led a webinar in November 2020 entitled "Wade in the Water: Preaching about Race and the Church." The webinar's purpose was to help preachers assess their congregation's readiness to hear a sermon on racism and equip pastors to develop such sermons in their contexts. In sharing about their congregations, one participant's comment was echoed by many in the group: "I live in a rural, white, conservative community. Our church is very small and exclusive. We have lost members over some very trivial things. I feel like preaching anti-racism in our church could be the final nail in our coffin. How do we balance keeping our doors open with speaking the truth of anti-racism?" Another shared, "There is a small group in my church that is focusing on being an anti-racist church, but we are struggling to bring the rest of the congregation along."

Are these isolated examples of what preachers are facing if they choose to address racism and white supremacy in their sermons and teaching? Or are these comments indicative of a larger matrix of demographic, cultural, and ecclesial factors? If this is the case, what insights might emerge if we systemically and methodically surveyed clergy about their experiences preaching about racism and other social issues, and how might we use these insights to help unmask and deconstruct white hegemony in churches?

These are the kinds of questions my research team and I have discussed and which I have asked myself as a preacher and homiletics professor. These have led me to conduct a longitudinal research project studying the preaching patterns of mainline Protestant clergy with survey waves in 2017 and 2021. I approach this empirical research as a white, female minister ordained in the Evangelical Lutheran Church in America who served two predominantly white congregations and one predominantly black congregation. I have wrestled with the challenges of addressing race in both contexts. Now as a professor of preaching and worship, I am tasked with helping seminary students address social issues such as racism in their sermons and ministries.

My initial assumption about the survey data was that it would reveal an overall reticence on the part of white Protestant clergy to address racism in their preaching. However, the situation is more nuanced and complex. As this chapter will demonstrate, the data shows an increasing number of preachers are taking up the task of addressing racism, which is encouraging. But my team and I also examined variables such as gender, length of time at a congregation, and the church's setting (rural vs. cities and suburbs) and found that these factors appear to affect clergy willingness to preach sermons addressing racism and whiteness.[1] Specifically, the data shows that the lack of racial diversity of congregations correlates with preachers' hesitancy to engage racism in their sermons. In this chapter, I will make the case that while pastors are becoming more willing to preach sermons about racism, they need more education, training, support, and accountability within theological education and denominational structures if white Protestant Christianity in the United States is to make serious progress with unmasking and deconstructing homiletical whiteness.

CHURCHES AND CLERGY AWAKENING TO THE CALL TO ADDRESS RACISM

In her book *Preaching About Racism: A Guide for Faith Leaders*, Carolyn Helsel observes that for preachers, the task of addressing racism with and within white congregations is daunting yet necessary. Issues around race often seem "too complicated and too divisive" for preachers to address in predominantly white congregations.[2] Yet, she also sounds a hopeful note: "If you are white, there may be times when racism remains utterly hidden from your consciousness. However, that is starting to change."[3] Indeed, the mere existence of a book like *Preaching About Racism* and its companion volume, *Anxious to Talk About It: Helping White Christians Talk Faithfully about Racism*, indicates that clergy and congregations are seeking and using tools for having forthright conversations about the structures and sins of racism in the United States.[4]

Helsel's books have been especially helpful for clergy and congregations grappling with the police murder of George Floyd and other high-profile murders of black citizens such as Ahmaud Arbery and Breonna Taylor in 2020 which spurred the country into a tumultuous awakening regarding the brutality against black bodies in the United States. Churches that had not previously engaged issues of race in America were moved to begin talking about it with study groups springing up to discuss books such as *Dear Church: A Love Letter from a Black Preacher to the Whitest Denomination in the U.S.*,[5] *How to be an Anti-racist*,[6] *White Fragility: Why It's So Hard for White People to Talk about Racism*,[7] and *Between the World and Me*,[8] to name just a few.

My own research confirms Helsel's assertion that "things are starting to change."[9] There are indications of a small but growing shift in the number of white mainline Protestant pastors who are willing to address racism in their preaching. As the data will show, many of these preachers have consistently recognized the importance of speaking about racial issues in their sermons. When comparing the data between surveys in 2017 and 2021, we see an increase in the number of pastors intending to address racial issues. However, there are many variables that affect white mainline Protestant pastors' willingness to address race. When we examine these factors, we can more clearly identify the barriers to preaching about racism and, in turn, think about how to effectively direct our energies toward removing, reducing, or going around these barriers.

METHODOLOGY

In the first two months of 2017, I conducted a solo research project to survey clergy in the United States assessing how preachers were approaching their sermons during that divisive time in our nation's history. The SurveyMonkey questionnaire ran for six weeks, from mid-January to the end of February, spanning the transition from the Obama administration to the incoming Trump administration. I received responses from more than 782 mainline Protestant clergy representing eight denominations in forty-five states.[10] The survey, which allowed respondents to remain anonymous, explored a range of topics, including the difference the 2016 presidential election made in preachers' willingness to address social issues in the pulpit, topics clergy intended to address in the six months following the presidential election, and reasons clergy gave for either engaging or avoiding certain social issues in their sermons.

Four years later, I assembled a team to design and conduct a second survey of clergy during the transition from the Trump administration to the Biden administration, from January to February in 2021. This time we received more than 2,600 respondents, who, as with the 2017 survey, were allowed to remain anonymous.[11] This chapter will focus on the 80% of respondents who identified as mainline Protestant ($N = 1,919$).[12] We will further narrow our focus to the 90% of respondents in both surveys who identified racially as white (2017 $N = 596$, 2021 $N = 1,719$) so as to examine how this subset of clergy chose to deal with issues around racism in 2017 and 2021. There are several questions to explore, including:

- How many white mainline Protestant preachers reported addressing racism in the years leading up to the election, 2016 vs. 2020?
- How high a priority was it for preachers to address racism as the presidential administrations in 2017 and 2021 began?
- How did factors such as gender, length of time at a congregation, community setting, and the racial diversity of a congregation appear to impinge on a preacher's willingness to address issues of race in the pulpit?

Admittedly, because this survey involves self-reporting by clergy, the questionnaires risk the classic problem of eliciting "socially desirable rather than objective responses from their subjects."[13] As Clifton F. Guthrie has noted, "Asking preachers via surveys about their own preaching can be like asking folks to calculate their own tax deductions: there is always the temptation to claim too much."[14] However, the surveys were not intended to yield data on the *actual content* of the preachers' sermons. Rather, we were testing for *attitudes*, *opinions*, and *expressions of underlying feelings and concerns* of clergy. The surveys were designed this way in order to provide information that may be useful in the pedagogical task of helping preachers discover and effectively exercise their prophetic voice.

The data we gathered demonstrates noticeable contrasts between the 2017 and 2021 surveys and indicates that addressing race in sermons is complexified by variables around a preacher's perceptions of vulnerability, risk, and safety. It also reveals noticeable patterns between congregational diversity and preachers' willingness to address race—patterns that confirm other scholars' assertions that white communities tend to reinforce their insularity when considering whiteness as a concept and racism as an issue.

CLERGY ATTITUDES REGARDING PREACHING ABOUT SOCIAL ISSUES: AN OVERVIEW

Before delving into the data regarding preaching and racism, it is helpful to get a sense of clergy attitudes toward preaching about social issues in general. The surveys indicate that overall, white mainline Protest clergy have shown an increasing willingness to address social issues in their preaching when comparing the data in the 2017 and 2021 surveys. In the 2017 survey, for example, respondents indicated that when it comes to frequency of engaging social issues in their preaching, 77% said they do so "sometimes" or "frequently." But in the 2021 survey, that number rose to 84%, a 7-point increase.

What are the driving reasons for pastors wanting to address social issues? In both surveys, the top three reasons ranked as the most important rationales for tackling controversial justice issues were 1) connecting scripture/faith with issues that affect people's lives; 2) Jesus and/or the Bible speak about social issues; and 3) to provide moral, biblical, or theological perspectives on an issue. These reasons also coincide with clergy attitudes regarding if—and how—the church, congregations, and preachers themselves should engage public issues.

Generally, white mainline Protestant clergy in 2021 indicated that when it comes to the church's role in the public square, they favor engagement over avoidance of social issues.[15] Ninety-two percent strongly or moderately agreed that the church should host educational dialogues about social issues and faith, and 91% strongly or moderately agreed that churches should put their faith into action through advocacy and social justice. Similarly, when it comes to clergy engaging social issues with their congregations, 96% either strongly or moderately agreed that clergy should help congregants think about social issues biblically and theologically. This indicates that, as a whole, white mainline Protestant clergy lean heavily toward having their congregations and themselves engage in social issues to some degree.

This does not mean, however, that white mainline Protestant preachers are addressing social issues such as racism en masse. There are certain key factors that affect whether a preacher is willing to tackle racism in the pulpit. One of these factors is a preacher's willingness to navigate the tension between unity and prophetic disruption and its implications for preaching about social issues such as racism. Many pastors avoid preaching about topics that might alienate members of their congregation, cause controversy, negatively impact their ability to provide pastoral care, or make anyone want to leave the church. In fact, the number one reason clergy gave for avoiding social issues in their sermons was to *maintain unity and avoid divisiveness*. In both 2017 and 2021, more than half of the respondents (55% and 52%, respectively) indicated that keeping their congregations together was either very or somewhat important.

However, is the desire for unity sometimes used as an excuse not to tackle the difficult but necessary issues around racism in America's churches? As Robert P. Jones observes, "American Christianity's theological core has been thoroughly structured by an interest in protecting white supremacy."[16] Jones's research indicates that "the genetic imprint of this legacy [of white supremacy] remains present and measurable in contemporary white Christianity, not only among evangelicals in the South but also among mainline Protestants in the Midwest and Catholics in the Northeast."[17] The data from my own surveys of white mainline Protestant clergy bears out this imprint of white supremacy, as we will see below. Yet, the data also indicates that while these clergy and congregations are far from where they need to be in the work of deconstructing racism, the work has begun and is making incremental progress. But first, let's consider the obstacles that prevent or block clergy from addressing social issues in their sermons.

BARRIERS TO PREACHING ABOUT SOCIAL ISSUES

One of the most telling questions in the 2021 survey was whether preachers felt inhibited about addressing social issues in their pulpits.[18] Overall, the majority of clergy (62%) indicated that they have no problem engaging social issues and feel free to do so in their contexts. However, 35% of clergy said that while they would like to engage social issues in their preaching, they *feel inhibited*.[19] Digging deeper, when we overlay factors such as gender, length of time in a church, and congregational setting, our research team found that there is a certain constellation of characteristics that indicates which white mainline Protestant clergy feel *most inhibited* when it comes to addressing hot-button social issues in their sermons. The data indicates that white female clergy who are new to their churches (<three years) and serve white congregations in rural areas expressed an inhibition rate of 56%. But only 44% of males in that same category expressed feelings of inhibition. Similarly, 37% of white males with at least four years at their church in rural areas expressed inhibition, compared with 45% of white female clergy in that same category. And white male clergy serving congregations in cities or suburbs with at least four years at their church have only a 25% inhibition rate, while females in this same category show slightly higher inhibition, 29%.

In other words, those white mainline Protestant pastors who are male, have tenure at their congregation, and serve in non-rural contexts appear to be much less inhibited when it comes to addressing social issues. The data suggests that clergy with certain levels of privilege due to their gender, their tenure, and their congregational setting feel more at ease in addressing potentially volatile issues. This is most likely because these privileges afford them higher levels of authority, respect, deference, and protection compared to their clergy colleagues without the benefit of these privileges. Further on, we will offer suggestions to support, equip, and encourage clergy in more vulnerable positions who *do* want to address social issues.

EFFECTS OF CONGREGATIONAL RACIAL DIVERSITY ON PREACHERS FEELING INHIBITED TO ADDRESS SOCIAL ISSUES

In 2021, one of the most dramatic markers for pastors feeling inhibited about engaging social issues in their preaching and teaching was the racial diversity of the congregation.[20] Eighty-three percent of white pastors serving congregations with at least a 25% racial/ethnic diversity rate said they have no problem engaging social issues in their preaching/teaching and feel free to do so in their contexts. But the same does not hold true for pastors who serve predominantly white congregations. For that group, 40% reported feeling inhibited about addressing social issues, compared with only 17% of pastors in more diverse congregations. We must note that the subset of clergy serving racially diverse congregations is small: in the 2021 survey, only 201 white mainline Protestant clergy said they served churches with at least a 25% racial/ethnic diversity rate which represents only 12% of congregations in the 2021 survey. Nevertheless, it appears that the "white gaze at the preacher," as HyeRan Kim-Cragg puts it, influences the preacher's choice of sermon topics and whether or not to tackle issues that challenge their whiteness.[21] We might hypothesize from this data that there is significant pressure on white pastors from white congregants *not* to address thorny issues such as race in their sermons.

There are many reasons why white pastors might implicitly collude with their white congregations to avoid talking about race. Helsel notes that many clergy are hesitant to talk about racism in white congregations because they fear "making listeners feel ashamed or guilty."[22] Robin DiAngelo contends that these feelings are a result of "white fragility," "a state in which even a minimum amount of racial stress . . . becomes intolerable, triggering a range of defensive moves . . . such as anger, fear, and guilt and behaviors such as argumentation, silence, and leaving the stress-inducing situation. These behaviors, in turn, reinstate white racial equilibrium."[23] Robert Jones suggests that all of this is part of white Christianity's efforts to "maintain an unassailable sense of religious purity that protects white racial innocence."[24] White Christians and their white-dominant society have, in essence, colluded in "deflecting any attempt to trace this ideology to its religious source."[25]

It stands to reason, then, that when white preachers choose to preach an anti-racism sermon, they strike at the very heart of white identity both within themselves and within their congregations. We can detect traces of the deflection and avoidance Jones writes about when we examine specifically how racial diversity in congregations affects white pastors' choices to address or avoid the specific topic of racial issues in their preaching. As we will see, there are patterns that demonstrate whiteness circles itself in defensiveness in order to protect itself from detection and prophetic interrogation. But first it is necessary to establish some basic data points about clergy addressing racism in their sermons.

WHITE MAINLINE PROTESTANT CLERGY ADDRESSING RACISM IN SERMONS: 2017 VS. 2021

This overview of general attitudes around preaching social issues has ramifications for the specific topic of addressing racism in white mainline Protestant churches in the United States. In the 2017 survey, participants were given a list of thirty-eight topics and asked to mark which ones they had addressed in their sermons in the previous year.[26] Three of those topics were related to racism: racial and/or ethnic tensions, white privilege/white supremacy, and environmental racism. For the purposes of this chapter, we are clustering those under the general topic of racism. Of the 625 white mainline Protestant pastors who answered that question, 489 (78%) said they addressed racial issues in their preaching in 2016.

Four years later in the 2021 survey, participants were given a list of twenty-six topics and asked which ones they had addressed in a sermon in 2020.[27]

In this survey there was one general category for racial issues: Racism/White supremacy/Black Lives Matter. Seventy-one percent of preachers said they had addressed that issue in 2020. While this is 7 points lower than what preachers reported in 2017, this drop might be partially explained by the fact that the topic of COVID-19 was present on the list of choices where it had not existed in 2017. COVID-19 was the number one social issue addressed in sermons in 2020 (87%) followed by economic issues (77%) and racism (71%). However, when we examine other variables affecting this data, such as congregational diversity, we see a more nuanced picture about clergy willingness to address race.

Preaching in Predominantly White Congregations vs. More Diverse Congregations

The racial demographics of the congregation a pastor serves appear to affect their willingness to address issues around race. In 2016, 480 of the white clergy in the survey served predominantly white congregations. Only fifty-one served diverse congregations.[28] However, of the clergy who served white congregations, 76% of them said they addressed racial issues in their preaching compared with 90% of those serving more diverse churches. The pattern holds true for 2021 where 73% of white pastors serving white congregations said they addressed race in their sermons, compared with 87% of pastors in diverse congregations. As was stated earlier and bears repeating, white clergy serving predominantly white congregations showed less willingness to address race in their sermons in 2016 and 2020 than their colleagues serving more diverse congregations.

Questions in the survey about intent to address or avoid topics further verify this pattern. For example, in both 2017 and 2021, respondents were asked to indicate which issues they would be *very hesitant* to preach about in the coming six months, as well as the topics they *intended to address*. Again, we see a pattern. In 2017, 21% of white clergy preaching to predominantly white congregations said they intended to *avoid* racial issues, compared with only 2% of pastors serving more diverse congregations. In terms of topics they *intended to address*, 48% of white pastors in white congregations said they wanted to preach about race in 2017. But for white pastors serving more diverse congregations, that number was higher: 54%.

Not surprisingly, the pattern holds in 2021 as well. Only 3% of pastors serving more diverse congregations indicated that they would avoid preaching about race, while 10% of white preachers serving white congregations expressed aversion. Note, however, that white preachers' level of hesitancy around preaching about race in white congregations was significantly lower than it was in 2017, dropping from 21% to 10%.

This same change is noticeable in the topics white preachers intended to address in 2021 as well. The majority of white pastors, regardless of the diversity level of their congregation, ranked racial issues as their number one priority to address in 2021, with more than half of them (56%) intending to address this topic. For white pastors serving predominantly white congregations, race was virtually tied with COVID-19 at 58%. But for white clergy serving more diverse congregations, there is a +10-point difference: 68% said they intended to address racial issues in 2021. Yet, it is worth noting that both groups—white clergy serving white congregations and white clergy serving more diverse congregations—demonstrated a 10% increase in willingness to address racial issues in their preaching compared to 2017.

Thus, there is reason to hope that, at least in 2021, things appeared to be moving in the right direction when it comes to white mainline Protestant clergy addressing racism. Racism is the number one issue that all white mainline Protestant clergy said they intended to address in 2021, with more than half (56%) of clergy serving congregations all along the political spectrum choosing that topic. Even more encouraging is that 60% of clergy serving "purple" churches (more politically mixed) rank the issue as number one. This indicated that clergy intended to offer an increased number of sermons about racism in 2021 as compared to 2017, if their self-reporting accurately reflects their intentions. However, while it is good news to see white clergy demonstrating more willingness to address race in both white-dominant and more racially diverse congregations, there are other variables we must consider that complicate this picture.

COMPLICATING FACTORS FOR CLERGY ADDRESSING RACIAL ISSUES

Two variables that affect preachers' willingness to address racial issues are the community setting of the congregation (rural vs. city/suburbs) and the political orientations of the congregation. For example, in 2021, the constellation of factors that characterize those with the most hesitancy in addressing race appears to be pastors serving smaller congregations (worship attendance <100) in *rural areas* who are new to their churches (three years or less).[29] These pastors are twice as hesitant to address race than their colleagues with at least four years in their churches serving larger congregations (worship attendance >100) in *cities or suburbs* (16% vs. 8% hesitancy rate, respectively). We can surmise, then, that pastors in small, rural congregations just beginning their calls might benefit from support, resources, and training offered by denominations and seminaries for preaching about racial issues.

Yet even clergy who have the benefit of certain privileges such as being male, having longer tenure, or serving as lead pastors in large congregations are not immune to pushback when it comes to preaching about race. According to both the 2017 and 2021 surveys, the most common forms of negative responses clergy received when addressing social issues in their preaching were angry words, letters, and/or emails (53% in 2017 and 48% in 2021). Running a close second was parishioners staying away from worship services (51% in 2017 and 48% in 2021). The biggest shift from 2017 to 2021 was in the number of clergy reporting members withdrawing from the church. In 2017, that number was 27%, but in 2021, it rose 10 points to 37%.

In other words, pastors are self-reporting numerous negative consequences when they choose to address social issues such as racism in their sermons. Loss of pastoral relationships, loss of worship attendance and financial giving, and even loss of one's position, though rare, are all possibilities when choosing to preach about hot-button social issues. This is even more exacerbated when white clergy choose to preach about racial issues in predominantly white congregations. Yet, as the data indicates, an increasing number of clergy are reporting that they are willing to step up to the challenge of addressing race in their preaching even with all the risks this entails. So we might ask how denominations, seminaries, pastoral colleague groups, and local anti-racism coalitions can offer or increase support to encourage and equip even more clergy to address racism in the pulpit.

RECOMMENDATIONS

If U.S. mainline Protestant Christianity is going to make real progress in dismantling racism, then denominations, seminaries, and teachers of preaching are going to have to increase the training, resources, support, and accountability for both new and experienced clergy. The data analysis in this chapter suggests that a strategic way to do this is to focus attention on those clergy who are most vulnerable when attempting to preach about race. Surveys such as the ones conducted for this study can help identify which pastors are most at risk and what resources and support they might find most useful.

Some may argue that there are already many resources available for equipping preachers and congregations to address racism; they just need to gather up their courage and do the work.[30] But unless these books are read and their methods practiced by clergy; unless they are taught in seminary preaching courses; unless they are offered by denominations and seminaries as part of continuing education for clergy, they will be like tools gathering dust in a toolbox. Further, mainline Protestant clergy need support from denominational structures so that their positions are not in jeopardy when they choose to preach on race from a biblical and theological perspective.

As Rev. Key and I were developing our "Wade in the Water" webinar, we stressed to the participants that dismantling racism in American mainline Protestant Christianity will not happen with the occasional sermon. This must be an ongoing process in which clergy are taught by homileticians trained in this work, supported by denominational staff who "have their backs" when pastors receive negative pushback, and encouraged by fellow preaching colleagues who covenant with each other in the task of addressing the structures and sins of racism in their congregations and society. So, we developed a model of "homiletical accompaniment" for working with pastors wanting to preach about racism and the church.[31] The model has tools for clergy to assess their own levels of engagement with anti-racism work, as well as those of their congregation, to determine the most prudent approach to preaching on racism in their context. Key to this work is that we continue to meet with and coach clergy over a series of weeks and months as they preach sermons about anti-racism so that they are supported, challenged, and companioned both by Rev. Key and me, as well as their preaching colleagues. Our hope is that this model of homiletical accompaniment for preaching about racism (and other challenging social issues) might be replicated in other denominations and within theological education.

CONCLUSION

As we think of the challenges that clergy face in preaching to unmask, confront, deconstruct, and expel the demon of white supremacy and racism as well as our own homiletical whiteness, Helsel reminds us that "as people of faith, we are all called to attend to the suffering of one another. In order to attend to this suffering, we need to first acknowledge that it exists. Racism continues to exist, and refusing to name it will not make it go away."[32] Indeed, preachers have a moral, ethical, and spiritual responsibility to name this suffering so that congregations can begin—or continue—the process of reckoning with the painful and shameful history of the church and its racist legacy. More specifically, clergy in predominantly white congregations are especially obligated to "take responsibility for educating one another. . . . We need to do our own work, and we need to do it in our faith communities."[33]

As Jones argues, when it comes to addressing racism in America, contemporary white Christians must take up this work of confronting the church's role in constructing and upholding white supremacy, "not just because it is morally right or politically prudent but also because it is the only path that can salvage the integrity of our faith, psyches, and legacies. . . . It's no exaggeration to say our very identities—our souls, to put it theologically—are at stake."[34] The data from the longitudinal surveys of white Protestant clergy explored in this chapter demonstrates that the church has important work to do in supporting its *preachers* in this task of addressing racism and white supremacy in the United States. Our hope is that data in this and future surveys about clergy and preaching will reveal the unique challenges preachers face when addressing race whiteness, white privilege, and white supremacy. In turn, denominations, churches, and seminaries may more effectively utilize their resources for equipping clergy for this essential work that, ultimately, may lead to the liberation of racially minoritized bodies.

NOTES

1. The team members were Rev. Dr. Amanda Wilson Harper, associate professor of Sociology at Tarleton State University; Dr. Wayne Thompson, professor of Sociology at Carthage College; and Rev. Dr. Katie Day, Charles A. Schieren Professor Emerita of Church in Society at United Lutheran Seminary.

2. Carolyn Helsel, *Preaching About Racism: A Guide for Faith Leaders* (St. Louis, MO: Chalice Press, 2018), 1.

3. Helsel, *Preaching About Racism*, 1.

4. Carolyn Helsel, *Anxious to Talk About It: Helping White Christians Talk Faithfully about Racism* (St. Louis, MO: Chalice Press, 2017).

5. Lenny Duncan, *Dear Church: A Love Letter from a Black Preacher to the Whitest Denomination in the U.S* (Minneapolis, MN: Fortress Press, 2019).

6. Ibram X. Kendi, *How to Be an Anti-Racist* (New York: One World, 2019).

7. Robin DiAngelo, *White Fragility: Why It's So Hard for White People to Talk About Racism* (Boston, MA: Beacon Press, 2018).

8. Ta-Nehisi Coates, *Between the World and Me* (New York: Spiegel & Grau, 2015).

9. Helsel, *Anxious*.

10. The 2017 denominations were (in order of the number of respondents): Lutheran (419); United Methodist Church (174); Christian Church (Disciples of Christ) (118); Episcopal Church (100); Presbyterian Church, USA (100); United Church of Christ (70); American Baptist (29); and Other (90).

11. Both the 2017 and 2021 surveys were distributed via social media networks (Facebook, Twitter), one-to-one sharing, and via newsletters and emails from state councils of churches, denominational offices, seminary student and alumni listservs, clergy peer groups, and organizations such as Alban, Backstory Preaching, and the Clergy Emergency League.

12. The 2021 denominations were (in order of the number of respondents): United Methodist Church (542), Lutheran (ELCA) (416), Christian Church (Disciples of Christ) (385), United Church of Christ (196), Presbyterian (USA) (161), Episcopal (118), and Other (101).

13. Clifton F. Guthrie, "Quantitative Empirical Studies in Preaching: A Review of Methods and Findings," *Journal of Communication and Religion* 30 (2007): 73.

14. Guthrie, "Quantitative," 76.

15. This question was not addressed in the 2017 survey.

16. Robert P. Jones, *White Too Long: The Legacy of White Supremacy in American Christianity* (New York: Simon & Schuster, 2020), 6.

17. Jones, *White Too Long*, 6.

18. This question was not asked in the 2017 survey.

19. Three percent of clergy indicated that they have *no interest* in engaging social issues in their preaching and teaching.

20. Another factor that affected preachers' willingness to preach about social issues was the political configuration of the congregation. The more conservative a congregation, the less comfortable most pastors felt addressing "hot topics" in their sermons. For example, more than half of pastors serving conservative congregations (54%) indicated that they felt inhibited preaching about social issues. In comparison, 36% of preachers in "purple" (politically diverse) churches felt inhibited, and only 15% of preachers in progressive churches felt inhibited.

21. HyeRan Kim-Cragg, *Postcolonial Preaching: Creating a Ripple Effect* (Lanham, MD: Lexington Books, 2021), 55.

22. Helsel, *Preaching*, 2.

23. DiAngelo, *White Fragility*, 103.

24. Jones, *White Too Long*, 20–21.

25. Ibid.

26. We must note that the survey did not specify parameters for what "addressing" meant for the preachers. For some, it may be an entire sermon devoted to the topic. For others, it may be only listing the topic as an example of sin without directly engaging the topic itself. As noted earlier, however, the surveys were not testing for actual *content* of sermons, but, rather, attitudes, opinions, and feelings of preachers about these topics.

27. The reader will note that there were fewer topics listed in the 2021 survey than the 2017 survey. This is because the research team decided to combine some subtopics into larger subjects in order to reduce "decision fatigue" in the survey.

28. Recall that for the purposes of this survey, we defined "diverse" as a congregation with at least a 25% racial/ethnic diversity rate.

29. There was no statistical difference when controlling for gender in this subset.

30. Frank A. Thomas's *How to Preach a Dangerous Sermon* (Nashville, TN: Abingdon Press, 2018), and Lisa Cressman's *The Gospel People Don't Want to Hear: Preaching Challenging Messages* (Minneapolis, MN: Fortress Press, 2020) are two such books.

31. Roberto S. Goizueta articulated a "theology of accompaniment" in *Caminemos con Jesús: Toward a Hispanic/Latino Theology of Accompaniment* (Maryknoll, NY: Orbis Books, 1995), which was further developed by María Pilar Aquino in "Theological Method in US Latino/a Theology: Toward an Intercultural Theology for the Third Millennium," in *From the Heart of Our People: Latino/a Explorations in*

Catholic Systemic Theology, edited by Orlando O. Espín and Miguel H. Díaz, 6—48 (Maryknoll, NY: Orbis, 1999).
32. Helsel, *Preaching*, 4.
33. Ibid, 4–5.
34. Jones, *White Too Long*, 24.

BIBLIOGRAPHY

Aquino, María Pilar. "Theological Method in US Latino/a Theology: Toward an Intercultural Theology for the Third Millennium." In *From the Heart of Our People: Latino/a Explorations in Catholic Systemic Theology*, edited by Orlando O. Espín and Miguel H. Díaz, 6–48. Maryknoll, NY: Orbis, 1999.

Coates, Ta-Nahisi. *Between the World and Me*. New York: Spiegel & Grau, 2015.

Cressman, Lisa. *The Gospel People Don't Want to Hear: Preaching Challenging Messages*. Minneapolis, MN: Fortress Press, 2020.

DiAngelo, Robin. *White Fragility: Why It's So Hard for White People to Talk about Racism*. Boston, MA: Beacon Press, 2018.

Duncan, Lenny. *Dear Church: A Love Letter from a Black Preacher to the Whitest Denomination in the U.S.* Minneapolis, MN: Fortress Press, 2019.

Goizueta, Roberto S. *Caminemos con Jesús: Toward a Hispanic/Latino Theology of Accompaniment*. Maryknoll, NY: Orbis Books, 1995.

Guthrie, Clifton F. "Quantitative Empirical Studies in Preaching: A Review of Methods and Findings." *Journal of Communication and Religion* 30 (2007): 65–117.

Helsel, Carolyn. *Anxious to Talk About It: Helping White Christians Talk Faithfully about Racism*. St. Louis, MO: Chalice Press, 2017.

———. *Preaching About Racism: A Guide for Faith Leaders*. St. Louis, MO: Chalice Press, 2018.

Jones, Robert P. *White Too Long: The Legacy of White Supremacy in American Christianity*. New York: Simon & Schuster, 2020.

Kendi, Ibram X. *How to Be an Anti-Racist*. New York: One World, 2019.

Kim-Cragg, HyeRan. *Postcolonial Preaching: Creating a Ripple Effect*. Lanham, MD: Lexington Books, 2021.

Thomas, Frank A. *How to Preach a Dangerous Sermon*. Nashville: Abingdon Press, 2018.

Chapter 6

Civility and the "Purple Church"

An Insufficient Response to White Supremacy

Andrew Thompson Scales

INTRODUCTION: "PURPLE CHURCH" AND THE PROBLEM OF RACISM

Many pastors in majority-white mainline denominations acknowledge that the political polarization that afflicts the United States has also divided congregations along partisan lines. Since the acrimonious presidential election in 2016, some mainline congregations have described their life together as a "purple church." "Purple church" pastors and church leaders seek to navigate tensions around controversial political issues with civility, dialogue, and discovery of common ground for mission and worship despite the different political convictions of the congregation's members.

After the summer of 2020, a season marked by extreme police and vigilante violence against black people, white Christians have a responsibility to do more than engage in dialogue about racism. This is a critical moment to repent of the ways we have not committed ourselves to confronting racism and white supremacy in our communities, our congregations, and also ourselves. Union Presbyterian Seminary president Brian Blount made it plain soon after the killing of George Floyd when he wrote: "White Christians are not witnessing. Not enough."[1]

This chapter seeks to wrestle honestly with Blount's judgment by examining the phenomenon of "purple churches" and the limitations of civility for confronting racism and white supremacy within mainline congregations. The first section offers a brief description of what a "purple church" looks like as it has been represented in national media profiles and recent scholarship in practical theology. The second section interrogates the high value placed on "civility" in "purple church" contexts in light of how civility has been invoked throughout American history to impede progress on civil rights. The third section considers the troubling findings of a 2018 study by the Public Religion Research Institute (PRRI) about racism among white Evangelicals, Protestants, and Catholics in the United States. Finally, we will also consider Blount's call for white Christians to bear witness to the crucified Christ by moving beyond dialogue and prayer to prophetic actions that confront racist violence in America.

A SKETCH OF "PURPLE CHURCH" AND WHITE CIVILITY IN THE NEWS

We begin with a brief sketch of the distinctive commitments of "purple churches," particularly the themes of civility and structured dialogue around controversial issues. "Purple church" often describes majority-white Protestant congregations or congregations within majority-white mainline denominations. These communities seek to hold together members with differing political convictions despite increasing polarization in American society. The "purple" imagery symbolizes the deliberate rejection of identifying the congregation's identity only with "red" (conservative/Republican) or "blue" (liberal/Democratic) political commitments. Instead, these churches represent some mixture or blending of the two "colors" (i.e., "purple").

The concept of "purple churches" received national media attention when Revs. Scott Black Johnston and Patrick H. O'Connor wrote an editorial for CNN after praying with President-elect Donald Trump in January 2017. Johnston and O'Connor described their respective churches—Fifth Avenue Presbyterian Church and First Presbyterian Church, Jamaica, Queens—as communities that self-identify as "'purple churches'—congregations that are economically, racially, and politically diverse, strong in faith, active in community."[2] Both churches are part of the PC(USA). Fifth Avenue is a majority-white congregation, and First Presbyterian's membership is comprised of "African Americans, and Afro-Caribbean, African, and Latino immigrants."[3]

Johnston and O'Connor offered a brief prayer during their meeting with President-elect Trump: "Deliver us, living God, from rancor and cynicism. . . . Encourage us to kindness. Teach us to mend the tattered places in this society. Give us hope and holy perspective for the living of these days."[4] This prayer represents many of the themes that arise from online searches for examples of "purple churches": lament for hurtful and angry words, petition for healing from division, a desire for respect between persons with differing viewpoints, a repair of what has been broken or lost.

"Purple churches" were featured in the national media again in April 2019 when National Public Radio broadcast a profile of White Memorial Presbyterian Church in Raleigh, North Carolina, titled "Pastoring a Purple Church: 'I Absolutely Bite My Tongue Sometimes.'" Pastor Christopher Edmonston described the tensions of preaching about controversial issues in a polarized political climate: "People are coming to our church with their political ideas already formed. . . . That puts pastors in a precarious place, because when you speak against that, given the options for people to practice their Christian faith, they will simply go and find a place where the pastor will agree with them."[5] For White Memorial, NPR correspondent Tom Gjelten observes, keeping the congregation together despite partisan differences means that "worshippers . . . have learned to avoid some subjects for the sake of maintaining harmony."[6]

The NPR profile on White Memorial also explores White Memorial's pragmatic approaches to bringing up controversial issues as a congregation. Edmonston stressed that civility is a common theme in his preaching life, and that it may be easier to maintain civility at White Memorial because of its racial and socio-economic "homogeneity." Despite representation across a wide spectrum of political viewpoints, White Memorial's membership is, as the article describes, "almost entirely white and upper middle class."[7] One of the strengths of maintaining civility in the congregation is that there are many ways they can join together in common mission that are not about issues that they consider controversial. When the congregational leadership decides to consider a controversial issue, White Memorial hosts listening sessions, and opportunities for education and dialogue to remind members that they belong together as people of faith despite disagreement.

PREACHING IN THE PURPLE ZONE: INVITATION TO DIALOGUE ABOUT CONTROVERSIAL ISSUES, MUTUAL DISCERNMENT, AND COMMUNAL PROCLAMATION OF BELIEFS

"Purple churches" stress that maintaining civility and unity can help congregations discuss controversial topics. Nevertheless, many white preachers consider sermons that confront racism and white supremacy too controversial for their pulpits and members. Leah D. Schade's *Preaching in the Purple Zone: Ministry in the Red-Blue Divide* explores a survey she conducted in January 2017 of mainline pastors about preaching on categories that she describes as "controversial justice issues." Eight-nine percent of the 1,205 respondents were white,[8] and 68% of the respondents answered that they hesitate to preach on controversial issues out of "concern about creating controversy and conflict within the membership."⁹ Schade also shares feedback from pastors after the violent white nationalist rallies in Charlottesville in August 2017 about how preaching about race has led to the departure of members and fears of being forced out of pastoral leadership.¹⁰

Schade proposes that pastors apply a "sermon-dialogue-sermon" process for addressing controversial justice issues. A "sermon-dialogue-sermon" approach prepares listeners for a difficult conversation with an introductory sermon, allows the voices of members to be heard in a moderated forum, and then reflects the convictions of the membership back to them in another sermon. Schade notes that an important question for discerning how to develop a preaching and education program on a controversial issue is the problem of "power differentials": acknowledgment of voices that are not present or feel uncomfortable expressing themselves because of a position of vulnerability.¹¹

Preaching in the Purple Zone offers helpful methods for pastors and congregations that want to discern and understand the community's different stances on a controversial justice issue. The pattern of "sermon-dialogue-sermon" is an effective method for discovering and describing a congregation's beliefs. These processes can reflect the values of the community back to its members and even create the opportunity for a pastor to ask curious questions and invite further reflection or deeper dialogue.

The "sermon-dialogue-sermon" process, however, does not explain how to confront white supremacy when members reveal racist convictions. Schade is very careful to distinguish between preaching about a controversial justice issue, and prophetic preaching that "critiques the present reality of injustice and provides an alternative vision of God's future."¹² Throughout the three stages of the "sermon-dialogue-sermon" process, Schade warns preachers that they must not "take a stand on the issue" in the initial sermon that invites people to dialogue,¹³ or while moderating a deliberative dialogue,¹⁴ or in the second sermon that represents the views of the community.¹⁵

Schade's "sermon-dialogue-sermon" method is grounded in trust that a faith community can discern together how to reflect theologically with *agape* love on a controversial issue.¹⁶ The majority of white Christians, however, dismiss the existence of systemic racism or systemic police brutality toward black people. Allen Hilton's book *A House United: How the Church Can Save the World* is an example of how white church leaders reinterpret issues around race as a political issue for which both sides of conservatives and liberals are to blame. Whereas Schade's methods can help members discern together what their beliefs and convictions are, Hilton holds up an ethics of civility that obscures the violence and oppressive systems that threaten black neighbors.

A HOUSE UNITED AND THE PROBLEM OF "BOTH SIDES" EQUIVALENCIES IN "PURPLE CHURCH" DISCOURSE

Within the first chapter of *A House United*, Allen Hilton makes an astonishing claim about American society since the 2016 election: "partyism has surpassed racism among our prejudices."[17] Hilton pairs this lament for an intensifying division of public life into stark polar opposites with nostalgia for moments in American history that he considers less divisive:

> Gone are the days of Lincoln's "Team of Rivals," which brought disparate voices into conversation for the country's good, or even the days when Republican president Ronald Reagan and Democratic congressman Tip O'Neill struck deals across the aisle. Across this present divide, compromise is anathema.[18]

According to *A House United*, the problems of intolerance in the contemporary political landscape are also present in religious divisions between the binaries of conservative and liberal or fundamentalist and progressive. Hilton traces a dialectic of both sides being equally responsible for discord throughout church history, including Paul and James on faith and works, Gnostics and Irenaeus of Lyons, Martin Luther and the Catholic Church during the Reformation, fundamentalists and liberals at Princeton Theological Seminary in the early twentieth century, and presently Rob Bell and John Piper on doctrines about hell and universal salvation.

The theological themes that *A House United* proposes for overcoming this dialectical tension of conservatives and liberals are Jesus's prayer for the unity of his disciples and Paul's criticism of divisions within the Corinthian church.[19] The solution to resolving conflict in congregations, as well as extreme tensions and violence in American society, is to reorient one's perspective on inclusion from a begrudging obligation to "the realm of enlightened self-interest."[20] Rather than entrenching in one's camps of division and difference, Hilton calls Christians to practice a counterintuitive generosity toward their opponents, not only for the opponent's benefit, but also for their own growth and development in faith.

By welcoming whomever a distinct group perceives as the "they" (i.e., "the other"), Christian communities establish a creative tension in which the opposing participants bless one another and the world around them. Practices like reading the Bible together or partnering in mission projects can bring people together across divides in a way that even transforms surrounding communities.[21] Hilton also recommends that churches host moderated discussions about controversial issues, organized by "ground rules that would guide respectful dialogue, asking us to *testify* rather than to *campaign*."[22]

Commitment to the work of dialogue and partnership across differences is the way forward, the book concludes, to achieving Christ's vision of reconciliation, healing, and peace: "Against all odds, by God's grace, through God's Spirit, the church can save this divided world."[23]

A House United represents American society as a stark binary of left and right, liberal and conservative, blue and red, with an assumption that both sides deserve equal blame for contemporary national tensions and incidents of violence. A strong nostalgia for less divisive periods of Christian and American history pervades each chapter, but the author simultaneously traces the binary of conservative/liberal intransigence through the earliest days of Christianity and the American Republic.

Another characteristic of "purple church" ministry that *A House United* affirms is an unfailing confidence that dialogue will bring about deeper mutual understanding and cooperation despite difference. Structured dialogue that acknowledges the values of both perspectives on an issue appears to be the resolution of conflict, rather than the discernment of the anatomy of the conflict (i.e., better understanding of what convictions participants hold and why). Shared mission projects that are not focused on controversial issues can draw people together, as can discussion about common ground and shared beliefs about their faith.

The grave error of *A House United*, and I would also argue of many mainline proponents of "purple church" values, is the uncritical assumption that the power dynamics of structured conversations and congregational life are equal for every participant. The affirmation of all perspectives as inherently and equally valid in the context of structured dialogue—without an acknowledgment of imbalances of power—can contribute to relational dynamics that silence or exclude the congregation's most vulnerable members.

Rhetoric about everyone remaining civil when talking about controversial issues reinforces an assumption that the stakes are the same for every participant. When moderators or preachers emphasize not expressing too much anger, or not holding people accountable too strongly for their convictions, these dialogues can unintentionally inhibit communal progress toward understanding the painful effect some perspectives can have on others. For example, when someone denies the existence of systemic racism or considers the growing list of black people killed by police to be unconnected incidents, it is a denial of the very real fear and danger that African Americans experience daily.

It is a mistake to treat the *representation* of different viewpoints as a *resolution* of conflict or the *restoration* of a beloved community gathered around Jesus. I propose that the high cost of maintaining civility despite profound divisions is not the greatest strength of "purple churches," but rather their fatal flaw. Civility presumes another person's good faith participation, and it demands reticence with respect to holding others accountable for the consequences of their views. Some views may deny or diminish the painful realities that so many neighbors face in America during this time of political division and violence. Representation of differing viewpoints is not the same as practicing spiritual discernment to call people to change, to repent, to recognize some commitments as destructive toward their neighbors, or even morally evil.

In contrast to Hilton's nostalgia for more civil times in American political discourse, I propose that the legacy of civility in American politics is not necessarily an ideal that deserves emulation. In fact, in many instances, civility has served as a powerful inhibitor to social justice. As the following examples demonstrate, powerful politicians have used the ideals of civility to thwart the passage of anti-lynching legislation, reinforce Jim Crow segregation, and deprive black Americans their right to vote throughout the history of the American legislative process.

Perhaps the most incisive critique of civility in American politics can be found in Robert Caro's multi-volume presidential biography *The Years of Lyndon Johnson*. Caro has often described his exhaustive work on figures like Lyndon Johnson and Robert Moses as a study about *power:* "about how power is obtained, about how power is used and how it's abused."[24] Far from offering an easy binary of liberals and conservatives, Caro dives deep into personal letters, transcripts of conversations, newspaper clippings, and thousands of interviews to bring powerful politicians to life. Caro exposes some of the most influential politicians in modern American history—such as Georgia senator Richard Russell (the namesake of the Russell Senate Office Building) and President Lyndon Johnson—as flawed human beings who were frequently vain, vehemently prejudiced, and most often unwilling to change their views about race without considerable political pressure.

Caro's third volume in the *Years of Lyndon Johnson* series, *Master of the Senate*, doubles as a biography of the ferocious Texan politician, and as a history of the Senate's centuries of reactionary policy regarding race in America. Caro describes the rules of civility and decorum on the Senate floor that prohibited any negative representation of fellow senators. During the 1940s and 1950s, the evocation of Rule 19 could silence a speaking senator for attacking a colleague's personal reputation or political record.[25]

Through extensive reliance on the rules regarding civility and a parliamentary loophole known as the filibuster, Southern senators like Russell and their allies defeated proposals for federal anti-lynching legislation in 1938,[26] and again in 1948.[27] In both campaigns to intimidate black voters through refusal to control white supremacist violence, opponents like Senator Bankhead of Alabama spoke with fastidious grace and magnanimity toward senatorial colleagues, while also using the most vicious racial slurs to describe black citizens who sought to exercise their right to vote.[28]

Civility often looms large in American media and public discourse as one of our nation's most precious common virtues. A great lament of our present political climate is the increasing polarization that divides friends, families, and communities along political lines. In the pursuit of healing divisions, many community leaders have sought a restoration of civility in our relationships as a corrective to violent and dehumanizing rhetoric. But civility can also, as Robert Caro observes, be a set of rules and expectations that maintains power structures and inhibits progress. Civility can be a tool for white supremacists to maintain power and coerce silence.

When white mainline churches employ rhetoric around maintaining civility while talking about controversial issues, it is worthwhile at least to ask the question of whether or not civility is covering over deeper issues of exclusion and prejudice. The following section of this chapter considers the results of a 2018 survey from the PRRI, which found that white Christians in America were far more likely than Americans at large to deny the realities of systemic racism toward black people. The PRRI study suggests that "purple churches"—majority-white mainline congregations committed to civility—are not helping alleviate racism and white supremacist violence in America. White mainline Protestants are actually some of the most vocal deniers of systemic racism and police brutality.

THE PROBLEM OF RACISM IN AMERICAN MAJORITY-WHITE CONGREGATIONS

The evils of racism are not simply "out there" in the world. Racism and white supremacy retain an idolatrous grip on majority-white congregations around the country. In 2018, the PRRI developed a "Racism Index" that assessed survey respondents' attitudes toward questions regarding structural or systemic racism in America. A brief review of the PRRI study is a disheartening exposé of racist attitudes held by Americans who identify as Christians. Robert P. Jones, the founder of PRRI, argues in a recent opinion article for NBC News that, contrary to the idea that participation in church communities makes white Christians less racist, "the relationship between holding racist views and white Christian identity is actually stronger among more frequent church attenders than among less frequent church attenders."[29]

The survey asked respondents about whether they believed that killings of black people by police were "isolated incidents" or "part of a broader pattern of how police treat African Americans." In 2018, two years before the massive civic mobilizations and public demonstrations after the killing of George Floyd by police officer Derek Chauvin, 53% of Americans in general considered police killings of black men as evidence of systemic racism. By contrast, 71% of white evangelical Protestants regarded police killings of black people as isolated incidents, as did 63% of white Catholics and 59% of white mainline Protestants.[30]

CONCLUSION: MOVING FROM PURPLE CHURCH CIVILITY TO REPENTANCE AND WITNESS

In this particular season of police and vigilante violence against black people in America, we return to Brian Blount's assertion: "White Christians are not witnessing. Not enough."[31] Blount offered this refrain throughout his statement from May 31, 2020, on the death of George Floyd. The horror of watching police officer Derek Chauvin kneel with his knee on George Floyd's neck for 8 minutes and 46 seconds has provoked an unprecedented wave of protests around the United States and the world. We have learned about the growing litany of names of murdered black people: Breonna Taylor, Ahmaud Arbery, Dominique Rem'mie Fells, and so many others. The crisis of state-sponsored violence against black people—when they are stopped by police, when they protest in the streets—reveals how radically different our society is from the Reign of God that Jesus talked about throughout his ministry.

Blount, a New Testament scholar and expert on Revelation, calls white Christians to bear witness to the crucified Jesus, who reigns even now above all earthly powers. This crisis is a moment to put faith into practice, "Not just spiritually. Tangibly. Not just with well-intentioned prayer. With concrete action. Not just from the pulpit and in the sanctuary. Out in the world, on the streets of their cities, in the corridors of their power."[32] Civility will not save us. We must repent of our tolerance of racism and turn again to the One who breaks down every dividing wall.

As a pastor and preacher, I know both the threats and opposition that come from talking about racism with fellow white Christians. Nevertheless, all of us, pastors and church members alike, must repent with the resolve to move beyond dialogue toward anti-racist action. The high value that "purple churches" place on the maintenance of civility is too costly when it avoids reckoning with dehumanizing violence that hurts our neighbors. The denial of racist violence and white supremacist influence in American society is pervasive in white Evangelical, mainline Protestant, and Catholic communities. Dialogue that does not acknowledge the complicity of white Christians in the brutal consequences of American white supremacy is insufficient to confront the evils of racism.

This radical reorientation toward solidarity with black neighbors may result in the death of the ideals that constitute a "purple church." We belong to a Messiah whose death was profoundly uncivil, shocking, and scandalous.

Christ crucified confronts and judges even our noblest impulses toward civility when that civility demands silence about the oppression of our neighbors. We worship a God who leads people and communities through death into a promise of life with the risen Lamb. When white Christians join in the work of confronting white supremacy with words and actions, we witness to the risen Christ and his radical solidarity with our black neighbors.

NOTES

1. Brian Blount, "Statement from President Blount on the Death of George Floyd," *Union Presbyterian Seminary,* May 31, 2020, https://www.upsem.edu/newsroom/statement-from-president-blount-on-the-death-of-george-floyd/ (accessed on October 20, 2020).

2. Scott Black Johnston and Patrick H. O'Connor, "We Prayed with Donald Trump," *CNN Opinion*, January 19, 2017, https://www.cnn.com/2017/01/19/opinions/we-prayed-with-donald-trump-johnston-oconnor/index.html (accessed on October 19, 2020).

3. Johnston and O'Connor, "We Prayed."

4. Ibid.

5. Tom Gjelten, "Pastoring a Purple Church: 'I Absolutely Bite My Tongue Sometimes,'" *National Public Radio*, April 6, 2019, https://www.npr.org/2019/04/06/703356844/pastoring-a-purple-church-i-absolutely-bite-my-tongue-sometimes (accessed on October 21, 2020).

6. Gjelten, "Pastoring."

7. Ibid.

8. Leah D. Schade, *Preaching in the Purple Zone: Ministry in the Red-Blue Divide* (New York: Rowman & Littlefield, 2019), 20.

9. Schade, *Preaching*, 22.

10. Ibid, 23.

11. Ibid, 80.

12. Ibid, 18.

13. Ibid, 85.

14. Ibid, 105.

15. Ibid, 124.

16. Ibid, 125.

17. Allen Hilton, *A House United: How the Church Can Save the World* (Minneapolis: Fortress Press, 2018), 9.

18. Hilton, *A House United*, 15.

19. Ibid, 101.

20. Ibid, 102.

21. Ibid, 126–38.

22. Ibid, 188.

23. Ibid, 223.

24. David Marchese, "Robert A. Caro on the Means and Ends of Power," *The New York Times Magazine*, April 1, 2019, https://www.nytimes.com/interactive/2019/04/01/magazine/robert-caro-working-memoir.html (accessed on October 21, 2020).

25. Robert A. Caro, *The Years of Lyndon Johnson: Master of the Senate* (New York: Vintage Books, 2002), 95.

26. Caro, *The Years*, 97.

27. Ibid, 101.

28. Ibid, 98.

29. Robert P. Jones, "Racism among White Christians is Higher than among the Nonreligious. That's No Coincidence," *NBC News*, July 27, 2020, https://www.nbcnews.com/think/opinion/racism-among-white-christians-higher-among-nonreligious-s-no-coincidence-ncna1235045 (accessed on October 23, 2020).

30. Alex Vandermaas-Peeler, Daniel Cox, et al., "Partisan Polarization Dominates Trump Era: Findings from the 2018 American Values Survey," *Public Religion Research Institute*, October 29, 2018, https://www.prri.org/research/partisan-polarization-dominates-trump-era-findings-from-the-2018-american-values-survey/ (accessed October 23, 2020).

31. Brian Blount, "Statement from President Blount on the Death of George Floyd."

32. Ibid.

BIBLIOGRAPHY

Black Johnston, Scott and Patrick H. O'Connor. "We prayed with Donald Trump." *CNN Opinion*, January 19, 2017, https://www.cnn.com/2017/01/19/opinions/we-prayed-with-donald-trump-johnston-oconnor/index.html (accessed on September 25, 2021).

Blount, Brian. "Statement from President Blount on the Death of George Floyd." *Union Presbyterian Seminary*, May 31, 2020, https://www.upsem.edu/newsroom/statement-from-president-blount-on-the-death-of-george-floyd/ (accessed on September 25, 2021).

Caro, Robert A. *The Years of Lyndon Johnson: Master of the Senate*. New York: Vintage Books, 2002.

Gjelten, Tom. "Pastoring a Purple Church: 'I Absolutely Bite My Tongue Sometimes.'" *National Public Radio*, April 6, 2019, https://www.npr.org/2019/04/06/703356844/pastoring-a-purple-church-i-absolutely-bite-my-tongue-sometimes (accessed on September 25, 2021).

Hilton, Allen. *A House United: How the Church Can Save the World*. Minneapolis, MN: Fortress Press, 2018.

Jones, Robert P. "Racism among White Christians Is Higher Than among the Nonreligious. That's No Coincidence." *NBC News*, July 27, 2020, https://www.nbcnews.com/think/opinion/racism-among-white-christians-higher-among-nonreligious-s-no-coincidence-ncna1235045 (accessed on September 25, 2021).

Marchese, David. "Robert A. Caro on the Means and Ends of Power." *The New York Times Magazine*, April 1, 2019, https://www.nytimes.com/interactive/2019/04/01/magazine/robert-caro-working-memoir.html (accessed on September 25, 2021).

Schade, Leah D. *Preaching in the Purple Zone: Ministry in the Red-Blue Divide*. New York: Rowman & Littlefield, 2019.

Vandermaas-Peeler, Alex, Daniel Cox, et al. "Partisan Polarization Dominates Trump Era: Findings from the 2018 American Values Survey." *Public Religion Research Institute*, October 29, 2018, https://www.prri.org/research/partisan-polarization-dominates-trump-era-findings-from-the-2018-american-values-survey/ (accessed on September 25, 2021).

Chapter 7

Resisting White Fragility

Preaching toward Indigenous-Settler Reconciliation in Canada

Sarah Travis

Canada's first prime minister, John A. Macdonald, was a purveyor of blatant anti-Indigenous racism.[1] In the late 1800s, he was the ideological architect of the country's residential schools program, which separated thousands of Indigenous children from their families with the primary goal of assimilation. Children were removed from their homes and relegated to unsafe communal living situations where they were cleansed of their Indigenous practices and abused—many died.[2] The aim of this partnership between church and state was the complete assimilation of Indigenous peoples and the eradication of their cultures.

Macdonald's image is captured on the Canadian ten-dollar bill and countless statues in the public square. He has been honored as a hero of Confederation and early nation-building. Today, there is a debate about how to approach his legacy as both a "nation-builder" and a racist. For example, the town of Kingston, Ontario, is the hometown of the late prime minister and has wrestled with the legacy of its "favorite son." Some have argued that the process has left them feeling "like the city is being personally attacked" because of the many negative comments about Macdonald's racism.[3] This kind of defensiveness is an example of white fragility, which refers to a variety of counterproductive reactions of white people when they encounter issues of race. It also relates to settler fragility, which is the tendency of settlers to become uncomfortable and defensive when confronted with their own participation in colonialism. Canada is in the midst of a conversation about how to remember and honor its nation-builders vs. the honoring of the tragic historical realities faced by Indigenous peoples which were caused by the white supremacy of Canada's leaders. Settler-Indigenous relations are, or should be, a serious concern for Canadians, especially given the patterns of racism and white supremacy that continue. Fragility is a barrier to transformation and reconciliation in the preaching process.

This chapter critically engages the concepts of "white fragility" and "settler fragility" in terms of their function as barriers to preaching toward reconciliation among white settler Canadians and Indigenous peoples in Canada. First, I briefly trace the meaning and context of reconciliation in the Canadian context. Second, I explore white fragility as it is described by Robin DiAngelo, critically evaluating its usefulness for preaching in the context of white supremacy and colonialism. I explore the concept of settler fragility as a means to create a more complete picture of the fragility of some preachers and listeners. Third, I consider the implications of white and settler fragility for preaching in white settler congregations in Canada as they move toward reconciliation. I propose that sermons may challenge fragility as it occurs in both preacher and listener primarily through a decolonized process of capacity-building. As we build the capacity of white people to resist both settler and white fragility, decenter whiteness, and avoid denial, we are also building capacities for the hard work of reconciliation.

COLONIALISM AND RECONCILIATION IN CANADA

From its beginnings, Canadian land has been contested. The nation emerged as an act of colonial fiat that settled a land that was declared "people-less' by the British and French monarchies, despite the existence of Indigenous peoples.[4] As Elaine Enns and Ched Myers observe, Canada, along with the United States, Australia, and South Africa, is a "settler colonial" state, which represents "a distinct type of colonialism that functions through the replacement of indigenous populations with an invasive settler society that, over time, develops a distinctive identity and sovereignty."[5] Settler Canadians are those who are non-Indigenous. Indigenous peoples are diverse groups which claim primacy in the land that is now Canada and whose occupancy of the land preceded European colonialism. Indigenous people are tremendously affected, and in negative ways, by the manifestations of colonialism that continue in Canada. Settler Canadians and Indigenous peoples are all caught up in the social, political, economic, and cultural repercussions of colonialism, with or without their knowledge.

Canadian self-understanding includes a belief that the nation is welcoming and tolerant of others, resulting in a multicultural nation that is inclusive and free of racism. This "myth of tolerance" is an important facet of national identity and is supported by the way that Canadians remember and tell stories about their national origins.[6] For instance, only recently have students learned about the existence of residential schools. In reality, Canadian society is divided by race, rooted in white supremacy, and complicit in atrocious acts against Indigenous populations. Indigenous peoples face barriers to education, health care, jobs, and basic sanitation. National and local governments have failed to provide for the material, physical, and intellectual well-being of Indigenous peoples.

In recent years, a truth and reconciliation process has sought to address the injustices faced by Indigenous peoples in Canada. The Canadian Truth and Reconciliation Commission conceptualizes reconciliation as being "about establishing and maintaining a mutually respectful relationship between Aboriginal and non-Aboriginal peoples in this country. For that to happen, there has to be awareness of the past, acknowledgement of the harm that has been inflicted, atonement for the causes, and action to change behaviour."[7] Thus, reconciliation has prerequisites—the past must be acknowledged and atoned for, behavior must change before these mutually respectful relationships can be established and maintained. In other words, truth-telling and accountability precede the possibility of reconciliation.[8]

Theologian Willie Jennings acknowledges that reconciliation is a problematic concept because of its misuse in Western Christianity, although it is not irretrievable. However, reconciliation may be beyond the capacity of many Christians: "In truth, it is not at all clear that most Christians are ready to imagine reconciliation."[9] If Jennings is correct, then a task of preaching may be to prepare and equip listeners to imagine reconciliation. This includes building capacity within our listeners to resist fragile responses and begin to acknowledge and atone for wrongs that have been committed. A typical fragile response would be to say, "I had nothing to do with these wrongs which were committed by my ancestors." In order to capacitate listeners to engage in the pre-work of reconciliation, we might encourage them to understand that (a) the wrongs are ongoing, contemporary, as well as historical; and (b) the church, as the body of Christ in the world, must take responsibility for its own action and inaction in regard to Indigenous peoples.

To preach reconciliation is a high calling for Canadian churches, especially settler churches with white preachers. We have the shared task of interrogating and exposing white supremacy, white privilege, and white colonial domination, particularly paying attention to the role of race in colonial systems. The preaching of the church is essential if reconciliation is to be enacted; it is an urgent and imperative task. As a matter of course, we can only preach *toward* reconciliation, highlighting the historical and contemporary racism that has prevented Indigenous peoples from finding safety in Canadian society. White fragility and settler fragility recognize the reality that white settlers have a really difficult time acknowledging and critically engaging the concept of race, especially as it is steeped in the problem of colonialism.

WHITE FRAGILITY AND SETTLER FRAGILITY

In 2018, sociologist Robin DiAngelo published *White Fragility: Why It's So Hard for White People to Talk about Racism*. It jumped to the top of the *New York Times* bestseller list following the racial uprisings in the summer of 2020, after the murder of George Floyd. DiAngelo describes a phenomenon in which white people experience extreme "racial stress" when they are confronted with the reality of racism and their own complicity. Part of this reluctance emerges from an implicit belief that good people are not racist. All whites are motivated to maintain the racial status quo that places white people at the top of a societal hierarchy and relegates all people of color to "other." DiAngelo writes: "Whiteness rests upon a foundational premise: the definition of whites as the norm or standard for human, and people of color as a deviation from that norm."[10] Acknowledging the history and reality of whiteness places individuals in a state of psychosocial stress, which then triggers a range of defensive responses.[11] As DiAngelo argues, these defensive responses include the "Outward display of emotions such as anger, fear, and guilt and behaviors such as argumentation, silence, and leaving the stress-inducing situation. These behaviors, in turn, reinstate white racial equilibrium."[12] For example, DiAngelo points out the tendency for white women (especially) to cry when they are confronted with their own racist behavior, which then re-centers the white person (woman) as the object of concern and detracts from the possibility of learning from that experience of racist behaviors or attitudes. White fragility, then, is a means for white people to wield power by maintaining the status quo. DiAngelo writes that white fragility is more than just defensiveness or whining, instead it may be "conceptualized as the sociology of dominance: an outcome of white people's socialization into white supremacy and a means to protect, maintain, and reproduce white supremacy."[13] When this maintenance and protection is threatened, when disequilibrium occurs, white fragility restores equilibrium by reinstating self-image, control, and white solidarity. Individuals might become angry, exhibit hurt feelings such as guilt, or shut down completely. These strategies are frequently subconscious, but not benign.[14]

These behaviors prevent white people from actively resisting racism—by being angry, guilty, or avoiding the situation altogether. Marcus Woolombi Waters, in 2016, argues that if one has been raised in a world that reinforces whiteness and white superiority, settlement and colonization via "invasion and genocide," fear arises if these "truths" are challenged. The fear is that "this 'truth' will destroy or diminish an identity you cherish, and because you have no understanding of a world beyond whiteness, you have no culturally acceptable way to articulate what you perceive as a crisis."[15] Katy Waldman, in her review of *White Fragility* in the *New Yorker*, likens white fragility to a virus: "Like a mutating virus, racism shape-shifts in order to stay alive; when its explicit expression becomes taboo, it hides in coded language. . . . It just looks for ways to avoid detection."[16] White fragility results in hidden racism, since it is culturally inappropriate for racist attitudes to be spoken out loud. Instead, individuals respond in a variety of ways to maintain their distance from people of color, as well as maintaining the status quo.

Once educated about white fragility, according to DiAngelo, white people will find themselves in a position of discomfort, which is a key to growth and therefore desirable.[17] Her advice is to get informed: "to consider it a matter of life and death and do your homework."[18] If white fragility surfaces, DiAngelo suggests that one should breathe, listen, and reflect, seeking advice when necessary, and eventually return to the situation in which the fragile response occurred.[19]

While DiAngelo's work has helped to educate some people about race, it is not without its critics. The key critique of this work is that it re-centers whiteness—black people are described two-dimensionally and frequently appear in the book merely as a foil to teach white people a lesson. DiAngelo also tends to homogenize whiteness, without truly accounting for diversity within the white population and without acknowledging that white people belong to a variety of cultures.[20] It is important to keep in mind that settler congregations are not themselves homogenous—there are a variety of races, socio-economic statuses, and every other category of difference.

White fragility is an interesting and useful concept for understanding the challenges that might arise when preaching about racism to settler congregations. It is productive when white preachers are able to recognize white fragility in themselves and their congregations. White settler Christians are likely to be affected by some degree of white fragility which may or may not resemble DiAngelo's analysis entirely. It is enough to premise that white people often feel defensive or fearful when they are confronted with the concept of racism and their own complicity in racist systems.

Settler fragility is a recent and related concept which identifies the inability of settlers to talk about their own social, racial, and geographical privilege.[21] As with white fragility, white supremacy is also at the root of settler fragility, but it relates more to European cultural and religious superiority than to the concept of white racial superiority. Fragile individuals distance themselves from implication in colonial systems in order to avoid the guilt of complicity. Settlers move toward "innocence" as if their presence on the land is unrelated to violence and genocide. Settlers may argue that they too have experienced racism, even though they are white, and thus avoid the conversation. Some will argue that they have played no role in the settling of the land. Others will claim that history is irrelevant—the present population bears no responsibility for what has happened in the past. Settler fragility is helpful for thinking about reconciliation, as it exposes the tendency of settlers to avoid the topic altogether, without perceiving that there is a need for confession and reparations. Unlike white fragility, settler fragility can also be experienced by persons of color. The outcomes are similar to those of white fragility, as are the potential responses of the preacher. From this point on, I will refer simply to "fragility" as it incorporates both white and settler tendencies.

FRAGILITY AS A BARRIER

What is a Canadian settler preacher to do with the existence of fragility? Specifically, in the Canadian context, we are invited to preach toward reconciliation. Fragility becomes a barrier to preaching toward reconciliation, insofar as it continually seeks to keep whiteness at the center and is motivated to reduce racial and colonial stress. Fragility is complicated by the "myth of tolerance" described above. If Canadians see themselves as welcoming and tolerant culture, it will come as an unwelcome shock to confront a Canada that is actually founded upon white supremacy. Even the way that race is codified and understood within the national dialogue is problematic. In 1995, the word "racist" was declared "unparliamentary language" in the Manitoba Legislative Assembly, meaning that it was not a word to be used in legislative debates.[22] This is an example that highlights the barriers to preaching about racism in a country that does not want to talk about racism at the level of government nor the level of community life. Canada is struggling to talk about race, yet acknowledging and confessing racism and privilege are essential aspects of moving toward reconciliation.

Jeffrey Denis writes about Indigenous-settler relations in Canada. He perceives that Canada's tendency is toward "laissez-faire" racism, a concept originally developed to talk about white attitudes of superiority toward African Americans in the post-civil rights era.[23] In the Canadian context, this involves stereotyping Indigenous persons, blaming contemporary Indigenous problems on the Indigenous themselves rather than on systematic or structural factors, and resistance to policy changes that would make a meaningful difference to Indigenous communities.[24] In other words, there is an appetite to maintain the status quo vis-à-vis the group positioning of settler vs. Indigenous communities. How might a preacher challenge the status quo in the face of white fragility? An important task of preaching toward reconciliation is to decenter whiteness, something which both white and settler fragility resist wholeheartedly.

There are significant pastoral implications of white and settler fragility. When preaching against racism or colonialism, preachers in white congregations are speaking to a roomful of people who may feel afraid and threatened. They will be uncomfortable if we talk about race. They might react in a variety of predictable and unpredictable ways. As preachers and pastors, do we coddle the frail tendencies of our white folks or do we challenge them? What is our responsibility as preachers toward the discomfort which white people experience? This may be an unpopular question, as it again centers white people's emotions in our response to racism. Yet we must be aware that this is an uncomfortable process, especially as it is likely to limit the ability of listeners to absorb or respond to our message of racial reconciliation. Mathias explains that "because of the hegemonic power of whiteness, racial dialogues falls short when emotionalities of whiteness such as guilt, defensiveness, silence, or sadness are held above emotionalities of anger, frustration, sadness, and humiliation felt by people of Color when deconstructing race."[25] It is essential to remember that the discomfort felt by white people in these situations is not comparable to the pain experienced by Indigenous persons. While we as preachers have a responsibility to protect and care for all listeners, it is important not to draw a false dichotomy between "pastoral" preaching and "prophetic." It is not pastoral to keep those who do harm comfortable in that harm. Disrupting the narratives that hurt and divide us is a pastoral and prophetic act.

Preachers are also affected by fragility. I see it in myself in my hesitation to talk about race, and my fear that my words, approach, and attitudes in relation to race may be inappropriate, offensive, or unintentionally damage the very relationships I want to enrich. I stumble over the language of race. As a preacher, I also fear the responses of others who are suffering from this frailty of spirit. I recall preaching a sermon about settler-Indigenous relations. As I was greeting people at the door, one man was visibly angry and took me to task for referring to residential schools as "cultural genocide." He was offended that I would accuse his nation of such an action, and angry that I was trying to overturn the status quo. On another occasion, I was criticized for preaching about Indigenous issues. The individual cited a "need to move on" and argued that his own white Irish ancestors were just as oppressed as Indigenous peoples today.

PREACHING AS CAPACITY-BUILDING

Fragility is highly problematic, and it stands as a clear barrier to preaching toward reconciliation insofar as it causes white people to avoid fruitful responses to racism and colonialism. In Canada, fragility must not only be identified as an issue, but also addressed and pronounced to be dangerous to the project of reconciliation. White individuals may respond in a variety of negative ways—consciously and unconsciously, to sermons about racism. In reality, preachers addressing settler-Indigenous relations might have to hurt settler-colonial feelings. Sermons may indeed trigger fragile responses, and it is not possible to avoid such responses. It may be most appropriate to deem this kind of preaching as resistance to fragility. Homiletician Christine Smith has written about preaching as resistance:

> Resistance is not just our reaction to the evil we experience and participate in, it is our stand against it. It is not an act of standing still and defending ourselves against the evil that surrounds us, but it is a movement into it and through it, with speech and presence and action. The church's resistance to evil needs to be strong and compelling. If preaching is to be a transforming act, then the power and integrity of our proclamations will surely be measured by their ability to mobilize communities to resist the evil that confronts us.[26]

Preaching should actively attempt to reform and transform the community, and this includes attempting to strengthen the capacity of listeners for the work of reconciliation. Sermons address whole communities of people, and in order to be mobilized for action, communities must also build capacity both to resist white fragility and equip to engage with issues of race and reconciliation.[27] This capacity-building involves offering skills and frameworks by which settler listeners might be able to bring white fragility to consciousness and act to respond in more productive ways. This is a journey of reformation of self and society.

There are a number of ways that preaching can contribute to this formation work. Enns and Myers invite us into a "discipleship of decolonization."[28] In the context of settler-Indigenous relations, it is helpful to employ tools of decolonization to dismantle white fragility. Decolonization involves "critically examining the historical, social, economic and political patterns and systems of power that have been formative in developing one's own and one's ancestors' worldview, and working to dismantle and transform one's way of being in the world."[29] This is an inner work of transformation that is both liberating and demanding.[30] The goal, of course, is for transformation of whole communities, yet the work must begin at the individual level.

This process begins with the preacher themselves, with self-formation and self-understanding. It is necessary for preachers to search themselves for fragile responses to the issue of race. Fragility must be addressed at the personal level of the preacher before it can be addressed from the pulpit. The following are acts of resistance against white fragility, which can be performed both in sermon preparation and in the delivery of sermons. These build the capacity of communities to respond to racism and engage in reconciliation. These acts of resistance are frequently overlapping and interrelated.

EXPOSURE TO DISCOMFORT

In DiAngelo's words, "to interrupt white fragility, we need to build our capacity to sustain the discomfort of not knowing, the discomfort of being racially unmoored, the discomfort of racial humility." Sermons are spaces in which settlers can be exposed to the uncomfortable history and legacy of settler-Indigenous relations, including contemporary wrongdoing against Indigenous peoples. Merely telling the stories of Indigenous peoples and the crimes committed against them by church and state will cause white people to be profoundly uncomfortable. Through repeated exposure in sermons, listeners may be caused to confront their own discomfort. A closely related goal is education. In sermons, we can learn the history of Indigenous people and be exposed to the proper names of Indigenous communities. It is also a time when intercultural competencies can be modeled. If we are to preach reconciliation, we must first confront the historical and contemporary realities that create the conditions for the divide in the first place. As noted above, reconciliation is not possible until there is confession and accountability. In sermons, the preacher is able to confess wrongs committed by the Christian community, of which some listeners may not even be aware.

DECENTERING WHITENESS

In naming a history of racial oppression and marginalization, we also deny that white people are special or more valuable than people of color. We must confront the denial of white people that racism does not exist or that they personally have no role to play. This has the positive consequence of naming the agency of settler individuals to engage in the work of reconciliation. In other words, they are necessary agents of change, who can choose to participate in the process of reconciliation. In Canada, preaching can work to debunk the national "myth of tolerance," acknowledging that white supremacy is alive and well in Canadian culture.[31] It is also important to tell the stories of Indigenous peoples in their own words.

PRACTICING RESTORATIVE SOLIDARITY

Restorative solidarity refers to the act of "making things right."[32] Enns and Myers choose the language of "response-ability" to engage the issue of restorative solidarity between settlers and Indigenous peoples, which they define as "a commitment to repair past harms and restore justice in our shared present."[33] White fragility inhibits our response-ability and our ability to engage in the work of decolonization. This may involve transforming unconscious settler shame into a useful kind of guilt that inspires action. It is useful for preachers to name concrete ways for settlers to participate in acts of reconciliation.

Through this kind of preaching, we acknowledge that building capacity to combat fragility is good news for both settler and Indigenous communities, although the good news may first sound like bad news for settlers. It is uncomfortable and disorienting to be exposed, educated, decentered, confronted, and urged toward solidarity. For preachers to address these issues will not make them popular, and they themselves will be intensely uncomfortable especially as fragility is triggered. To be liberated from fragility is gospel news. Sermons can strengthen white people to resist their tendency toward fragility, so that they may become active and willing participants in the work of reconciliation.

NOTES

1. Canada occupies the northernmost portion of North America. Thirty-five million Canadians live in a land area of approximately 4 million square miles. It is important to note that Canadian identity is not monolithic. Canada's Indigenous peoples are diverse and represent a variety of geographic, historic, and social locations.

2. It is unclear how many children died. In May 2021, a mass grave was discovered outside of the Residential School in Kamloops, British Columbia, with the bodies of 215 children. Although the true number is unknown, it is estimated to be in the thousands.

3. Eric Andrew-Gee. "In Kingston, an Agonizing Question: What to Do about Sir John A. Macdonald?" https://www.theglobeandmail.com/canada/article-in-kingston-an-agonizing-question-what-to-do-about-sir-john-a/ (accessed on February 19, 2021).

4. Maria A. Wallis, *Colonialism and Racism in Canada: Historical Traces and Contemporary Issues* (Toronto, ON: Nelson Education, 2010), 1.

5. Quoted in Elaine Enns and Ched Myers, *Healing Haunted Histories: A Settler Discipleship of Decolonization* Center and Library for the Bible and Social Justice Series Book 2 (Eugene, OR: Cascade Books, 2021), Kindle Edition, 68.

6. Wallis, *Colonialism and Racism in Canada*, 23–24.

7. Canada, Truth and Reconciliation Commission, Volume 6, http://www.trc.ca/assets/pdf/Volume_6_Reconciliation_English_Web.pdf (accessed on June 18, 2021).

8. Canada. Truth and Reconciliation Commission, http://trc.ca/assets/pdf/Calls_to_Action_English2.pdf (accessed February 26, 2021).

9. Willie James Jennings, *The Christian Imagination: Theology and the Origins of Race* (Hartford: Yale University Press, 2010), Kindle Edition, 9.

10. Robin J. DiAngelo, *White Fragility: Why It's So Hard for White People to Talk about Racism* (Beacon Press, 2018), Kindle Edition, 25.

11. DiAngelo, *White Fragility*, 101.
12. Ibid, 103.
13. Ibid, 113.
14. Ibid, 106.
15. Marcus Woolombi Waters, "White Fragility, White Fear: The Crisis of Racial Identity in Australia, and Beyond," *The Guardian*, November 23, 2016, https://www.theguardian.com/commentisfree/2016/nov/23/white-fragility-white-fear-the-crisis-of-racial-identity-in-australia-and-beyond (accessed on February 11, 2021).
16. Katy Waldman, "A Sociologist Examines the 'White Fragility' that Prevents White Americans from Confronting Racism," *The New Yorker*, July 23, 2018, https://www.newyorker.com/books/page-turner/a-sociologist-examines-the-white-fragility-that-prevents-white-americans-from-confronting-racism (accessed on February 5, 2021).
17. DiAngelo, *White Fragility*, 142.
18. Ibid, 143.
19. Ibid, 147–48.
20. See Raluca Bejan, "Robin DiAngelo's 'White Fragility' Ignores the Differences between Whiteness," *The Conversation*, August 27, 2020, https://theconversation.com/robin-diangelos-white-fragility-ignores-the-differences-within-whiteness-143728 (accessed on February 11, 2021). See John McWhorter, "The Dehumanizing Condescension of 'White Fragility,'" *The Atlantic*, July 15, 2020, https://www.theatlantic.com/ideas/archive/2020/07/dehumanizing-condescension-white-fragility/614146/ (accessed on February 6, 2021).
21. See Dina Gilio-Whittaker, "Settler Fragility."
22. Elsa Kaka, "Why Is Being Called 'Racist' More Offensive than Racism Itself? White Fragility Silences Voices, Says Advocate | CBC News." *CBC*, June 20, 2020, https://www.cbc.ca/news/canada/manitoba/pov-racism-white-fragility-1.5619647 (accessed on February 17, 2021).
23. Jeffrey Denis, *Canada at a Crossroads: Boundaries, Bridges, and Laissez-Faire Racism in Indigenous-Settler Relations* (Toronto, ON: University of Toronto Press, 2020), 9.
24. Denis, *Canada at a Crossroads*, 9.
25. C. E. Matias, "Decolonizing the Colonial White Mind," in *Feeling White. Cultural Pluralism Democracy, Socio-Environmental Justice & Education*. SensePublishers, Rotterdam, 2015, 68, https://doi-org.myaccess.library.utoronto.ca/10.1007/978-94-6300-450-3_11 (accessed on February 17, 2021).
26. Christine Smith, *Preaching as Weeping, Confession and Resistance*, 5.
27. DiAngelo, *White Fragility*, 14.
28. Enns and Myers, *Healing Haunted Histories*, 44.
29. Marchand-Lafortune, quoted in Enns and Myer, 43.
30. Enns and Myers, *Healing Haunted Histories*.
31. With thanks to Ben Travis-Miller for this and other insights. Personal Correspondence, June 18, 2021.
32. Enns and Myers, *Healing Haunted Histories*, 41.

33. Ibid, 43. Carolyn Helsel has also used this language in relation to preaching against racism: "Authentic relationships require this kind of response-ability: being able to hear the frustration and the pain another person has experienced, without feeling as if we need to run in and 'fix it' or save them. Instead, we are called to respond by being witnesses, accompanying our brothers and sisters and supporting them in whatever ways we can." Carolyn Helsel, https://reflections.yale.edu/article/lets-talk-confronting-our-divisions/white-fragility-and-response-ability-carolyn-b-helsel (accessed on February 22, 2021).

BIBLIOGRAPHY

Andrew-Gee, Eric. "In Kingston, an Agonizing Question: What to Do about Sir John A. Macdonald?" https://www.theglobeandmail.com/canada/article-in-kingston-an-agonizing-question-what-to-do-about-sir-john-a/ (accessed on February 19, 2021).

Bejan, Raluca. "Robin DiAngelo's 'White Fragility' Ignores the Differences within Whiteness." *The Conversation*, http://theconversation.com/robin-diangelos-white-fragility-ignores-the-differences-within-whiteness-143728 (accessed on February 19, 2021).

Canada, House of Commons Debates (May 9, 1883), 1107–08.

Church, Jonathan. "The Problem with 'White Fragility' Theory." *Quillette*, https://quillette.com/2018/08/24/the-problem-with-white-fragility-theory/ (accessed on August 24, 2018).

Denis, Jeff. *Canada at a Crossroads: Boundaries, Bridges, and Laissez-Faire Racism in Indigenous-Settler Relations*. Toronto, ON: University of Toronto Press, 2020.

DiAngelo, Robin J. *White Fragility: Why It's So Hard for White People to Talk about Racism*. Boston: Beacon Press, 2018.

Enns, Elaine and Ched Myers. *Healing Haunted Histories: A Settler Discipleship of Decolonization*. Center and Library for the Bible and Social Justice Series. Eugene, OR: Cascade Books, 2021.

Gilio-Whittaker, Dina. Beacon Broadside: A Project of Beacon Press. "Settler Fragility: Why Settler Privilege Is So Hard to Talk About," https://www.beaconbroadside.com/broadside/2018/11/settler-fragility-why-settler-privilege-is-so-hard-to-talk-about.html (accessed on June 22, 2021).

Helsel, Carolyn B. "White Fragility and Response-Ability – by Carolyn B. Helsel | Reflections." https://reflections.yale.edu/article/lets-talk-confronting-our-divisions/white-fragility-and-response-ability-carolyn-b-helsel (accessed on February 19, 2021).

Jennings, Willie James. *The Christian Imagination: Theology and the Origins of Race*. Hartford: Yale University Press, 2010.

Kaka, Elsa. "Why Is Being Called 'Racist' More Offensive than Racism Itself? White Fragility Silences Voices, Says Advocate | CBC News." *CBC*, June 20, 2020, https://www.cbc.ca/news/canada/manitoba/pov-racism-white-fragility-1.5619647 (accessed on February 19, 2021).

McWhorter, John. "The Dehumanizing Condescension of 'White Fragility.'" *The Atlantic*, July 15, 2020, https://www.theatlantic.com/ideas/archive/2020/07/dehumanizing-condescension-white-fragility/614146/ (accessed on February 19, 2021).

Smith, Christine M. *Preaching as Weeping, Confession, and Resistance: Radical Responses to Radical Evil*, 1st ed. Louisville, KY: Westminster John Knox Press, 1992.

Waldman, Katy. "A Sociologist Examines the 'White Fragility' That Prevents White Americans from Confronting Racism | The New Yorker," https://www.newyorker.com/books/page-turner/a-sociologist-examines-the-white-fragility-that-prevents-white-americans-from-confronting-racism (accessed on February 19, 2021).

Wallis, Maria A. *Colonialism and Racism in Canada: Historical Traces and Contemporary Issues*. Toronto, ON: Nelson Education, 2010.

Waters, Marcus Woolombi. "White Fragility, White Fear: The Crisis of Racial Identity in Australia, and beyond | Marcus Woolombi Waters." *The Guardian*, November 23, 2016, sec. Opinion. https://www.theguardian.com/commentisfree/2016/nov/23/white-fragility-white-fear-the-crisis-of-racial-identity-in-australia-and-beyond (accessed on February 19, 2021).

Chapter 8

Through a Glass Dimly

White Preaching and Epistemological Ignorance

Christopher M. Baker

INTRODUCTION: BLACK LIVES, WHITE OPINIONS

When, on May 25, 2020, Derek Chauvin was filmed kneeling on a motionless George Floyd, slowly suffocating him until he was dead, the footage was so shocking that for a brief moment it seemed like there might be some small consensus on race in the United States. *This*, at least, was so blatant a murder, so patently indefensible that no one could deny or defend it. Floyd's cry, "I can't breathe"—echoing Eric Garner and countless other victims of white asphyxiation—galvanized a growing global protest movement.[1] In the middle of a pandemic sweeping the face of the globe, protestors from all around the world—galvanized by the initial protests in the Twin Cities of Minneapolis and Saint Paul—took to the streets demanding a justice far beyond the mere question of criminal accountability for Chauvin.

Once again, "I Can't Breathe" and "We Can't Breathe" became the rallying cries of continually suffocated peoples, even as, too often, they choked on the tear gas of militarized police forces hell-bent on proving the protestors right. These protests so captured the public imagination that as the COVID-19 pandemic raged, American Psychological Association president Sandra L. Shullman placed George Floyd's murder alongside the killings of Ahmaud Arbery, Breonna Taylor, Eric Garner, Philando Castile, Trayvon Martin, and a countless list of other victims of anti-black racist violence, and said, "We are living in a racism pandemic."[2] This juxtaposition of pandemic with pandemic articulated well what protestors themselves were saying. While the whole world was facing the threat of COVID-19, that threat was neither evenly distributed racially nor the only pressing threat to black lives.

But while for a moment there seemed to be a consensus that Derek Chauvin's murder of George Floyd was, well, murder, that consensus, and along with it, white support for Black Lives Matter, quickly dissipated. From June 2020 (toward the beginning of the mass protests) to September 2020, according to Pew Research Center, white support for the Black Lives Matter movement (or the Movement for Black Lives) dropped rapidly, from 60% to 45%,[3] a decline that has since fallen to 37% as of April 2021.[4] Meanwhile, as white support for Black Lives Matter has fallen, American trust in the police to "promote justice and equal treatment of all races"—which fell sharply after the murder of George Floyd—has risen from a low of 56% in June 2020 all the way to 69% in March 2021.[5] There are many possible reasons why white support for Black Lives Matter plummeted from its high point shortly after George Floyd's murder, but key among them may well be narrative contestation. While the protests themselves, and initial news coverage, highlighted police violence against black people—a narrative that was confirmed by brutal police overreactions to the protests themselves—a counter-narrative soon emerged, rooted in cultural tropes of innate black criminality.[6] "Protestors" were often re-framed as "looters," justifying egregious, violent police crackdowns and reinforcing "law and order" motifs that cast police violence as a necessary constraint on black criminality.

This contest of narratives, in which different stories compete against each other to define the meaning of a moment, is not a new one, nor is narrative contestation a new idea for preachers. In concert with Hans Frei's crucial intervention in biblical hermeneutics[7] and subsequent trends in postliberal theology, "narrative"—not just as story, but also and especially as epistemology and theological method[8]—has long been a watchword in homiletics. Further, as method, "narrative" is a matter of collaborative worldmaking, in which storytellers "prompt interpreters into the process of co-creating narrative worlds,"[9] manufacturing realities that resemble and help us process and interpret our own world. Let me say that again, more clearly: Stories manufacture realities. Stories, as bell hooks noted of movies, "make real."[10]

This understanding of narrative contestation, placed in the context of this flashpoint in the global movement for racial justice, has significant implications for white preaching—especially white preaching as white preaching—on race. It is into this contest of narratives that white preachers who wish to preach on race must enter. And my concern is that when white preachers do enter into this contest, they do so from a position of ignorance.

In this chapter, drawing from resources in the emerging field of Philosophy of Race,[11] I will first argue that white preaching is preaching shaped by the socio-political production of whiteness. This is not quite the same thing as "preaching that happens to be done by preachers who happen to be white," but there is a tremendous amount of overlap between the two. Next, I will argue that whiteness is characterized in part by a particular kind of ignorance, a strategic unknowing and mis-knowing, especially on matters of race and whiteness. Finally, I will argue that in order to be able to preach adequately on race, white preachers (or any other preacher shaped by whiteness) need to understand white epistemological ignorance and need to take steps to correct it by learning both global and local racial histories

THE WHITENESS OF WHITE PREACHING

A main reason white preaching cannot adequately address "race" and "whiteness" is precisely because it is white. This is not merely a matter of standpoint epistemology, as that would cast "white" as a standpoint among standpoints, a perspective from which one may know, fail to know, or "know" falsely. But whiteness is neither a standpoint nor a perspective, but rather is a power structure that shapes the production of knowledge.

Sociologist Joe R. Feagin describes "whiteness" as a kind of "racial frame"—by which he means a way of constructing and organizing knowledge and experience in ways that make meaning and provide structure—"that provides an overarching and generally destructive worldview" broadly common to white people across the bounds of "class, gender, and age."[12] This frame is a hegemonic frame, and of such central importance that it "is more than just one significant frame among many; it is one that has routinely defined a way of being, a broad perspective on life, and one that provides the language and interpretations that help structure, normalize, and make sense out of identity."[13] As such, it is an enduring frame, one "deeply held and strongly resistant to displacement,"[14] shaping the bounds of knowledge, establishing the most basic, default assumptions about the white self, the world, and the role of the white self in the world, even when whiteness itself—in post-racial form—is kenotic, self-emptying, rendering itself invisible to itself.[15]

Linda Martín Alcoff describes whiteness as a "mythically rendered" group identity formation.[16] It is a group identity formation in that it binds a group together with a common social identity, forming the group as the group, however provisional and fluid the identity of that group and the content of its members may be. It is "mythically rendered" both in that it is in and of itself a socially constructed fiction (there is no objective reality to "race," and thus no objective reality to "whiteness" as either a racial formation or a norm that transcends the fiction of "race") and especially in that the fictional narrative of whiteness is "historically truncated to foreground the good bits."[17] If, as Richard Dyer argues, whiteness is a symbolic claim to both aesthetic and moral superiority (where the two amount to the same thing), it must craft narratives of itself to justify itself as such.[18] This shapes the contours and content of collective memory, determining what gets remembered, what gets forgotten, and what gets misremembered.

WHITE EPISTEMOLOGICAL IGNORANCE, STORYTELLING, AND COUNTER-STORYTELLING

This dimension of whiteness—the erasure of true (or at least honest) narratives and metanarratives and the construction of politically convenient false ones—can be best understood through the category of "epistemologies of ignorance." As Shannon Sullivan and Nancy Tuana note, "epistemology of ignorance" may seem like an oxymoron, as "epistemology" is the study of knowledge and "ignorance" describes the state of *not* knowing.[19] But this risks fundamentally misunderstanding ignorance. While the word does describe "a gap in knowledge" that constitutes "an epistemic oversight" or "an accidental bi-product of the limited time and resources that human beings have to investigate and understand their world," often ignorance is neither accidental nor innocent.[20] This is especially true when it comes to issues of race, where "a lack of knowledge or an unlearning of something previously known often is actively produced for the purposes of domination and exploitation."[21]

White racial ignorance, coupled with and serving to ignore and/or legitimize racial oppression, is a species of what Alison Bailey calls "strategic ignorance."[22] Rather than being a matter of simply not knowing, ignorance, for Bailey, is "often an active social production" emerging out of and helping to maintain a dominant social position.[23] Sometimes this ignorance is imposed on oppressed persons, such as the cultural genocide that is the erasure of Indigenous knowledges and languages. Sometimes it is the strategic rewriting of history. And sometimes it is smaller, more individual, a psychological defense mechanism whereby the white person (whose position as white is a morally impermissible position of privilege that undermines the moral and ontological innocence at the heart of the symbol "white") refuses to learn that which is painfully obvious.

While the language may be relatively new,[24] José Medina notes that epistemologies of ignorance—whether understood as such or not—"have always been a key theme of race theory, and they have featured prominently in the philosophies of race of classic authors such as Sojourner Truth, Anna J. Cooper, W.E.B. Du Bois, Alain Locke, and Frantz Fanon, to name a few."[25] It is, or ought to be, impossible to seriously study race and not notice the key role that the manufacture of ignorance plays in the construction and maintenance of racial oppression. Further, this manufactured ignorance is what Medina calls an "*active* ignorance,"[26] a "will *not* to believe."[27] This *active* ignorance is differentiated from *passive* ignorance. Where *passive* ignorance (like all forms of ignorance) includes both the "absence of true belief" and the "presence of false belief," these are a neutral matter of simply not knowing or knowing wrongly.[28] *Active* ignorance is also a matter of not knowing or knowing wrongly, but it is decidedly not neutral. It entails "cognitive resistances," "affective resistances," "bodily resistances," and "defense mechanisms and strategies," *active* ways of refusing to know.[29] Further, these happen both in white individuals and white communities, and make it difficult to unlearn false racial narratives and learn true ones.

Unlearning false narratives and learning true ones is one of the greatest challenges in engaging race, because race itself is a false narrative, and one that renders all narratives about the modern liberal world false. The entire field of CRT, going all the way back to its roots in the appropriation and critique of CLS, is built precisely on this observation. All legal structures, all politics, and all accounts of history within the unfolding of the liberal democratic project are built on false narratives about universal ideals and rights that do not hold up under a critical historical gaze. Discourses on, say, freedom fall apart when one realizes that as "freedom" becomes an ideal, the freedom for some (wealthy white male landowners) is purchased by the enslavement and subjugation of others. And this, according to Charles W. Mills, pertains to every aspect of the modern world.

"White supremacy," Mills argues, "is the unnamed political system that has made the modern world what it is today."[30] That this is such a jarring statement indicates just how successful the project of white epistemological ignorance has been. A modern, liberal, global paradigm built on imperialism, colonialism, slavery (chattel and otherwise), and genocide becomes the story of the emergence of order from chaos, of civilization from barbarianism, of Enlightenment from the Dark Ages, of universal progress of both the technological and moral sense.[31] But those—the story of slavery and genocide and the story of freedom and progress—are in fact the same story, told from different sides. They are competing narratives aiming to define the meaning of the same broad events. White epistemological ignorance is what allows one version of the tale, a race-neutral version, to become hegemonic.

While this may all seem theoretical, at a moment in which many states are moving to ban the teaching of CRT (without any apparent concept of what CRT even is); ban the use of the 1619 Project in schools; and preserve a hagiographic account of the United States, its founders, and its founding ideals, theory can be a pressing political problem.[32] But racial storytelling and counter-storytelling and how it is shaped by white epistemological ignorance is not just a global phenomenon. It is also and especially a local problem, and for a white preacher to preach adequately on race, she must go beyond understanding the ways in which white ignorance shapes storytelling; she must actively learn local racial history, the main site of contestation in the congregation.

CASE STUDY: WILMINGTON, NORTH CAROLINA

In *Blood Done Sign My Name*, historian Timothy B. Tyson recalls his childhood growing up in North Carolina in the early 1970s, the son of Rev. Vernon Tyson, a white Methodist minister who wanted to work for racial justice.[33] While the main tale told in the book is the story of the 1970 lynching of Henry Marrow in Oxford, North Carolina, the book—like a good Southern story—meanders through both the racial history of North Carolina and the exploits of the Tysons. Toward the end, young Tim Tyson finds himself as one of "the first white students to attend Williston Ninth Grade Center" in a desegregating Wilmington.[34] There he encountered startling racial violence:

> Fistfights were common. To go to the bathroom, especially alone, was to risk being beaten up, or worse. One boy cut another with a straight wire. Several others bashed another boy's head with a brick. Someone shot and wounded two boys in a racial clash after a basketball game. Many students carried knives and brass knuckles. Full scale riots erupted several times a year; we would be sitting in the cafeteria, hear a loud crash of silverware and plastic trays clattering to the floor, and the bloodhounds of race would come flying off their leashes. We grimly referred to early spring as "riot season," as though it were a varsity sport.[35]

The racial violence Tyson encountered in the school mirrored the racial violence erupting outside it. In response to this, Tyson's father Rev. Vernon Tyson—who had an established history of racial liberalism if not quite radical anti-racism—decided to try "to ease the violence and nurture interracial community."[36] This, Tyson notes, was not unfraught. "Like many white liberals, of course, Daddy was still mired up to his ankles in racial paternalism."[37] Most white attempts at anti-racism, after all, are paternalistic, coming at the "problem" (often framed as a "race problem" as though it were a neutral matter) from a generally unstated position of moral superiority, aiming (consciously or not) to be the white savior captured so well in popular film.[38] But Rev. Tyson, unlike so many white liberals, was willing to both speak honestly and listen attentively. So he began speaking with local black leaders and community members.

In the conversations that followed, he "heard African American parents make bitter references to 'what happened' and 'what caused all of this'—as if the causes of Wilmington's racial turmoil were self-evident."[39] And they were self-evident. To black people. White Wilmington residents, however—no matter how long they had lived in the city or how well they thought they knew the area—could only offer "quizzical expressions and vacant nods."[40] If "what happened" was "what caused all of this," white folk had no idea "what happened." And "what happened" was the Wilmington Insurrection of 1898, the ghosts of which were still haunting the city.

Jeanette Rodríguez and Ted Fortier have developed a concept of "cultural memory" to describe the way that memory is both preserved by and helps shape the "culture" of a given group, the "collective knowledge" of that group that "ensures cultural continuity" from generation to generation, allowing each new generation to both preserve and "*reconstruct* their cultural identity."[41] This memory is often preserved in narrative form,[42] in which the people are the carriers of story but also in which the story—as cultural memory, that memory that is a condition of possibility for culture and for a people—is in a sense the carrier of the people.

For Rodríguez and Fortier, "cultural memory" helps establish the identity of a people and to help that people "reconstruct the past in order to exist in a meaningful manner in the present."[43] In its narrative form, it functions very much like myth,[44] in that it is an organizing narrative that "has a historical basis" and "can be transformative."[45] Like myth, too, it often reflects conscious choices to both preserve memory and to lend it significance, "to give those memories precedence in communal remembrance."[46] It helps marginalized cultures preserve themselves against the "ravages of colonialism," as narratives and meta-narratives become tools for resisting the erasure of that culture and its people as a people via cultural genocide.[47] Stories are preserved. They are told and retold and retold again in countless ways as part of a narrative, epistemological contestation of meaning. "Cultural memory," in other words, is the exact opposite of white epistemological ignorance.

This—the contestation of meaning via competing memories and narratives—is what was at work in Wilmington when Rev. Tyson tried to figure out the cause of all the violence. The "cultural memory" was a *racial* memory, a memory of and about race, preserved in the black narrative memory while strategically erased from the white narrative memory. White people in Wilmington had collectively forgotten the single most important and traumatic event in Wilmington's entire history, and black people were no longer going to let them keep forgetting.

In the 1897 Wilmington municipal election, a Fusionist coalition of the Populists and Republicans helped create a multi-racial government.[48] In a city in which, at that time, the black population outnumbered the white population, this exacerbated white racial anxiety, threatening not just the myth of white supremacy but the reality of white racial rule.[49] Thus, on November 10, 1898, white rioters staged a coup against the legitimately elected multi-racial government and massacred many in the majority black population. While no one knows the exact death toll, as one black mother told Rev. Tyson, "They say the river was full of black bodies."[50]

It is important to note that the Wilmington Insurrection was part of a pattern of white racial violence at the end of the nineteenth and beginning of the twentieth centuries in the United States. As with massacres in Atlanta in 1906, East St. Louis in 1917, Omaha and Chicago in 1919, and Tulsa in 1921, black progress—whether political, economic, or both—was met with violent white backlash, snuffing out countless black lives. These events, historian H. Leon Prather Sr. notes, have often been euphemistically called "race riots," a dishonest phrase that tries to make largely one-sided massacres seem like something other than what they were: "white massacre[s] of defenseless blacks with a macabre mixture of carnage and carnival."[51] This kind of false framing is an essential part of the production of white epistemological ignorance, and any white preacher who wishes to preach honestly and responsibly on race must pay close attention to it and contest it whenever and wherever it arises.

CONCLUSION

Where does that leave the white preacher, then, standing in the pulpit at a moment in history in which the centrality of race is impossible to honestly ignore? As white views on race and policing swirl and eddy, flowing this way then that, how does a white preacher preach a good word to a largely white congregation? As a white theologian who has preached for almost two decades now, often on race, and often in white congregations, the only answer I have to offer is a difficult one. White preachers must unlearn so much of what they have always thought they have known, understanding that whiteness has shaped the very contours of thought, memory, belief, and done so in a way that is almost wholly invisible to white people. As George Yancy has put it, "for white people, whiteness is the transcendental norm in terms of which they live their lives," and thus our whiteness is, for us, so normal that we do not notice it.[52]

White preachers must then learn that whiteness manufactures a particular kind of epistemological ignorance, characterized by both the absence of true belief and the presence of false belief. This is an active ignorance, one that white people strategically participate in and benefit from. This ignorance manufactures false narratives that must be contested by true ones. The crafting of compelling, true narratives is one of the primary tasks in preaching, for preaching is always a site of narrative contestation. To preach responsibly on race, then, white preachers must—like Rev. Vernon Tyson—take the time and effort to listen and learn, to be uncomfortable and sit attentively in their discomfort. They must learn both global and local narratives. And they must always question anything that makes them feel better. When it comes to race, convenient, comforting narratives are always a lie. And one of the most profound lies is the symbolic conflation of whiteness with goodness and innocence.

At the end of each class I teach, I leave my students with a charge: "Your hands will never be clean, so choose your dirt wisely." I leave a similar charge now to white preachers. In this mortal life, we see always only ever through a glass dimly. Our gaze is clouded, distorted by sin, and by whiteness. If, then, you must see the world through a layer of dirt and dust, choose that dirt wisely.

NOTES

1. A theological and liturgical account of this white asphyxiation is developed in: Andrew Wymer and Chris Baker, "Drowning in Dirty Water: A Baptismal Theology of Whiteness," *Worship* Volume 90 (July 2016): 319–44.

2. American Psychological Association, "'We Are Living in a Racist Pandemic,' Says APA President," news release, May 29, 2020, https://www.apa.org/news/press/releases/2020/05/racism-pandemic (accessed on September 25, 2021).

3. "Support for Black Lives Matter Movement Down since June," Pew Research Center, https://www.pewresearch.org/fact-tank/2020/09/16/support-for-black-lives-matter-has-decreased-since-june-but-remains-strong-among-black-americans/ft_2020-09-16_blm_01 (accessed on September 16, 2021).

4. Alex Samuels, "How Views on Black Lives Matter Have Changed – And Why that Makes Police Reform So Hard," *FiveThirtyEight*, April 13, 2021, https://fivethirtyeight.com/features/how-views-on-black-lives-matter-have-changed-and-why-that-makes-police-reform-so-hard/ (accessed on September 16, 2021).

5. Samuels, "How Views."

6. On "blackness" and "criminality" in the United States, Khalil Gibran Muhammad argues persuasively that the very idea of "criminal," going back to the early twentieth-century origins of criminology, is a kind of racial ontology manufactured in order to condemn black people by casting blackness as criminal. In a more global setting, Falguni A. Sheth makes a similar observation, as the process of "racialization" casts racialized populations as "unruly" and thus in opposition to and beyond the protections of "law." See Khalil Gibran Muhammad, *The Condemnation of Blackness: Race, Crime, and the Making of Modern, Urban America* (Cambridge, MA and London: Harvard University Press, 2010) and Falguni A. Sheth, *Toward a Political Philosophy of Race* (Albany, NY: State University of New York Press, 2009).

7. Hans W. Frei, *The Eclipse of Biblical Narrative: A Study in Eighteenth and Nineteenth Century Hermeneutics* (New Haven, CT and London: Yale University Press, 1974).

8. Most clearly articulated in Terrence W. Tilley, *Story Theology* (Collegeville, MN: The Liturgical Press, 1985) and William C. Placher, *Narratives of a Vulnerable God: Christ, Theology, and Scripture* (Louisville, KY: Westminster John Knox Press, 1994)

9. David Herman, et al., *Narrative Theory: Core Concepts and Critical Debates* (Columbus, OH: The Ohio State University Press, 2012), 14.

10. bell hooks, *Reel to Real: Race, Class and Sex at the Movies* (New York and London: Routledge, 1996), 1.

11. While "critical race theory" has become a catchall for any critical approach to "race," it is important—especially at a time in which "critical race theory" is a vacuous boogieman weaponized by conservatives in the United States—to understand the similarities and differences between various critical approaches to "race." Critical Race Theory (CRT) emerged in the field of legal studies in the 1970s in the wake of two perceived failures: The failure of the Civil Rights Movement to secure sufficient, lasting, material change, and the failure of Critical Legal Studies (CLS) to adequately address race.

Philosophy of Race, sometimes called Critical Philosophy of Race, by contrast, began to emerge in the field of philosophy in the 1990s, as a reaction to the realization that much of the Western canon is steeped in racism. Any attempt to come up with an adequate account of "race" using the tools of Post-Enlightenment thought would be limited by the very tools being used.

CRT has had a significant influence on Philosophy of Race. CRT and Philosophy of Race have a number of common features, most notably an account of "epistemic privilege," which recognizes that groups negatively affected by racism are more likely to recognize and understand racism than those groups that benefit from it. They are each also deeply critical of liberalism (broadly) and especially the racial liberalism of the Civil Rights Movement. However, they exist in different fields of study, deploy different tools and methods, and have different projects.

12. Joe R. Feagin, *The White Racial Frame: Centuries of Racial Framing and Counter-Framing*, 2nd ed. (New York and London: Routledge, 2013), 10.

13. Feagin, *The White Racial Frame*, 11.

14. Ibid, 12.

15. George Yancy has also recently applied the Christian doctrine of "kenosis" to whiteness, but he does so in a very different way than I am doing here and have done elsewhere. For Yancy, the "kenosis" is not a matter of whiteness emptying itself of form (as I assert here), but rather a matter of white people emptying themselves of whiteness. See George Yancy, *Across Black Spaces: Essays and Interviews from an American Philosopher* (Lanham, MD, Boulder, CO, New York, and London: Rowman & Littlefield, 2020), 126–27.

16. Linda Martín Alcoff, *The Future of Whiteness* (Malden, MA: Polity Press, 2015), 22.

17. Alcoff, *The Future*, 22.

18. Richard Dyer, *White* (New York: Routledge, 1997), 70.

19. Shannon Sullivan and Nancy Tuana, "Introduction," in *Race and Epistemologies of Ignorance*, edited by Shannon Sullivan and Nancy Tuana (Albany, NY: State University of New York Press, 2007), 1.

20. Sullivan and Tuana, "Introduction," 1.
21. Ibid.
22. Alison Bailey, "Strategic Ignorance," in *Race and Epistemologies of Ignorance*, edited by Shannon Sullivan and Nancy Tuana (Albany, NY: State University of New York Press, 2007), 77–94.
23. Bailey, "Strategic Ignorance," 77.
24. Charles W. Mills's 1997 book *The Racial Contract* offers one of the first if not the first robust accounts of race and epistemological ignorance. Charles W. Mills, *The Racial Contract* (Ithaca, NY and London: Cornell University Press, 1997).
25. José Medina, "Epistemic Injustice and Epistemologies of Ignorance," in *The Routledge Companion to Philosophy of Race*, edited by Paul C. Taylor, Linda Martín Alcoff, and Luvell Anderson (New York and London: Routledge, 2018), 247.
26. Medina, "Epistemic Injustice," 247.
27. Ibid, 248.
28. Ibid, 250.
29. Ibid, 205.
30. Mills, *The Racial Contract*, 1.
31. Meant in the broadest sense, as that which flows from "[t]he anti-feudal egalitarian ideology of individual rights and freedoms that emerged in the seventeenth and eighteenth centuries to oppose absolutism and ascriptive hierarchy." Charles W. Mills, *Black Rights/White Wrongs: The Critique of Racial Liberalism* (New York: Oxford University Press, 2017), 28.
32. The 1619 Project is an ongoing, interactive, project of longform journalism developed by Nikole Hannah-Jones and the *New York Times* that understands the history of the United States through the lens of chattel slavery. The name comes from the year that the first enslaved Africans arrived in the British American colonies that would become the United States.
33. Timothy B. Tyson, *Blood Done Sign My Name: A True Story* (New York: Three Rivers Press, 2004).
34. Tyson, *Blood Done*, 258.
35. Ibid, 258–59.
36. Ibid, 263.
37. Ibid.
38. See Hernán Vera and Andrew W. Gordon, *Screen Saviors: Hollywood Fictions of Whiteness* (Lanham, MD: Rowman & Littlefield Publishers, Inc., 2003) and Matthew W. Hughey, *The White Savior Film: Content, Critics, and Consumption* (Philadelphia, PA: Temple University Press, 2014) for some of the ways in which Hollywood motifs and white racial formation dovetail to create a kind of soteriological whiteness.
39. Tyson, *Blood Done*, 271.
40. Ibid.
41. Jeanette Rodríguez and Ted Fortier, *Cultural Memory: Resistance, Faith, and Identity* (Austin, TX: The University of Texas Press, 2007), 1.
42. Rodríguez and Fortier, *Cultural Memory*, 7.
43. Ibid, 14.
44. Ibid, 12.

45. Ibid.
46. Ibid.
47. Ibid, 110.
48. H. Leon Prather Sr., *We Have Taken a City: The Wilmington Racial Massacre and Coup of 1898*, 3rd ed. (Southport, NC: Dram Tree Books, 2006), 30.
49. Prather, *We Have Taken*, 31.
50. Tyson, *Blood Done*, 271.
51. Prather, *We Have Taken*, 11.
52. George Yancy, *Look, a White!: Philosophical Essays on Whiteness* (Philadelphia, PA: Temple University Press, 2012), 7.

BIBLIOGRAPHY

Alcoff, Linda Martín. *The Future of Whiteness*. Malden, MA: Polity Press, 2015.
Dyer, Richard. *White*. New York: Routledge, 1997.
Feagin, Joe R. *The White Racial Frame: Centuries of Racial Framing and Counter-Framing*, 2nd ed. New York and London: Routledge, 2013.
Frei, Hans W. *The Eclipse of Biblical Narrative: A Study in Eighteenth and Nineteenth Century Hermeneutics*. New Haven, CT and London: Yale University Press, 1974.
Herman, David, et al. *Narrative Theory: Core Concepts and Critical Debates*. Columbus, OH: The Ohio State University Press, 2012.
hooks, bell. *Reel to Real: Race, Class and Sex at the Movies*. New York and London: Routledge, 1996.
Hughey, Matthew W. *The White Savior Film: Content, Critics, and Consumption*. Philadelphia, PA: Temple University Press, 2014.
Mills, Charles W. *Black Rights/White Wrongs: The Critique of Racial Liberalism*. New York: Oxford University Press, 2017.
———. *The Racial Contract*. Ithaca, NY and London: Cornell University Press, 1997.
Muhammad, Khalil Gibran. *The Condemnation of Blackness: Race, Crime, and the Making of Modern, Urban America*. Cambridge, MA and London: Harvard University Press, 2010.
Placher, William C. *Narratives of a Vulnerable God: Christ, Theology, and Scripture*. Louisville, KY: Westminster John Knox Press, 1994.
Prather, H. Leon, Sr. *We Have Taken a City: The Wilmington Racial Massacre and Coup of 1898*, 3rd ed. Southport, NC: Dram Tree Books, 2006.
Rodríguez, Jeanette and Ted Fortier. *Cultural Memory: Resistance, Faith, and Identity*. Austin, TX: The University of Texas Press, 2007.
Sheth, Falguni A. *Toward a Political Philosophy of Race*. Albany, NY: State University of New York Press, 2009.
Sullivan, Shannon and Nancy Tuana, eds. *Race and Epistemologies of Ignorance*. Albany, NY: State University of New York Press, 2007.
Taylor, Paul C., Linda Martín Alcoff, and Luvell Anderson. *The Routledge Companion to Philosophy of Race*. New York and London: Routledge, 2018.

Tilley, Terrence W. *Story Theology*. Collegeville, MN: The Liturgical Press, 1985.

Tyson, Timothy B. *Blood Done Sign My Name: A True Story*. New York: Three Rivers Press, 2004.

Vera, Hernán and Andrew W. Gordon. *Screen Saviors: Hollywood Fictions of Whiteness*. Lanham, MD: Rowman & Littlefield Publishers, Inc., 2003.

Wymer, Andrew and Chris Baker. "Drowning in Dirty Water: A Baptismal Theology of Whiteness." *Worship* 90 (July 2016): 319–44.

Yancy, George. *Across Black Spaces: Essays and Interviews from an American Philosopher*. Lanham, Boulder, CO, New York, and London: Rowman & Littlefield, 2020.

———. *Look, a White!: Philosophical Essays on Whiteness*. Philadelphia, PA: Temple University Press, 2012.

RESISTANCE AND POSSIBILITIES
IN HOMILETICS

Chapter 9

Multitasking Preaching

The Liberating Power of Unmasking Whiteness from the Pulpit

HyeRan Kim-Cragg

Unmasking whiteness in multitasking preaching involves constantly scanning preachers' own biases and prejudices when they read, write, see, speak, hear, teach, and research for preaching. Multitasking preaching exposing this thick and complex mask of whiteness is hard work. It requires heavy lifting at times. However, it is ultimately a liberating work, because wearing this mask may distort the beautiful faces of people and harm communities and societies. This work of unmasking whiteness is empowering, because it aims to dismantle the tangled oppression of racism so as to recognize the agency and the dignity of all people regardless of race. It seeks to articulate a goal of preaching as repentance and turning to God.

A CONCEPT OF WHITENESS AND ITS CONNECTION TO PREACHING

A growing body of scholarship shows how "whiteness circulates as an axis of power and identity around the world."[1] Kamal Al-Solaylee in *Brown: What Being Brown in the World Today Means* showcased how whiteness is pervasive in the commercialization of the cosmetics industry, especially for women. One example is "whitening" products that encourage dark-skinned and non-white consumers to believe that white skin is more beautiful.[2] Whiteness is not only a concept or a racial ideological socio-historical construct, but also a materialistic capitalist and sexist problem. Whitening products are a great example of how race, gender, class, and capitalism as well as colonialism intersect. Here we come to one more category, religion, and more specifically Christian preaching.

Evidence of how gender, race, and colonialism were tied together in Christian preaching is found in the book called *Men and Books: Studies in Homiletics*, where Austin Phelps makes an analogy of the preacher using military imagery: "The pulpit should be a battery, well-armed.... The gunner who works it must know what and where the vulnerable spots are.... He must be a man."[3] According to Phelps, the preacher targets people and weaponizes the gospel as a system of truth.

Daniel Coleman's research on Canada and its project of Anglo nation-building demonstrates how the rhetorical expression of "muscular Christianity" was often used in preaching and functioned powerfully to inculcate normative ideals of British civility during the era of national expansion into the prairie west. Coleman writes, "The figure of the muscular Christian, with his untiring and virile physical body balanced by his spiritually sensitive heart, made a perfect representation of the ideal Canadian who could carry out the hard physical work of territorial expansion.... This figure was fundamental to the establishment of the British Protestant ethnic norm in Canada."[4]

The writings of Phelps, and the research of Coleman, demonstrate how closely the white, Anglo, manly, military approach to preaching is connected with the project of colonial nation-building in the United States and Canada. This history is still in our imaginary, and it is difficult to dismiss it. Taking the concept of whiteness and its connection to preaching into consideration, let us examine the different aspects of multitasking preaching, first, turning to preaching as reading.

PREACHING AS READING WITH EYES OPENED

Then the eyes of both were opened. (Genesis 3:7a)

The Bible has often been used to propagate the idea that it is "the transcendental text which all people in all cultures at all times in all circumstances should obey."[5] Such idea of the Bible has been oppressive and has done much harm. Yet, to say that the Bible serves as a tool of oppression is not to deny the importance of the Bible as a tool to resist and liberate. Without question, readers and communities of faith who have suffered many forms of oppression have also found the Bible to be a source of freedom and hope. The Bible readily lends itself to transcultural readings even as it is often used to repress affirmations of difference.[6] It is necessary to be aware of this ambivalence of the biblical interpretation and its impact.

Here, I propose using a postcolonial reading optic[7] in terms of exposing the colonial whiteness within the text through a contrapuntal reading.[8] This reading strategy was developed by Edward Said who writes that contrapuntal reading is reading with "awareness both of the metropolitan history that is narrated and of those other histories against which (and together with which) the dominating discourse acts."[9] The goal of a contrapuntal reading for preaching is not to be content with the dominant and obvious point of view but to reveal the hidden and less obvious stories and issues of the colonized that are intermeshed and embedded in the text.

HOMILETICAL EXEGESIS: A POSTCOLONIAL CONTRAPUNTAL READING OF THE BOOK OF ESTHER 1

Chapter 1 in the book of Esther is outside the lectionary. There are many great questions looking at the first chapter in Esther as we use a contrapuntal reading of the text by highlighting places, words, and events. Reading contrapuntally means taking account of different perspectives simultaneously and seeing how the text interacts with historical or biographical contexts.[10] Let me highlight a few perspectives as a way of probing whiteness overshadowing sexism, racism, and colonialism by using a three "B" homiletical exegesis: "Behind, Between, and Before."[11] Each "B" represents a different aspect of biblical interpretation, using chiefly historical, literary/linguistic, and reader-response criticism, respectively.

Behind

The "behind" exegesis mainly focuses on the background of the biblical text, its culture, its context, its authorship, and its purpose, often employing historical criticism. Chapter 1 in the book of Esther indicates that this empire under the regime of Ahasuerus was powerful, occupying the land from "India to Ethiopia" (1:1). It implies that people in these places have their own language (1:21) and also signals that the empire was prosperous as it highlights "the great wealth" (1:4). The text goes into some detail: "There were couches of gold and silver on a mosaic pavement of porphyry, marble, mother-of-pearl, and colored stones" (1:6). The fact that the king was able to throw a big banquet for many days leads us to question where this wealth came from and how it was accumulated and whose labor was used (exploited) to amass these precious things. The extravagant display of wealth continues in the party by way of listing all the fancy drinks. Amid these lavish banquets going on among all high-class male officials, including seven eunuchs, and sages, at the table,

Vashti appears and throws a party for women. "Queen Vashti gave a banquet for the women in the palace of King Ahasuerus" (1: 9). In the meanwhile, the king is drunken and summons Vashti to come before him, "wearing the royal crown, in order to show the peoples and the officials her beauty; for she was fair to behold" (1: 11). Vashti defies the order. A contrapuntal reading of this particular text implicitly highlights not only the feminist issues of the injustices of patriarchy but also the apparently shameless accumulation of wealth from other lands—an aspect of empire building in the ancient time.

Between

The message between the lines of text is something preachers must pay attention to. Here, "between" points to literary functions of the text, by noting vocabulary, translation, genre, plots, and other devices. The verses 11 and 12 are read: "to bring Queen Vashti before the king, wearing the royal crown, in order to show the peoples and the officials her beauty; for she was *fair* to behold. But Queen Vashti refused to come at the king's command conveyed by the eunuchs. At this the king was enraged, and his anger burned within him."

The word "fair" in English has a racial connotation which conflates "lighter skin" with beauty. Western art often portrays Vashti as white. The Hebrew, however, is תָבוֹט (tō-w-ḇaṯ) which simply means "good," as in good looking. Yet, both **NRSV** and **KJV** versions of the Bible translate the Hebrew word as "fair." Attention to the translation of "fair" is a good example of how a hidden (between the lines) agenda to normalize whiteness and tie whiteness with beauty may be sneaking in homiletical exegesis.

Before

The key to exegesis "before" is to take the readers' interpretive context seriously. The "before" exegesis makes the point that the text must be read through the multiple identities and different social locations of the readers. The "before" exegesis also takes popular cultural and literary work outside the scope of Christian biblical interpretation seriously. Hebrew Bible scholar Linda Day examines how Vashti has been represented in English literary works of the eighteenth and nineteenth century. She was surprised to discover the high degree to which attention was paid to the figure of Vashti in English novels, poetry, and plays during this period and concludes that such intensified interest was connected to the rising movement for women's rights of the nineteenth century in the United Kingdom (UK), USA, and Canada.[12] Yet, Vashti in this European and North American countries' suffrage movement is represented as a white woman's work for white women's benefit at the expense of advancing the abolition movement. This is where the race and gender issues intersect and where anti-racism movements and feminist movements are in tension. It is imperative, hence, that we preach on Vashti, and when we preach on Vashti, we have to do so in a way that goes beyond the ways she was important for white suffragettes. Preachers need to proclaim by lifting up her strong will to refuse, while contesting the representation of portraying Vashti as white.

Preaching unmasking whiteness through homiletical exegesis that uses a contrapuntal reading must involve opening eyes wide enough to notice embedded colonial presence and unveil a racially charged white supremacist interpretation of the Bible. Let us turn to the second aspect of multitasking preaching which is integral to the work of unmasking whiteness.

PREACHING AS WRITING WITH KEEN SELF-AWARENESS

They knew that they were naked. (Genesis 3:7b)

Who has written about whiteness in preaching? Is there a robust scholarship of whiteness in homiletics? If the answer is "no" to these questions one may arguably and regrettably have to admit that academic publishing culture of homiletics breeds white invisible normativity. For this invisibility manifests itself as absence in academic publications as argued elsewhere.[13] Whiteness is a structural power and its presence is most prevalent in its invisibility.[14] Andrew Wymer notes that the fact that white homiletical discourse in journal articles and books is silent about whiteness is evidence that whiteness is pervasive.[15]

To flip the coin, unmasking whiteness includes appreciating writings and contributions of non-white scholars because their lived experience of racism could powerfully confront the sin of whiteness. Yet, the well-intentioned effort of including non-white scholars ends up further ghettoizing and tokenizing their voices. That is why the late Dale Andrews who was asked to write "the African American" chapter for a handbook of practical theology writes, "We have not escaped the marginalization of studying the marginalized" in *Opening the Field of Practical Theology*, edited by two white scholars.[16] Courtney Goto who was asked to write "the Asian American" chapter in the same volume noticed that none of the white scholars were asked to write their own ethnic and racial chapters. Instead, they were invited to address approaches that are central (meaning foundational or well-studied) in the field. After Goto vocally raised the concern of the racial parceling out of volumes and subject matter, a chapter entitled "the white practical theology" was added. Yet, Goto notes that the whole structure of the book, which included fifteen chapters in total, "assumes that the field is divisible into broad approaches that are seemingly untouched by race, while the work of addressing issues of race is assigned to isolated chapters coded as such."[17] This is not just a problem of practical theology but it is the problem found in other theological disciplines as well.[18]

Turning to textbooks in homiletics in terms of preaching as writing with keen self-awareness, we note that there are very few textbooks that are written by non-white scholars in homiletics. There are also very few textbooks, decentering whiteness, that are deployed in mainline theological education. The reality is dire when one looks at Haddon Robinson's *Biblical Preaching*, which is the most sold textbook (over 300,000 copies) in homiletics in the twentieth and twenty-first century in North America.[19] Robinson's book has been republished (in its eighth printing, 2007) and has been translated into other languages for use in different parts of the world. Yet, it too mainly reflects and represents the European and white North American experiences and understandings of homiletics.

It is a painful evidence that whiteness is not an issue as far as scholarly writings are concerned. Or whiteness is ubiquitous in academic publication culture. Sharon Fennema puts it this way, "Whiteness comes with a sense of culturelessness because it is 'just there,' the atmosphere backdrop against which other cultures appear as exotic and unique." That is why "it may be hard to imagine overt manifestations of the power and privilege that constitute whiteness."[20]

That is why preaching as writing with keen self-awareness is crucial. Barbara Blaisdell puts it this way, "We must be honest about our own doubts, questions, and experiences as we prepare to write. This part of preaching is confessional. The final sermon need not be autobiographical, but it must reflect the real issues and struggles of a person of faith."[21] Preachers and scholars of preaching, as writers who work with different authors in edited volumes, must be vigilant how non-white racialized authors may be singled out racially, and targeted or tokenized for work limited to a racial point of view.

Writing here is neither a leisurely hobby nor a luxurious profession that only wealthy intellectuals can afford. Preaching as writing in unmasking whiteness is a struggle, sharpening our pencil to pin down racism, vocalizing the chord to compose resistant sentences. Let us move to the third aspect of multitasking preaching.

PREACHING AS SEEING THROUGH ART AND SPACE IN WORSHIP

> . . . and the man and his wife hid themselves from the presence of the LORD God among the trees of the garden. . . . But the LORD God called to the man, and said to him, "Where are you?" (Genesis 3:8–9)

The location of the pulpit is essential to preaching. It is the place of sight and a space where the message gets across, so to speak. Preaching is on display as "the-flesh-and-blood, oral-aural, face-to-face synesthetic speech event of divine self-disclosure."[22] Susanne Langer speculates that human perceptions are affected by physical forms. She argues that architecture serves more than a functional purpose, because it shapes a space of "human relations and activities."[23] Yet, the discourse on the physical space, including the pulpit, its location, and its use, is never simple.[24] The location of the pulpit is more than utilitarian; it is a theological matter for it creates the environment of the theological encounter. James White puts it this way, the location of the pulpit is important "not because of the place itself but because what God does for humans in that place."[25] The pulpit as a liturgical object is not neutral but power laden. It communicates the preaching authority. It visibly exposes identities of the preacher from gender, body, age, ability, to race. Some young, non-white, and female preachers find that using the pulpit compensates for their marginal identities. However, the voices of those who opposed using the pulpit are also loud as they make a case that the elevated pulpit sets the preacher above and apart from the congregation, symbolizing a colonial theology that overvalues the authority of the preacher.[26]

Since preaching as seeing happens in worship, preachers must also investigate how whiteness is manifested in art related to the liturgical season, especially the ways in which light and darkness are employed in liturgy.[27] For example, the color white is associated with manifestation of the Divine presence, the *theophany*. The story of the transfiguration, for example, appearing in the liturgical season of Epiphany describes Jesus, "transfigured before them, and his face shone like the sun, and his clothes became dazzling white" (Matthew 17:2, NRSV). Celebrating the season by maximizing the use of white as a sign of the Divine presence is taken for granted. It is hard to preach against this visually charged dominant sign celebrated in liturgy. Christmas and Easter also use the color white as the liturgical color. Again, the color white communicates the meaning of goodness, joy, new life, and holiness in the Western liturgical symbolism and culture. Preaching against these significant liturgical seasons is like rowing a boat against a powerful current.

However, the color white does not mean the same thing in other cultures, as argued elsewhere.[28] White clothes in Western culture are associated with joyful celebrations (the wedding dress, for example), whereas the wearing of black is common when one is mourning. In other cultures, is needed, Korean, for example, people wear white during funerals, and red or multi-colors during joyful celebrations such as birthdays and weddings. The color white signifies death and sadness in Korean and other East Asian cultures. The color white may not be necessarily negative in these cultures, but it certainly communicates solemnity rather than joy and happiness. One may also point out that black does not have negative connotations in Western culture all the time. "Black tie," for example, denotes formality usually associated with very happy, special events such as weddings. Judges and academics have worn black gown, including the Geneva gown called preacher's gown, to emphasize their authority, which is something that is honored and respected.

However, it should be noted that a dark color, especially the color black, is negative in most cultures. The ubiquity of the color black as negative poses a serious problem. In the worst case, the color black associated with sinful, dirty, and dangerous meanings is used to stigmatize black and other racially minoritized people. Avoiding this negative association and switching it to something positive is one way to unmask whiteness in preaching as seeing. A more sustained examination of the color symbolism in liturgical art is necessary as preachers know the crucial impact of image, the power of seeing in making sermons. As a final element of multitasking preaching, the next section engages the use of language and the ways it is conveyed in a non-written form.

PREACHING AS HEARING THROUGH LANGUAGE

They heard the sound of the LORD God walking in the garden at the time of the evening breeze. (Genesis 3:8)

Whiteness embedded in liturgical art goes beyond the preaching space. It is also evident in preaching language. "Does language express racial bias?" David Buttrick asked in 1987.[29] We know it does to a degree. Black/white language in English demeans black and favors white. Christine Smith also poses a challenge: if the culture in which we live is white dominant, we should expect that our language is indispensable in transmitting that culture.[30]

It is possible and necessary for a certain community to perform preaching without using human voices (e.g., deaf community). In other words, preaching language includes sign language. However, preaching is the event of hearing *Shema* (Deut. 6:5) that requires the verbal and spoken language to communicate. In this regard, the questions of who speaks and what the language used are critical in unmasking whiteness in preaching. The English language normativity of the standard accent is masked by the white innocence of cultureless neutrality. Henry Giroux names this normativity as colonizing because it is "both invisible to itself and the norm by which everything else is measured."[31]

When I did qualitative research on racialized (non-white) women ordained preachers in the United Church of Canada, most participants shared the challenges they experienced around the language spoken in the pulpit. The following are a few comments they receive after they preached: "Thanks for the sermon. I am sure it was good. But I just did not understand your sermon due to your accent." "I can tell it is a good sermon. But I had a hard time understanding you because you speak so softly. Is this because you come from a patriarchal country?"[32]

While there is a vast variety of English accents spoken in Canada and the United States (and elsewhere), racialized preachers often receive this kind of comment on Sunday mornings, and it tends to be worse for women than for men. More than simply an issue of a linguistic barrier, there are clearly racial overtones in such complaints from the pews. The proof of this is in the fact that racialized ministers who are born in Canada and whose first language is English still get this kind of comment, while white immigrant preachers from Europe, some of whom are not even English speakers (i.e., German, Hungarian), do not.

As shown in the McGeachy research, racialization happens as an encounter with language. While everyone is racialized, racialization refers to "a process that categorizes people of color and Indigenous peoples according to white people's categories of race."[33] While such an encounter becomes a painful experience of deprivation and discrimination, Rey Chow argues that such an encounter also "offers a privileged vantage point from which to view the postcolonial situation, for precisely the reason that this language has been imposed from without."[34] On the other hand, language barriers do exist among racialized preachers who serve the predominantly white and English-speaking congregations.

Language is a medium of relationships. It enables people to build understanding, respect, and trust. The McGeachy research is instructive in this regard: "After a few years of serving an English-speaking congregation, one day a parishioner came to me after the service, 'I heard everything you said. You improved your English quite well.' So I answered, 'Thank you for the comment. I think you improved your hearing ability, too.'"[35] Kwok Pui-lan convincingly sums up well the importance of preaching as hearing through language: "If the aim of postcolonial preaching is to create a multivocal and dialogical faith community committed to justice, we have to attend to the issue of language in intercultural contexts. In urban global cities, it is increasingly common to have church members speaking different mother tongues and immigrants struggling with English or another colonial language. Many of them live in bicultural and bilingual worlds, speak the dominant language with an accent, and must negotiate and translate constantly between hybrid contexts."[36]

CAUTIOUS WORDS INSTEAD OF A CONCLUSION

Hagar named the Lord who spoke to her, "You are El-roi"(the one who sees)... and wandered about in the wilderness of Beer-sheba.... When the water in the skin was gone, she cast the child under one of the bushes.... And as she sat opposite him, she lifted up her voice and wept.... Then God opened her eyes and she saw a well of water. She went, and filled the skin with water, and gave the boy a drink. (Genesis 16: 13; 21: 14–16, 19)

The story of Hagar who named the one who sees is an example of double revelation as she sees the well spring of water as God's revelation which in turn reveals God's attention to her well-being. A similar example of revelation can be found in Genesis 3 which I have mentioned several times above. Feminist interpreters have challenged a dominant telling of Eve's action tempted by the serpent. In their view, the serpent reveals a truth, the tree of the knowledge of good and evil. And upon eating of the fruit, Eve's eyes were opened to wisdom.

Likewise, multitasking preaching involves discerning, self-locating, and naming as preaching involves reading, writing, seeing, speaking, and hearing. The verb "unmask" conjures the image of revealing someone's hidden face. The bottom line of unmasking whiteness in preaching is that the mask of whiteness exists by concealing a hidden reality like air. Whiteness in homiletics breathes deeply in the cultural norm of whiteness in academia and preaching practice as examined above. It is, thus, a time for whiteness to come out.

Preaching unmasking whiteness can be a sweaty exercise. It is a discipline. It requires practice every day in order to build up a muscular habit by naming our social locations, biases, and privileges. This naming is not limited to political correctness but a serious act of confession with humility and honesty. The homiletical task of unmasking whiteness requires vulnerability, exposing the preacher's own nakedness and weaknesses. Anna Carter Florence calls for the preaching as testimony as narrating one's life, a life that is inevitably shaped by colonialism, migration, and other difficult realities.[37] Or she put it more plainly, "What is it about your life and context that leads you to hear this in the text?"[38]

Unmasking homiletical whiteness is a daily and regular practice of repentance, wrestling with Scripture, and its various modes of interpretations involving the location and the identity of the preacher and the people while taking various critical engagements of issues pertinent to whiteness in the world

NOTES

1. Rasmussen Birgit Brander, Irene J. Nexica, and Matt Ray, eds., *The Making and Unmasking of Whiteness* (Chapel Hill: Duke University Press, 2001), 3.

2. Kamal Al-Solaylee, *Brown: What Being Brown in the World Today Means (to Everyone)* (New York: HarperCollins, 2017).

3. Austin Phelps, *Men and Books: Studies in Homiletics* (New York: Scribner's, 1892), 29, cited in Roxanne Mountford, *Gendered Pulpit: Preaching in American Protestant Spaces* (Carbondale: Southern Illinois University Press, 2003), 55.

4. Daniel Coleman, *White Civility: The Literary Project of English Canada* (Toronto: University of Toronto Press, 2006), 129–30.

5. Mary Ann Tolbert, "A New Teaching with Authority: A Re-evaluation of the Authority of the Bible," in *Teaching the Bible: The Discourses and Politics of Biblical Pedagogy*, edited by Fernando F. Segovia and Mary Ann Tolbert (Minneapolis: Fortress, 1998), 176.

6. Kathleen O'Connor, "Crossing Borders: Biblical Studies in a Trans-cultural World," in *Teaching the Bible: The Discourses and Politics of Biblical Pedagogy*, edited by Fernando F. Segovia and Mary Ann Tolbert (Minneapolis: Fortress, 1998), 328.

7. HyeRan Kim-Cragg, *Story and Song: A Postcolonial Interplay between Christian Education and Worship* (New York: Peter Lang, 2012), chapter 2.

8. The term "contrapuntal" has also been deployed by David Buttrick who introduced the same term in his discussion of sermonic moves. For him, the contrapuntal statement in a sermon creates room for doubt and questions. David Buttrick, *Homiletic: Moves and Structures* (Philadelphia: Fortress, 1987), 47.

9. Edward Said, *Culture and Imperialism* (London Vantage, 1993), 51.

10. HyeRan Kim-Cragg, *Postcolonial Preaching*, see chapter 6 (Lanham: Lexington, 2021), 111.

11. Kim-Cragg, *Postcolonial Preaching*, 112.

12. Linda Day, "Vashti Interpreted: Nineteenth and Twentieth Century Literary Representations of the Book of Esther," *Proceedings of the Eastern Great Lakes and Midwest Bible Societies* 23 (Grand Rapids, 2003): 1–14.

13. HyeRan Kim-Cragg, "Invisibility of Whiteness: A Homiletical Interrogation," *Homiletic* 46, no. 1, (2021): 28–39.

14. HyeRan Kim-Cragg, "The Emperor Has No Clothes!: Exposing Whiteness as Explicit, Implicit, and Null Curricula," *Religious Education* 114, no. 3 (2019): 239–51.

15. Andrew Wymer, "Knee-Deep Preaching: A Homiletical Engagement of White Bullshit," *Practical Matters* (July 2018): 7, found at http://practicalmattersjournal.org/wp-content/uploads/2018/07/Wymer-KneeDeep-Preaching.pdf (accessed on September 13, 2021).

16. Dale P. Andrews, "African American Practical Theology," in *Opening the Field of Practical Theology*, edited by Kathleen A. Cahalan and Gordon S. Mikoski (Lanham: Rowman & Littlefield, 2014), 27.

17. Courtney T. Goto, "Writing in Compliance with the Racialized 'Zoo' of Practical Theology," in *Conundrums in Practical Theology*, edited by Joyce Ann Mercer and Bonnie J. Miller-McLemore (Boston: Brill, 2016), 112.

18. Serene Jones and Paul Lakeland, eds., *Constructive Theology: A Contemporary Approach to Classical Themes* (Minneapolis: Fortress, 2005), cited in Ibid.

19. Haddon W. Robinson, *Biblical Preaching: The Development and Delivery of Expository Messages*, 2nd edition (Grand Rapids: Baker, 2001).

20. Sharon R. Fennema, "Postcolonial Whiteness: Being-With in Worship," in *Liturgy in Postcolonial Perspectives: Only One is Holy*, edited by Cláudio Carvalhaes (New York: Palgrave, 2015), 278–79.

21. Ronald J. Allen, Barbara S. Blaisdell, and Scott Black Johnson, *Theology for Preaching* (Nashville: Abingdon, 1997), 182.

22. Charles L. Bartow, "Performance Study in Service to the Spoken Word in Worship," in *Performance in Preaching: Bringing the Sermon to Life*, edited by Jana Childers and Clayton J. Schmit (Grand Rapids: Baker Academic, 2008), 215, 222.

23. Susanne Langer, "Feeling and Form," in *Art and Its Significance*, edited by Stephen Davis Ross (Albany: State University of New York Press, 1987), 235.

24. HyeRan Kim-Cragg, "Probing the Pulpit: Postcolonial Feminist Perspectives," *Liturgy* 34, no. 2 (2019): 22–25.

25. White, *Introduction to Christian Worship* (Nashville: Abingdon, 2000), 81.

26. Mountford, *Gendered Pulpit*.

27. Michael N. Jagessar and Stephen Burns, *Christian Worship: Postcolonial Perspectives* (Oakville: Equinox, 2011), 37–50.

28. Kim-Cragg, "Invisibility of Whiteness."

29. David Buttrick, *Homiletic: Moves and Structures* (Philadelphia: Fortress, 1987), 196.

30. Christine M. Smith, *Preaching as Weeping, Confession, and Resistance: Encountering Handicappism, Ageism, Heterosexism, Sexism, White Racism, Classism* (Louisville: Westminster John Knox, 1992), 131.

31. Henry Giroux, "Racial Politics and the Pedagogy of Whiteness," in *Whiteness: A Critical Reader*, edited by Mike Mill (New York: New York University Press, 1997), 305.

32. HyeRan Kim-Cragg, "Sharing the Feast and Hearing Complex Calling: A Study of Racialized Ordained Women Ministers of the United Church of Canada," report submitted to the McGeachy Senior Scholarship Committee, 2011, https://unitedchurchfoundation.ca/wp-content/uploads/Sharing-the-Feast-and-Hearing-Complex-Calling-HyeRan-Kim-Cragg.pdf (accessed on September 13, 2021).

33. http://www.aclrc.com/racialization (accessed on September 13, 2021).

34. Rey Chow, *Not Like a Native Speaker: On Languaging as a Postcolonial Experience* (New York: Columbia University Press, 2014), 14.

35. Kim-Cragg, "Sharing the Feast and Hearing Complex Calling."

36. Kwok Pui-lan, "Postcolonial Preaching in Intercultural Contexts," *The Homiletic: Journal of the Academy of Homiletics* 40, no. 1 (2015): 18.

37. Anna Carter Florence, *Preaching as Testimony* (Louisville: Westminster John Knox, 2007), xiii.

38. Anna Carter Florence, *Reshaping Scripture: Discovering God's Word in Community* (Grand Rapids: Eerdmans, 2018), 78.

BIBLIOGRAPHY

Al-Solaylee, Kamal. *Brown: What Being Brown in the World Today Means (to Everyone)*. New York: HarperCollins, 2017.

Allen, Ronald J., Barbara S. Blaisdell, and Scott Black Johnson. *Theology for Preaching*. Nashville: Abingdon, 1997.

Andrews, Dale P. "African American Practical Theology." In *Opening the Field of Practical Theology*, edited by Kathleen A. Cahalan and Gordon S. Mikoski, 11–29. Lanham: Rowman & Littlefield, 2014.

Bartow, Charles L. "Performance Study in Service to the Spoken Word in Worship." In *Performance in Preaching: Bringing the Sermon to Life*, edited by Jana Childers and Clayton J. Schmit, 211–23. Grand Rapids: Baker Academic, 2008.

Brander, Birgit, Rasmussen, Irene J. Nexica, and Matt Ray, eds. *The Making and Unmasking of Whiteness*. Chapel Hill: Duke University Press, 2001.

Buttrick, David. *Homiletic: Moves and Structures*. Philadelphia: Fortress, 1987.

Chow, Rey. *Not Like a Native Speaker: On Languaging as a Postcolonial Experience*. New York: Columbia University Press, 2014.

Coleman, Daniel Coleman. *White Civility: The Literary Project of English Canada*. Toronto: University of Toronto Press, 2006.

Day, Linda. "Vashti Interpreted: Nineteenth and Twentieth Century Literary Representations of the Book of Esther." In *Proceedings of the Eastern Great Lakes and Midwest Bible Societies* 23, Grand Rapids, 2003, 1–14.

Fennema, Sharon R. "Postcolonial Whiteness: Being-With in Worship." In *Liturgy in Postcolonial Perspectives: Only One is Holy*, edited by Cláudio Carvalhaes, 277–87. New York: Palgrave, 2015.

Florence, Anna Carter. *Preaching as Testimony*. Louisville: Westminster/John Knox, 2007.

———. *Reshaping Scripture: Discovering God's Word in Community*. Grand Rapids: Eerdmans, 2018.

Giroux, Henry. "Racial Politics and the Pedagogy of Whiteness." In *Whiteness: A Critical Reader*, edited by Mike Mill, 194–215. New York: New York University Press, 1997.

Goto, Courtney T. "Writing in Compliance with the Racialized 'Zoo' of Practical Theology." In *Conundrums in Practical Theology*, edited by Joyce Ann Mercer and Bonnie J. Miller-McLemore, 110–34. Boston: Brill, 2016.

Jagessar, Michael N., and Stephen Burns. *Christian Worship: Postcolonial Perspectives*. Oakville: Equinox, 2011.

Jones, Serene, and Paul Lakeland, eds. *Constructive Theology: A Contemporary Approach to Classical Themes*. Minneapolis: Fortress, 2005.

Kim-Cragg, HyeRan. "The Emperor Has No Clothes!: Exposing Whiteness as Explicit, Implicit, and Null Curricula." *Religious Education* 114, no. 3 (2019): 239–51.

———. "Invisibility of Whiteness: A Homiletical Interrogation." *Homiletic: Journal of the Academy of Homiletics* 46, no. 1, (2021): 28–29.

———. *Postcolonial Preaching*. Lanham: Lexington, 2021.

———. "Probing the Pulpit: Postcolonial Feminist Perspectives." *Liturgy* 34, no. 2 (2019): 22–30.

———. "Sharing the Feast and Hearing Complex Calling: A Study of Racialized Ordained Women Ministers of The United Church of Canada," report submitted to the McGeachy Senior Scholarship Committee, 2011, https://unitedchurchfou

ndation.ca/wp-content/uploads/ Sharing-the-Feast-and-Hearing-Complex-Calling-HyeRan-Kim-Cragg.pdf (accessed on September 13, 2021).

———. *Story and Song: A Postcolonial Interplay between Christian Education and Worship*. New York: Peter Lang, 2012.

Kwok, Pui-lan. "Postcolonial Preaching in Intercultural Contexts." *The Homiletic: Journal of the Academy of Homiletics* 40, no. 1 (2015): 8–21.

Langer, Susanne. "Feeling and Form." In *Art and Its Significance*, edited by Stephen Davis Ross, 224–39. Albany: State University of New York Press, 1987.

Mountford, Roxanne. *The Gendered Pulpit: Preaching in American Protestant Spaces*. Carbondale: Southern Illinois University Press, 2003.

O'Connor, Kathleen. "Crossing Borders: Biblical Studies in a Trans-Cultural World." In *Teaching the Bible: The Discourses and Politics of Biblical Pedagogy*, edited by Fernando F. Segovia and Mary Ann Tolbert, 322–37. Minneapolis: Fortress, 1998.

Robbinson, Haddon W. *Biblical Preaching: The Development and Delivery of Expository Messages*. 2nd ed. Grand Rapids: Baker, 2001.

Said, Edward. *Culture and Imperialism*. London: Vantage, 1993.

Smith, Christine M. *Preaching as Weeping, Confession, and Resistance: Encountering Handicappism, Ageism, Heterosexism, Sexism, White Racism, Classism*. Louisville: Westminster/John Knox, 1992.

Tolbert, Mary Ann. "A New Teaching with Authority: A Re-evaluation of the Authority of the Bible." In *Teaching the Bible: The Discourses and Politics of Biblical Pedagogy*, edited by Fernando F. Segovia and Mary Ann Tolbert, 168–89. Minneapolis: Fortress, 1998.

White, James. *Introduction to Christian Worship*, 3rd ed. Nashville: Abingdon, 2000.

Wymer, Andrew. "Knee-Deep Preaching: A Homiletical Engagement of White Bullshit." *Practical Matters Journal* (July 20, 2018). http://practicalmattersjournal.org/2018/07/20/knee-deep-preaching/.

Chapter 10

Wrestling with Whiteness in Homiletic Pedagogy

A Reflection on Teaching "Proclaiming Justice in the Church and Public Square"

Richard W. Voelz

HOMILETICAL PEDAGOGY AS A TECHNOLOGY OF WHITENESS

George Yancy helps conceptualize Whiteness through an imagined public confession during worship in the church he attends. A woman stands up and says:

> I have been thinking recently about how my whiteness is a site of power and privilege. I have been thinking about how, despite the fact that I define myself as a white anti-racist, I continue to incur white privilege, I continue to carry the weight of white racist training in my body. I notice how when I fight against white racism, it remains in place. I want you to pray for me so that I can become more aware of the complex and subtle ways that I am unfairly privileged because I am white in a society that privileges whiteness.[1]

Yancy describes this fictive liturgical utterance as "daring and *dangerous*" in the majority White congregation he attends because naming Whiteness and its effects would be out of the ordinary.[2]

Yancy's imaginative scenario prompts us to further raise questions about why this confession would be so out of character *as a liturgical act*. The rhetorical markers and content of Whiteness remain unchecked in majority White[3] Christian worship, despite the intentions of well-meaning White congregants. For Yancy, this is a "theological problem [that] lies in the ways in which White bodies have become normative bodies that are directly or indirectly involved in the oppression of non-normative bodies of color. The theological problem of whiteness is both a systemic problem and an embodied problem at the level of calcified embodied white racist practices; it is a problem of a politico-social and economic structural phenomenon, and it is a problem at the site of embodied white subject formation."[4] In other words, Whiteness is comprehensive and programmatic, a theological problem that manifests at multiple and intersecting points.

One of these intersections is in the field of homiletics, a field concerned with the theologies and practices of preaching, as well as the teaching of such. As Cleophus J. LaRue and Dale P. Andrews have highlighted in their work, the unmerited centering of White preaching practices, theology, and pedagogy has obscured Black preaching practices, theology, history, and pedagogy.[5] This is no less the case in homiletical works that articulate postcolonial/decolonial positions.[6] And while it would be valid to observe how Whiteness manifests in particular theologies and practices of preaching, as other chapters in this volume do, this chapter focuses on pedagogy because it often functions as a technology of Whiteness by shaping the habits and values of those who preach.

Indeed, for many, what it means to be a "preacher" is a social identity shaped by Whiteness, just as it has been shaped by what it means to be cisgendered male and heterosexual. And while the preaching classroom is not the first partner in shaping homiletical identity, it plays an indispensable and key role. Classrooms are sites of identity performance[7] for all in the learning community[8] and an attempt, in some measure, to form and reproduce certain kinds of identities. As Linda Martín Alcoff observes, "To say, then, that whiteness is involved in the constitution of the self means that our core set of routine perceptual and epistemic practices and our everyday habits of social interaction, interpretation, and judgement need to be analyzed in relation to a specific racialization process involving whiteness."[9] Applying this to homiletical pedagogy means attentiveness to the ways that the teaching and learning of preaching form a specific kind of self. This formation comes by way of the production and reproduction of an ecclesial practice (preaching) that has all too often and all too invisibly been shaped by Whiteness in theory, practice, and pedagogical strategy. When we begin to analyze the ways that this particular identity is formed and performed via pedagogy, we can begin to comprehend and unravel the ways that a multitude of oppressive forces manifest and persist in preaching. In short, in order to more fully "unmask White preaching," the homiletics classroom must also necessarily come under scrutiny.

Wrestling with Whiteness in the homiletics classroom, then, begins by recognizing the ways that Whiteness shapes the pedagogical environment, including how pedagogical commitments and strategies have functioned together as a technology of Whiteness, and then attempting to move in liberative directions. This process is not particular to the homiletics classroom. As Alcoff suggests, "Rendering our habits visible makes them accessible for reflection and evaluation. This is a possible route for change." Mark Perry notes that anti-racist teaching should be an "ongoing process of learning, exemplified in the equation experience + reflection = growth."[10] The rest of this chapter seeks to reflect on the work of unmasking Whiteness through a particular course by someone with a White social identity.[11] While this instance is specific, readers are invited to consider resonances with their own experiences as a teacher and/or student in any field of study, or in the learning of a practice beyond the classroom.

Institution, History, Geography

Attempts to unmask Whiteness in homiletical pedagogy account for the ways that institutional, historical, and geographical contexts are shaped by White supremacy and the social forces which have produced Whiteness. Therefore, a word is in order regarding the setting in which this course took place: Union Presbyterian Seminary in Richmond, VA. From 1830 to 1860, Richmond was the largest source of enslaved Africans on the East Coast of the United States.[12] In Richmond, historical sites of the slave trade were and are quite literally masked over with newer construction, in addition to the infamous monuments to Confederate figures on Monument Avenue and elsewhere. Although the seminary was located 70 miles southwest of Richmond on the campus of Hampden-Sydney College until 1898, Union professor Robert Louis Dabney was the highly influential architect of the Presbyterian Church's theological defense of slavery (and later helped found Austin Presbyterian Theological Seminary). In 1870, he published a textbook on sacred rhetoric, a record of his lectures on preaching. This text was taught at Union until 1908[13] and has been subsequently reprinted as late as 1979. Though only a brief historical snapshot, these glimpses form part of the backdrop for the seminary's historical context and, beyond that, the everyday frame of life in Richmond, VA. Life in Richmond grapples daily with racism and classism as a direct legacy of the slave trade, the Civil War, and civil rights struggles in the 1950s–1960s, especially in the areas of educational and housing justice, as well as conflicts over infamous Confederate monuments.

Further, the campus of Union Presbyterian Seminary itself forms a liminal geographical space, a functional dividing line between racial and class differences in Richmond's Northside neighborhood. The seminary sits in an area from which White flight took place in the 1950s as the residents of the predominantly Black Jackson Ward neighborhood, located closer to downtown, were displaced by the strategic construction of Interstate 95 through that neighborhood. Parts of Northside where White flight took place are now gentrifying, even as the seminary's direct neighbors are a predominantly White private school and historically high-priced homes on one side, and low income/subsidized housing with predominantly African American residents on the other. These are unavoidable and important considerations as to why I made specific pedagogical decisions to center Black/White racialized dynamics over a broader, more representational pedagogical strategy. I am fully aware that "unmasking White preaching" reaches beyond Black/White racial binaries, but this dynamic plays a very particular role in Union's educational context.

Students

Related to these institutional, historical, and geographical factors are the students themselves. Union Presbyterian Seminary remains a predominantly White institution. Most students, however, are highly cognizant of the complexities of Richmond[14] and have at least basic competency in social analysis of power. For this course in particular, most if not all students would have completed Introduction to Christian Ethics with Katie Geneva Cannon, whose work to help students engage in conscientization around identity and Christian ethics, and whose Womanist approach would have begun the interrogation of Whiteness, if it had not begun prior to this course. In addition to Professor Cannon, faculty colleagues and other aspects of community life attempt to deal honestly with Whiteness in such a way that provides a synergistic pedagogical environment. As Karen Teel notes, institutional support empowers social justice pedagogy; this is certainly true in my case.[15] The course consisted of seven students, with the following demographics represented: PC(USA)—two identifying as White male, one identifying as White female, one identifying as Black female. Mennonite—one identifying as White female, National Baptist—one identifying as Black female, Pentecostal—one identifying as White male. Further, it is important to note that perhaps only as many as three or four of these students were preparing for ministries of congregational leadership, while others were preparing for non-profit or parachurch ministries, chaplaincy, and/or academia. With these background factors in mind, I now turn to describing the pedagogical principles and strategies for unmasking Whiteness in homiletical pedagogy that stood at the core of the course.

PEDAGOGICAL PRINCIPLES AND STRATEGIES

Pedagogy that unmasks White preaching shifts centers of knowledge. One of the most obvious pedagogical decisions for the construction of the course was determining what would constitute the center of knowledge. While Karen Teel advocates for "diversifying the syllabus" in White anti-racist pedagogy, there is a substantive difference between diversifying and decentering, and I attempted to decenter White scholarship in the course.[16] Womanist Hebrew Bible scholar Nyasha Junior's Twitter hashtag #SyllabusSoWhite has popularized a sort of anti-mantra (or damning assessment) for syllabus design. Therefore, Kenyatta Gilbert's *A Pursued Justice*, Frank Thomas's *How to Preach a Dangerous Sermon*, and Leah Gunning Francis's *Ferguson and Faith* were three of the five main texts for the course. While Richard Lischer's *Preacher King* is written by a person identified as White, its focus on Martin Luther King Jr. helped center King as an exemplar. Essays by Teresa Fry Brown, Raphael Warnock, and Willie Jennings provided additional indispensable insights from African American scholars.[17]

I sought to carry this decentering work beyond the course texts. Each week, I wove insights from the class readings with a Scripture text that grounded a student's understanding of justice (a week one opening exercise) into an opening prayer for the class session. In this, I wanted to reinforce that not only were the class readings a source of our mutual *academic* learning, but that the insights from these scholars were a *spiritual* foundation for our work together, constituting a source of spiritual knowledge and a more holistic sense of our work. This sought to refuse a dualistic separation between the academic and the spiritual/emotional, which is built upon a racialized hierarchy in which what is rational is attributed to White racial formations and privileged over the spiritual/emotional, which is ascribed to non-Whites.[18] Instead, the work of anti-racist pedagogy recognizes that education is both a head and heart endeavor.[19]

In a course on preaching and public proclamation, this also meant incorporating sermons and public speeches from various settings. We watched and discussed a significant number of videos in the course. These included African American clergy such as Teresa Fry Brown, Yvette Flunder, Dale Andrews, William Barber II, Terri Hord Owens, Traci Blackmon, and Michael Curry. Additionally, for one of our class sessions, I facilitated a conversation with Rodney Sadler, who is a faculty colleague in the Bible department on our Charlotte, NC campus, an organizer/activist, and leads our seminary's Center for Social Justice and Reconciliation. With regard to the sermons and speeches students themselves produced, I considered that unmasking White pedagogy also means shifting the center of pedagogical resources for preparation and evaluation of sermons. As an initial step in this direction, I adapted the "homiletical brief" from Kenyatta Gilbert's book *Exodus Preaching* as a guide to help students prepare sermons and public speeches.[20] These attempts sought to disrupt the White normativity of bodies and voices who are often raised up as exemplars of theory and practice in preaching courses.

Pedagogy that unmasks White preaching shows anti-racism at work. Even as I attempted to center Black scholars, pastors, and activists, this was not a complete promise fulfilled, and intentionally so. For other readings and multimedia, I chose materials that either explicitly or implicitly showed anti-racism at work from White scholars and preachers.[21] Another Twitter hashtag underscores part of the underlying rationale for this pedagogical strategy: #WhiteChurchQuiet. This hashtag has voiced the criticism of the White church's silence regarding anti-racism and its resultant inaction. White students need to see anti-racism in action for their contexts and I take the hashtag to mean that students from racially and ethnically marginalized backgrounds do as well. So, while it was of utmost importance to decenter Whiteness by centering Black voices in much of the class materials, it was also crucial for all students to see the work of anti-racism modeled in both academy and church. As Dana Nichols notes, this helps White students "begin to forge new, proud, and positive antiracist identities."[22] And, perhaps, it suggested that Black students and communities would not have to bear the burden of anti-racist work as they saw their peers engage in it more deeply. In seeking this balance, Nora Tisdale's *Prophetic Preaching: A Pastoral Approach*, Richard Lischer's aforementioned work on King, an essay by David Schnasa Jacobsen, and my then in-process work *Preaching to Teach* served as additional core texts.

In terms of those who model anti-racism in their preaching and public proclamation, we analyzed sermons from Amy Butler, as well as a sermon from Nora Tisdale to complement discussion of her book. Contemporaneity played a significant role in these choices as well, which is why I used a segment of the summer 2018 "Reclaiming Jesus" conference. This showed White pastor Jim Wallis and African American bishop Michael Curry speaking back-to-back and exchanging a deep embrace in between, which provided a moment for us to analyze not only their words but also the ways in which embodiment accompanies proclamation. One of the timeliest sermons we reviewed together was a sermon preached by Texas Baptist minister George Mason in the wake of the murder of Botham Jean by a police officer. These examples of written work and proclamation serve as practical evidence of anti-racism at work among those identified as White.

Pedagogy that unmasks White preaching exhibits historical consciousness. Just as the history of my institution and the city of Richmond functioned as significant background, the course contends that pedagogy that wrestles with Whiteness in preaching should exhibit historical consciousness. As mentioned above, one of the core texts for the course was Kenyatta Gilbert's excellent book *A Pursued Justice*, which highlights African American preaching in the Great Migration and Civil Rights Movement eras. In using this text, I not only wanted to establish that proclaiming justice has been a historically and contextually situated act, as Gilbert's text so ably shows. But for Black students, I hoped that they would gain a greater familiarity with (and celebrate) the "cloud of witnesses" particular to Black preaching traditions, especially beyond isolating Martin Luther King Jr. as a central figure (a patriarchal move). I also hoped that the White-identifying students would deepen their understanding of how proclaiming justice in church and public square have long been central tasks in Black preaching traditions, and that they should learn from this history. For me to allow White-identifying students to remain naïve or unaware of these historical traditions would be to effectively render rich traditions of Black preaching invisible.[23]

To reinforce this point, one of the assignments that accompanied this reading was for students to prepare a 2–3 minute section of one of the sermons in the appendices and re-preach it to the class. This exercise intended to go beyond simple appropriation of words, instead forming a critical exercise intended to generate discussion about valuing a wider tradition rooted in the particularity of African American experiences in the Great Migration and beyond. "Trying on" someone else's words in this regard went beyond simply reading them, and we did not engage in performative mimicry. Rather, students were encouraged to re-perform these pieces in their own voices with raised historical sensitivity, attuned to how those words might have been experienced in context, what importance they might carry in the present, and how this performance affected the students' understandings of the history and task of proclaiming justice. Even if momentarily, this was an important act for White-identifying students to apprentice themselves to another's proclamation. In this sense, historical consciousness was another effort at decentering.

Pedagogy that unmasks White preaching fosters agency and considers intersectionality. In the beginning stages of course design, I wrestled with either choosing a specific thematic focus for the course on race/racism in Richmond or allowing students to pursue their own interests. Rather than limiting the scope of the class, I chose a more student-centered approach, allowing students to select their own justice issues to pursue through the semester. Mark Perry suggests that this student-centered approach is a hallmark of social justice pedagogy, and it meant that I had to give up some of my control and become a co-learner.[24] Since I was not managing the content and direction of the class at every level, I hope this too was shifting power relations and modeling anti-racist, antipatriarchal, and decolonizing pedagogy.

As a by-product of an approach that fostered agency in this way, students worked with their chosen issue and engaged in intersectional analysis, rather than operating on single axis thinking. Students looked at their justice issues through the prisms of race, ethnicity, class, gender, sexuality, and so on. The students also naturally connected their issues to local manifestations: White privilege, especially in the wake of the events of Charlottesville; public education in Richmond and surrounding areas; gentrification in Richmond's Northside; mass incarceration and integration of the formerly incarcerated among Black churches in Richmond; health care in Richmond; disability/neurodiversity among Richmond youth and young adults; and immigration policy stances among local politicians. Leah Gunning Francis's text *Ferguson and Faith*, which shows ministerial work from different perspectives in Ferguson, MO, was a crucial teaching text in this regard, even as it came near the end of the course. Analysis of these local manifestations demonstrated how "local history [functions] as powerful object lessons of how racial formation functions."[25] In this case, student agency led to powerful understandings of intersectionality and more complex understandings of the power and privilege of White social identity and its relationship to other social identities.

Pedagogy that unmasks White preaching is accountable to the public. The notion of a classroom that remains neutral, theoretical, and insular only serves the interests of Whiteness. Thus, the course attempted to be a formational space but it was not constructed to be a "safe space." While Anne Wagner describes "'safety' as an untenable goal" with regard to maintaining conflict-free notions of White identity and classroom discussion,[26] this lack of safety also translated to the nature of the major assignments for the course. Since the course was one of our "Church in the World" curriculum electives, two of the major assignments were what we call "community engagement" activities. The first required an interview with a local church pastor about proclaiming justice from the pulpit, with Nora Tisdale's text shaping the questions they asked. The second required students to report on a conversation/interview with a civic leader/elected official and/or a gathering associated with their selected issue (such as a protest, a rally, an organizing meeting, etc.). Students then analyzed how religious speech functions in those settings and described their understanding of how religious speech should function, in conversation with course readings and discussions. The other two major assignments were (1) a sermon for the seminary community on their justice concern and (2) a 7-minute public proclamation, in which the class took on the form of a public forum livestreamed over the internet. Having engaged in a variety of anti-racist instructional strategies inside the classroom setting, these assignments raised the stakes for a publicly accountable classroom. As the instructor, I was a participant in the live preaching and public forum as convener. This communicated that I was a participant as well and had some "skin in the game."

I also sought to model public accountability of unmasking White pedagogy through my Twitter account (@RevDrVoelz). Before each class session, I tweeted out a thread of the day's course readings and videos, tagging the authors/speakers (as available) to amplify their work, naming the major topics/questions we would be covering, and a screenshot of the day's prayer (described above). My Twitter following is not large, so I do not want to misrepresent the significance of this practice, but the "signal boost" for the underrepresented authors through Twitter sought to create an additional layer of public accountability for the pedagogical choices I made and to chip away at the White normativity of homiletic discourse in public, digital space.

PEDAGOGICAL OBSERVATIONS

I conclude with three observations about the course's challenges and discoveries. First, I remain modest in what this course achieved in terms of unmasking White preaching. This chapter seeks to name process and intentions, so I leave it to others to assess whether my attempts at wrestling with Whiteness in preaching and pedagogy were effective, and to what degree. Any course will have limited effects and effects that might not be realized among individuals, ministries, or wider social systems for quite some time, if at all.

Second, I remain attentive to the ways Whiteness shapes my pedagogy and remains yet to be "unmasked." For example, in one class session I planned an improvisational in-class assignment in which students were given 30 minutes to plan and deliver 3-minute remarks for a simulated local faith leader press conference, responding to the October 2018 act of White domestic terrorism at a Louisville, Kentucky Kroger grocery store.[27] In my estimation, this story had received less airtime than the shooting at the Tree of Life synagogue shooting in Pittsburgh that occurred three days later. My error was not in the nature of the assignment as a whole. But in trying to be responsive, I did not think through the implications of requiring each person in the class to respond to this event. More specifically, I did not consider the potential effect on two Black women students, and the emotional labor they might need to perform in order to complete the assignment. As the instructor I remain aware that this was a failing attributable to my own Whiteness, especially since the assignment and the scenario were unannounced, and I had not provided an alternative scenario should a student have decided that responding to the one I provided was an impossibility. I raise this instance here to say that wrestling with Whiteness in pedagogy is both fraught with complexity and an ongoing process.

Third and finally, while my course focused on preaching and this chapter has been highly self-referential, I do believe that the principles and practices highlighted above translate well to other pedagogical attempts to unmask Whiteness and work toward decolonization in other disciplines. Attempts to shift centers of knowledge, show anti-racism at work, exhibit historical consciousness, foster agency and consider intersectionality, and enact a publicly accountable classroom are all ways that learning communities can move toward anti-racist and decolonizing pedagogies. In this sense, the work of "unmasking" is not merely an analytical enterprise but simultaneously seeks to enact alternative futures for both pedagogy and whatever discipline or practice might be under consideration.

NOTES

1. George Yancy, *Christology and Whiteness: What Would Jesus Do?* (London, United Kingdom: Taylor & Francis Group, 2012), 3–4, http://ebookcentral.proquest.com/lib/upsce-ebooks/detail.action?docID=1024669 (accessed on September 25, 2021).

2. Yancy, *Christology*, 4.

3. With the exception of direct quotations, I have capitalized both Black and White, as well as Whiteness, throughout this chapter in keeping with larger cultural conversations about the visibility of Whiteness and the guidance of most style guides. See, for instance, https://cssp.org/2020/03/recognizing-race-in-language-why-we-capitalize-black-and-white/ (accessed on September 3, 2021).

4. Yancy, *Christology*, 7.

5. Cleophus J. LaRue, "Two Ships Passing in the Night," in *What's the Matter with Preaching Today?*, edited by Mike Graves (Louisville, KY: Westminster John Knox Press, 2004), 127–44; Dale P. Andrews, "New to Whom," in *Preaching Prophetic Care: Building Bridges to Justice*, edited by Phillis-Isabella Sheppard, Dawn Ottoni-Wilhelm, and Ronald J. Allen (Pickwick Publications, 2018), 299–301.

6. See, for instance, HyeRan Kim-Cragg, *Postcolonial Preaching : Creating a Ripple Effect* (Lanham, MD: Lexington Books, 2021); Justo L. Gonzalez and Pablo A. Jimenez, *Pulpito: An Introduction to Hispanic Preaching* (Nashville, TN: Abingdon Press, 2005); Kwok Pui-lan, "Postcolonial Preaching in Intercultural Contexts," *Homiletic (Online)* 40, no. 1 (2015): 9–20.

7. Although the author focuses solely on students, see, for instance, John T. Warren, "Doing Whiteness: On the Performative Dimensions of Race in the Classroom," *Communication Education* 50, no. 2 (April 2001): 91–108, https://doi.org/10.1080/03634520109379237 (accessed on September 25, 2021).

8. I use "learning community" here rather than a hierarchical understanding of the relationship between teachers and students.

9. Linda Martín Alcoff, *The Future of Whiteness* (Malden, MA: Polity Press, 2016), 85.

10. Mark Perry, *Walking the Color Line: The Art and Practice of Anti-Racist Teaching* (New York: Teachers College Press, 2000), 175.

11. "Proclaiming Justice in the Church and Public Square" was offered in the Fall 2018 semester at Union Presbyterian Seminary, Richmond, VA. A PDF copy of the syllabus can be found at https://drive.google.com/file/d/19JwWRmJROiSkOEAq0-56D0gicH_OabcX/view?usp=sharing (accessed September 25, 2021). For full

bibliographic references to class texts named throughout this chapter, please see the syllabus.

12. "Richmond Slave Trail," http://www.richmondgov.com/CommissionSlaveTrail/documents/brochureRichmondCityCouncilSlaveTrailCommission.pdf (accessed on July 3, 2019).

13. It is worth mentioning that Dabney's text was replaced with John Broadus's famous text, whose legacy as a slave owner and White supremacist is documented here: http://www.sbts.edu/wp-content/uploads/2018/12/Racism-and-the-Legacy-of-Slavery-Report-v3.pdf (accessed on September 25, 2021). Broadus's text was in use at Union at least until the 1928–1929 school year, when the records become inconclusive about which texts were used for the course. My thanks to UPSem reference librarian and archivist Paula Skreslet for assistance with this information.

14. For this distinction, see Michael Paul Williams, "Williams: We Remain Two Richmonds – RVA Blossomed While Richmond Is Being Left Further and Further Behind," *Richmond Times-Dispatch*, https://www.richmond.com/news/local/michael-paul-williams/williams-we-remain-two-richmonds---rva-blossomed-while/article_2c9d466f-c300-55fd-9ddb-7ba85bef339b.html (accessed on July 8, 2019).

15. Karen Teel, "Getting Out of the Left Lane: The Possibility of White Antiracist Pedagogy," *Teaching Theology & Religion* 17, no. 1 (January 2014): 19.

16. Teel, "Getting Out," 10.

17. Kenyatta R. Gilbert, *A Pursued Justice: Black Preaching from the Great Migration to Civil Rights* (Waco, TX: Baylor University Press, 2016), Frank A. Thomas, *How to Preach a Dangerous Sermon* (Nashville, TN: Abingdon Press, 2018), Leah Gunning Francis, *Ferguson and Faith: Sparking Leadership and Awakening Community* (St. Louis, MO: Chalice Press, 2015), Richard Lischer, *The Preacher King: Martin Luther King, Jr. and the Word that Moved America*, Revised edition (New York: Oxford University Press, 1997).

18. Chacour Koop, "Smithsonian Museum Apologizes for Saying Hard Work, Rational Thought Is 'White Culture,'" *Miami Herald*, https://www.miamiherald.com/news/nation-world/national/article244309587.html (accessed on June 21, 2021).

19. See also bell hooks, *Teaching to Transgress: Education as the Practice of Freedom* (New York: Routledge, 1994), 195.

20. Kenyatta R. Gilbert, *Exodus Preaching: Crafting Sermons about Justice and Hope* (Nashville, TN: Abingdon Press, 2018). To Gilbert's categories in the brief, I added "Emerging Perspectives," which asked students to "Identify some of the data, statistics, and/or narratives outside the biblical text that are shaping your thinking on this issue," as well as a category for "Intersectional Analysis," to be mindful of intersectional understandings of social identities and justice concerns, as well as "Homiletical Approach," which asked for a brief summary of how students were approaching their sermon design and any concerns/difficulties they were encountering along the way.

21. Dana Nichols, "Teaching Critical Whiteness Theory: What College and University Teachers Need to Know," 1, no. 1 (2010): 7ff, http://www.wpcjournal.com/article/view/5421 (accessed on September 25, 2021).

22. Nichols, "Teaching," 9.

23. See the section "Null Curriculum of Whiteness: The Violence of Forgetting of History," in HyeRan Kim-Cragg, "The Emperor Has No Clothes!: Exposing Whiteness as Explicit, Implicit, and Null Curricula," *Religious Education*, April 29, 2019, 6ff, https://doi.org/10.1080/00344087.2019.1602464.

24. Perry, *Walking the Color Line*, 182.

25. See Nichols, "Teaching," 7–8.

26. Anne E. Wagner, "Unsettling the Academy: Working through the Challenges of Anti-Racist Pedagogy," *Race Ethnicity and Education* 8, no. 3 (September 1, 2005): 265ff, https://doi.org/10.1080/13613320500174333 (accessed September 25, 2021).

27. "Kentucky Kroger Shooting Suspect Charged with Federal Hate Crimes," NPR.org, https://www.npr.org/2018/11/15/668476169/kentucky-kroger-shooting-suspect-charged-with-federal-hate-crimes (accessed on September 25, 2021).

BIBLIOGRAPHY

Alcoff, Linda Martín. *The Future of Whiteness*. Malden, MA: Polity Press, 2016.

Gilbert, Kenyatta R. *Exodus Preaching: Crafting Sermons about Justice and Hope*. Nashville, TN: Abingdon Press, 2018.

Gonzalez, Justo L. and Pablo A. Jimenez. *Pulpito: An Introduction to Hispanic Preaching*. Nashville, TN: Abingdon Press, 2005.

Graves, Mike. *What's the Matter with Preaching Today?* Louisville, KY: Westminster John Knox Press, 2004.

hooks, bell. *Teaching to Transgress: Education as the Practice of Freedom*. New York: Routledge, 1994.

Kim-Cragg, HyeRan. "The Emperor Has No Clothes!: Exposing Whiteness as Explicit, Implicit, and Null Curricula." *Religious Education*, April 29, 2019, 1–13. https://doi.org/10.1080/00344087.2019.1602464 (accessed on September 25, 2021).

———. *Postcolonial Preaching : Creating a Ripple Effect*. Lanham, MD: Lexington Books, 2021.

Koop, Chacour. "Smithsonian Museum Apologizes for Saying Hard Work, Rational Thought Is 'White Culture.'" *Miami Herald*. https://www.miamiherald.com/news/nation-world/national/article244309587.html (accessed on June 21, 2021).

Nichols, Dana. "Teaching Critical Whiteness Theory: What College and University Teachers Need to Know." 1, no. 1 (2010). http://www.wpcjournal.com/article/view/5421 (accessed on September 25, 2021).

NPR.org. "Kentucky Kroger Shooting Suspect Charged with Federal Hate Crimes." https://www.npr.org/2018/11/15/668476169/kentucky-kroger-shooting-suspect-charged-with-federal-hate-crimes (accessed on July 9, 2019).

Perry, Mark. *Walking the Color Line: The Art and Practice of Anti-Racist Teaching*. New York: Teachers College Press, 2000.

Pui-lan, Kwok. "Postcolonial Preaching in Intercultural Contexts." *Homiletic (Online)* 40, no. 1 (2015): 9–20.

"Richmond Slave Trail." http://www.richmondgov.com/CommissionSlaveTrail/documents/brochureRichmondCityCouncilSlaveTrailCommission.pdf (accessed on July 3, 2019).

Sheppard, Phillis-Isabella, Dawn Ottoni-Wilhelm, and Ronald J. Allen, eds. *Preaching Prophetic Care: Building Bridges to Justice*. Pickwick Publications, 2018.

Teel, Karen. "Getting Out of the Left Lane: The Possibility of White Antiracist Pedagogy." *Teaching Theology & Religion* 17, no. 1 (January 2014): 3–26.

Wagner, Anne E. "Unsettling the Academy: Working through the Challenges of Anti-racist Pedagogy." *Race Ethnicity and Education* 8, no. 3 (September 1, 2005): 261–75. https://doi.org/10.1080/13613320500174333 (accessed on September 25, 2021).

Warren, John T. "Doing Whiteness: On the Performative Dimensions of Race in the Classroom." *Communication Education* 50, no. 2 (April 2001): 91–108. https://doi.org/10.1080/03634520109379237 (accessed on September 25, 2021).

Williams, Michael Paul. "Williams: We Remain Two Richmonds – RVA Blossomed While Richmond Is Being Left Further and Further Behind." *Richmond Times-Dispatch*. https://www.richmond.com/news/local/michael-paul-williams/williams-we-remain-two-richmonds---rva-blossomed-while/article_2c9d466f-c300-55fd-9ddb-7ba85bef339b.html (accessed on July 8, 2019).

Yancy, George. *Christology and Whiteness: What Would Jesus Do?* London: Taylor & Francis Group, 2012. http://ebookcentral.proquest.com/lib/upsce-ebooks/detail.action?docID=1024669 (accessed on September 25, 2021).

Chapter 11

Of Handmaids, Mediatrixes, and Mothers

The Idealized Feminine and Rhetorics of Whiteness

Jerusha Matsen Neal

> *After breaking a few stained-glass ceilings, I am tempted to center myself as savior, heroine, and victim simultaneously . . . ,*
> A white ordained woman, discussing the dangers of patriarchal racism

THE PARADOX OF THE "HANDLESS MAIDEN": A PARABLE

There is a gruesome, European folktale of a young woman who loses her hands to the Devil. Her starving father makes a blind trade with a disguised Lucifer: prosperity in exchange for whatever stands behind his barn. He thinks he is giving away an apple tree, but on this day, his daughter stands beneath its boughs. The father begins an urgent negotiation over her fate. The Devil does not carry all the cards. Apparently, the young woman's skin must be caked with dirt in order for the Devil to touch her—and her tears keep falling onto her hands, washing them "pure white and clean." In a rage, the Devil forces the father to cut off his daughter's hands with an ax, but her tears keep falling, cleaning the stumps of her arms. Frustrated, the Devil storms away. The maiden's tears and white skin have protected her from the worst consequences of her father's betrayal. But they have also left her maimed. Handless, she leaves her home, depending on wild fruit trees to feed her.[1]

The folktale is a Jephthah-like story of patriarchal violence but, in a world where "pure" and "white" are adjectives twisted by the logic of white supremacy, it also becomes a parable about privilege. It describes the terrifying danger facing women whose future is up for barter. It also suggests that the danger is far greater for those whose tears do not translate into "whiteness." Indeed, it narrates a deep truth about what it means to be a white woman living in the intersections of patriarchal racism. It names tears and whiteness as strategies of survival.

For certain white women in my classroom, being denied their calls to preach by their denominations is not unlike having their hands removed. It is, perhaps, the first time their strategies for survival—their wells of emotion, their white skin, their ability to follow the rules of their fathers—could not save them from the Devil's maiming. Their eyes are haunted and their movements skittish. The rules and persons they thought would keep them safe have proved untrustworthy. And yet, their wounds are a sign of privilege as well as trauma, for their bodies are visible. They have not disappeared into some unseen underworld; they sit in a divinity school classroom. They have left their father's home but have managed to save their skin.

I'm grateful for those survivals.

There are other haunted eyes in these homiletic classrooms. There are the eyes of black women and men who are tired of the "ingenuities"[2] required in the predominately white halls of my institution. There are transgender eyes and undocumented eyes. There are eyes of students of every ethnicity, hungry because their school bills have eaten away their food budgets. The Devil is busy in all sorts of intersectional ways. But in this chapter, I talk about the eyes of handless maidens—particularly white, handless maidens—not because their eyes matter more, but because such women can themselves become dangerous. In searching for lost hands of privilege, a woman can play into the hands of a Devil she thought she had escaped.

"PROPER RHETORIC," "PROPER WOMEN," AND WHITENESS

In her work on the connections in Western thought between rhetoric's persuasive power and the female body, Jane Sutton traces the metaphor of "proper rhetoric" and "proper woman" from Ancient Greece through the Enlightenment. She compares the tradition's fear and fascination with rhetorical persuasion to its fierce categorization of the gendered body.[3] Rhetoric could be "wifely" or "whorish," submissive and hardworking, or overly adorned and promiscuous.[4] Women's bodies might not have been considered appropriate vessels for public speaking,[5] but as a trope, they haunt the rhetorical tradition. Calvin speaks of rhetoric as the "handmaid" of the Word.[6] Augustine uses treatises on female virginity and inappropriate cosmetic adornment to illumine his discussion of rhetorical style.[7] Socrates describes rhetoric as an "untamed filly" in Plato's *Gorgias*.[8] Proper women, like proper speech, are tamed, submissive to reason, beautiful—but not sexual. And it is no surprise that proper women are also aligned with structures of power. They are not "Other" women. When Dionysius of Halicarnassus critiques the rhetoric of his day as emerging from "some Asiatic deathhole," he maps categories of gender and sexual promiscuity onto categories of ethnicity. He describes good rhetoric as the Athenian wife and false rhetoric as an "Amazonian erotic woman."[9]

Of course, actual women were never intended to embody either rhetorical category. Instead, proper rhetorical practices were mapped onto female tropes which could then be properly embodied by men. Men played the part of the handmaid that lived in "subjection to the Word"[10] while wielding "hidden power which leaves nothing in man untouched."[11] Men offered their immaculate flesh to the preaching labor, believing that "perfectly pure, obedient humanity might utter divinity ... a transparent medium."[12] Men embodied the grammar of the church's mother tongue, drawing on patriarchal tropes of the feminine ideal to protect their theological traditions.

The dangers of the archetypal Feminine (with a capital "F") are well known to feminist thinkers. Such idealizations have been co-opted by patriarchal theologies and political agendas for centuries, excluding and regulating the bodies of actual women.[13] My own work has emphasized the theological dangers of such idealizations in the homiletic tradition, arguing that they outsource the work of the Spirit to human preachers—whether male or female—who can never live up to such pure, powerful, submissive, job descriptions.[14] But feminist rhetorician Krista Ratcliffe's work on "whiteness" in the rhetorical tradition gives another reason for concern. Ratcliffe's analysis reveals a similar functionality undergirding "whiteness" and the trope of the feminine ideal in the rhetorical tradition.

In her article "Eavesdropping as Rhetorical Tactic: History, Whiteness, and Rhetoric," Ratcliffe draws on Ruth Frankenberg's definition of "whiteness" as a set of practices that signify privilege and "foster stasis by resisting and denying differences."[15] Ratcliffe, a white academic, then describes the ways that she sees "whiteness" impacting practices of rhetoric in the contemporary moment and in her composition classroom. She posits that "whiteness," in its desire for stasis, works to circumscribe rhetorical agency across four sites: "discursive, authorial, readerly and cultural."[16] (1) "Whiteness" works to limit discursive agency in flattening and stabilizing a text's meaning, denying language play, and ignoring the relationality of binary categories (like whiteness and blackness) in textual interpretation. (2) "Whiteness" works to limit authorial agency by reducing concepts of "ethos" to individual ethical appeal. In celebrating the successful rhetor as an autonomous hero or heroine, for example, the cultural construction of "ethos" remains unexamined.

(3) "Whiteness" works to limit readerly agency in its relegation of readers to secondary importance in the making of meaning. (4) And "whiteness" limits cultural agency by denying the influence of cultural structures on everyday life, speech, and performance.

"In sum," she states, "whiteness (in its desire for stasis) celebrates discursive agency in which language is made literal, an authorial agency in which ethos is reduced to individualism, a readerly agency in which readers are relegated to secondary importance in the construction of meanings, and a cultural agency in which the influence of cultural structures on identity are occluded."[17]

Ratcliffe's description of rhetorical "whiteness" underscores the tradition's fascination with rhetoric that can be controlled, enclosed, objectified, and used for the perpetuation of a lineage. As such, the rhetorical tradition's fascination with the "proper woman" as a guide for "proper rhetoric" intersects and reinforces the impacts of "whiteness" on discursive/authorial/readerly/cultural agency. The question is less about origins and more about usage: both "whiteness" and the "proper woman" trope have worked to promote stasis in the tradition. A handful of examples suffice. In submission to the text's plain meaning, handmaid rhetoric has limited the text's generative agency.[18] In a desire to persuade, queen rhetoric has bent the listener to her will.[19] In its celebration of purity, immaculate rhetoric has insisted it can "fade away."[20] In its attempt to transcend divides, mediatrix rhetoric has tried to speak for all.[21] And in its desire to embody ecclesial tradition (note the singularity of the noun), mother rhetoric has passed down the church's mother tongue, taming the tongues of outsiders.[22] In each case, difference is denied or resisted.

The problem with practices that grow from such idealizations is that they become rigid and cold to the touch. They lose their relationality and vulnerability. They maintain stasis, rather than growth. And if such idealizations are rooted in the desire to protect privilege, stasis is deadly. Not only do such idealizations continue to amputate difference across lines of gender, race, sexual orientation, class, nationality, and theological conviction, they also project the tradition's fears onto the traditions and bodies of others, fueling new idealizations as attempts to resist negative representation. Chanequa Walker-Barnes understands the "StrongBlackWoman" archetype as a "racialized version of the cult of true womanhood—a White, middle-class ideal characterized by piety, purity, domesticity and submissiveness."[23] Walker-Barnes makes plain the heavy toll the "StrongBlackWoman" has had on the mental, physical, and spiritual health of black women, despite its attempt to reject racist caricatures.

In the "Handless Maiden" folktale, a prince finds the maiden in a forest. He falls in love and gives the woman a wedding gift: two silver hands. His gift is meant to make up for her loss. It is meant to show care and honor. It is a precious gift, meant to mirror the hands that have been removed. But of course, silver hands are different from real hands. My fear for the students in my classes—particularly those who receive the silver hands of "proper wifely rhetoric" along with their stoles—is that these silver hands will become the source of their confidence, security, and authority. As such, these practices of stasis and privilege (i.e., practices of "whiteness") will become idols.

RESISTING SILVER HANDS

The lure of silver hands can be particularly potent for white women in the context of patriarchal racism who have experienced the violence of patriarchy but who can still draw on the power of whiteness. White women who pursue a call to ministry no longer satisfy the criteria the "cult of true womanhood," but they have privilege left to wield and privilege left to lose. This can make the silver hands a difficult gift to turn down, no matter how heavy they hang on one's wrists. Women of color have observed this complicity as a recurring motif in the history of white feminism. Audre Lorde's famous response, "The Master's Tools Will Never Dismantle the Master's House"[24] was made at a conference where the experiences of white, straight women academics "resisted and denied differences."[25]

But even for white women who desire a better way, the question of how to avoid the "silver hands" of static, privileged practices is a difficult one. If practices that deny difference and promote stasis are considered "proper rhetoric," how else does a woman called to the work of holy wordsmithing fulfill her role? Can she, in good conscience, do this work at all? It is a dilemma feminist rhetoricians have been asking in the secular academy for more than fifty years. For Sutton, "It means I write with an eraser."[26]

The crisis is especially acute for me, a white female homiletician, because the teaching of rhetorical practices is in my job description. One does not need to scratch deeply beneath the surface of homiletic rhetorical history to find unholy ghosts. In *The Hidden History of Women's Ordination*, Gary Macy frames the preaching reforms of the late Middle Ages as responses to the fear that the exclusivity of the male priesthood was being threatened.[27] Claire Waters agrees, arguing that the influx of preaching handbooks at the time reflected anxiety around decentralization in pulpit authorization and women preachers who were exceeding many of their male counterparts in dynamism.[28] It is enough to give a homiletician pause. The first flurry of homiletic handbooks in church history served to centralize ecclesial power and exclude women and lay persons from the preaching task. And there are many similar examples. Rhetorical practices that protected privilege grew out of the explicit racism in elocutionary training in the nineteenth-century United

States[29]—or out of colonial agendas that shaped the language of theological education and the translation of scripture around the world.[30] *What does this mean for my classroom?* How do I teach rhetoric without reducing that work to handing over "silver hands" (i.e., practices that resist or deny difference)?

The following tactics of resistance have been proposed by secular rhetoricians who are also women of color.[31] After describing each tactic, I point to contemporary homileticians who employ similar techniques to subvert "whiteness" in their classrooms and in the pulpit.

Jacqueline Jones Royster and the Tactic of "Listening"

Revising her chair's address to the 1995 CCCC meeting, Jacqueline Jones Royster's classic article, "When the First Voice You Hear is Not Your Own," recounts three vignettes in which her contributions and particularity as an African American female rhetorician were ignored. Drawing on this personal testimony, Jones Royster notes how "listening" has been undervalued in the rhetorical tradition. For Jones Royster, relation and appropriate action are listening's goal, not submission and silence. She states, "The goal is not 'You talk, I talk.' The goal is better practices so that we can exchange perspectives, negotiate meaning . . . with the intent of being in a good position to cooperate."[32] Developing an "afrafeminist"[33] methodology for studying rhetorical history, Jones Royster teases out the contours and scope of deep, relational "listening."[34] Describing the work of "critical imagination," "strategic contemplation," "social circulation," and a "globalizing point of view," Jones Royster repurposes "listening" to animate the agencies of readers, texts, cultures, and communities. Her description of "strategic contemplation" serves as an example. Combining both scholarly inquiry with "an inward journey" that notices how researchers "process, imagine and work with materials," strategic contemplation attempts to "reclaim a genre of research and scholarship traditionally associated with processes of mediation, introspection and reflection."[35]

Donyelle McCray's homiletic work embodies practices of deep listening, particularly in regard to traditions that that have not "counted" as preaching. Her attentiveness is seen in her analysis of Harriet Power's quilting as sermonic speech[36] or the intercession of church mothers as pastoral labor.[37] Her honoring of strategic contemplation as a rhetorical practice, however, might be best exemplified in her book, *The Censored Pulpit: Julian of Norwich as Preacher.*[38] Reframing Julian's contemplation as rhetorical action reanimates silent corners of the homiletic tradition, past and present. It refuses to let speech obfuscate bodies, insisting that bodies speak. In an early paper on the subject, McCray speaks of the relationality of embodied rhetorical labor. "There is no objectivity. . . . Our broken bodies bind us to Christ and to one another and are full participants in the mystery and miracle of call."[39] This is not listening in which one's body fades away. It is listening that preaches.

Shirley Wilson Logan and the Tactic of "Speaking the Unspeakable"

As an African American female professor who teaches rhetoric in predominately white classrooms, Shirley Wilson Logan describes the difficulty of discussing racism with white students. A lifetime of instruction has convinced her of the truth of bell hooks's affirmation that "all knowledge is forged in conflict."[40] She has also seen how her presence in the classroom leads white students to "avoid topics that are controversial. It becomes safe to discuss only the 'them' not represented in the classroom."[41] The challenge for Logan is to find ways for students to "speak the unspeakable," to talk about the issues surrounding race, class, and gender so that students can analyze the assumptions that undergird their behaviors.[42] Her pressing of the conversation brings differences within the student body into view, as well as differences in how cultural scripts shape rhetorical practice. In both of these ways, she counters the resistance and denial of difference that marks "whiteness."

In her Nobel Prize Acceptance Speech, Toni Morrison describes the danger of speaking the unspeakable if one's goal is to tame or domesticate the trauma of racism as an issue. She notes the violence that lies beneath attempts to "monumentalize," "sum up," or "pin down" the depths of "slavery, genocide or war."[43] But the speaking that Logan describes is not for the purposes of coercion or domestication. It is similar to Morrison's description of reaching out one's hands to feel the hands of the listener.[44] The point is not harmony or conflict in its own right. The point is encounter and critical reflexivity.

Lis Valle's creative work in postcolonial liturgy is a beginning attempt to imagine rhetorical action that "speaks the unspeakable" through worship practices of tension, imagination, and connectedness.[45] While Valle refuses to create rigid binaries between colonized and colonizer, she is committed to bringing these categories and their communal impact into view. She draws on the pre-Columbian religion of the Taínos to create a Christian liturgy that makes space for complementary duality and encounter. This duality, performed in time, is not held in stasis. Interruption and tension, including spoken testimonies describing the impact of imperial violence and colonization, are the first step toward connection. It is worth noting that Valle shares Morrison's reticence about language's ability to sum up such pain or evoke meaningful hope. She quotes Walter Brueggemann's description of the preacher's goal as "not a grand scheme or a coherent system, but the voicing of a lot of little pieces out of which people can put life together in fresh configurations."[46] Her attention to movement, ritual, and celebration provides a depth of congregational resources to engage that work.

Ellen Gil-Gomez and the Tactic of "Piece-Making"

Ellen Gil-Gomez isn't sure what to make of "practices"—feminist or otherwise.[47] In her response to those attempting to construct feminist practices for the composition classroom, she notes the stress that the discussion of "practices" produces in her as a mestiza writer. In one way, the root of her discontent is related to the question that haunts my homiletic instruction: Is it possible to create a practice that liberates the classroom from its patriarchal roots? But for Gil-Gomez, the problem is greater than acknowledging that classrooms are patriarchal spaces. She fears that practices themselves produce false unities and static traditions. They ignore the "fragmentation" she understands as central to her identity—and indeed, central to what it means to be alive and human.[48] "Questioning the meaning and content of a practice *is* a feminist practice," she states.[49] Rather than standing in "the privileged status of truth-tellers . . . , we must be willing to reveal our pieces."[50]

Lisa Thompson's *Ingenuity: Preaching as an Outsider* speaks from the particularity of a black female preacher's experience. Her "pieces" are different than Gil-Gomez's. And yet, her struggle with the stability of communal practices that resist difference resonates with Gil-Gomez's description. Thompson describes an encounter with a woman who admits to not liking woman preachers. "But I like you," the woman continues, "You don't sound like a man, but you don't sound like a woman either."[51] Thompson admits to the discomfort this backhanded compliment brings her. She feels caught between her commitment to a community and the subject positions into which she is pressed by that community's expectations. "Doing or not doing whatever some think they mean by 'black preaching' or 'women's preaching' is risky business."[52] The "ingenuity" described by Thompson is fluid, committed, and vulnerable work. It requires embodied engagement and prayerful negotiation of one's role and one's voice. It requires a coming to peace with one's "pieces."

For Thompson, the work is also theological. It refuses to let static practices and silver hands substitute for the disruptive presence of the risen Jesus. When communal expectations become synonymous with a preacher's understanding of her role, "we potentially close off . . . the possibility of sacred in-breaking through the practice of preaching itself."[53] For Thompson and Gil-Gomez, something more than new practices are called for to counter the "whiteness" of rhetoric's "proper woman." Provisionality, vulnerability, and critical engagement are needed. Practices of flesh, moving in time and pieced together in relationship, are required.

HANDS OF FLESH

The folktale has a hopeful arc, for all its sorrow. The maiden's hands grow back. She leaves the palace with her silver hands in a box, and in the forest, her hands begin to reemerge. They appear first as a baby's hands, then as a young girl's hands, until miraculously, they become the hands of a woman. What ties together the tactics of these female rhetoricians is their commitment to the embodied relationality of language and their rejection of linguistic stasis. They desire hands of flesh for their students, even when those hands are vulnerable to the scarring of a cruel world.

The problem with the idealized Feminine has never been the rhetorical qualities that it celebrates. Power, submission, piety, and modesty are not dangerous, in and of themselves. Each can be appropriate in a given context. Neither is the disruption of tradition a universal good. Fijian sociologist Akanisi Tarabe notes the importance of reclaiming traditional practices in her Fijian context as a prophetic stance against Western globalization.[54]

The problem with the "proper woman" trope is her stasis, her lack of human limits, and her invulnerability to text, community, and world. Such rigid idealisms create practices requiring amputations. To draw on Frankenburg's definition, her "whiteness" is the problem. She is locked into a subject position that cannot admit fragmentation and multiplicity. And as such, she locks others into corresponding positions, restricting agency, encounter, and learning. Her flesh becomes statuesque or shadowy, a divinized "norm" that denies and resists difference—even the difference introduced by Christ's body and Christ's Word through the mediating work of the Spirit.

The white, female pastor quoted in this chapter's epigraph describes the temptation to center herself as "savior, victim and heroine" in her ministry. But "that is not the space I'm called to as a white woman," she continues. "The work is in the claiming of radical honesty, in the de-centering of white womxn, in the checking of my selfishness . . . in the ridding of ego . . . so that I may become more real . . . formed through intersectionality and women that don't look like me."[55] There is a cost to embracing hands of flesh, but there is also joy—the joy of genuine relationship.

Gil-Gomez ends her essay by challenging teachers of rhetoric to "risk our identities" alongside the risks of our students. "We cannot expect our students to challenge the stability of their . . . ideologies while we simply 'provide' . . . opportunities to do so."[56] In light of her call, I share a "piece" of myself.

When I was a young mother in my early thirties, I had a dream that I was presiding at the communion table with silver hands. It was a season when I didn't feel "real" in my ministry, and the role of "proper pastor" weighed heavy on my spirit. There were prophetic words I did not speak and questions I did not ask. Complicated fragments of my own identity were swept into corners. In my dream, those silver hands were a necessary grief. I had no idea how to serve at the table without them.

Ten years later, I was at an Anglican monastery at a writing retreat. My final morning, I came to the daily communion service assuming that one of the men who ran the retreat center would preside. I was surprised to find a woman behind the table instead. She was dressed in full priestly regalia, sporting a shock of hair that looked like snow. Her eyes snapped with humor. And when she raised her hands in blessing, I saw that she was missing a hand. There was a piece of thumb and half a palm, but not enough to lift the chalice and paten. A layperson stood beside her. Together they lifted the elements and poured the wine. Together—using one hand each—they lifted the bread and tore it in two. She showed us her "pieces"—dependent, unafraid, and real. And the fragments were re-membered as flesh.

NOTES

1. There are many versions of this story found across Middle and Eastern Europe, sometimes called "The Handless Maiden" or "Silver Hands." This version is a compilation found in Clarissa Pinkola Estés, *Women Who Run with the Wolves: Myths and Stories of the Wild Woman Archetype* (New York: Ballantine Books, 1992), 389–94. I follow Estés's telling, but not her interpretation.

2. Lisa L. Thompson describes "ingenuity" as a posture engaged by "outsider" preachers—and particularly African American women—to claim authority, connection, and voice in the exclusionary currents of congregational power structures, in *Ingenuity: Preaching as an Outsider* (Nashville: Abingdon Press, 2018).

3. Jane Sutton, "The Taming of the Polos/Polis: Rhetoric as an Achievement without Women," in *Contemporary Rhetorical Theory: A Reader,* edited by John Louis Lucaites, Celeste Michelle Condit and Sally Caudill (New York: The Guilford Press, 1998).

4. Alan of Lille praises rhetoric that avoids the "excessive coloration and adornment" that so disgusted Tertullian in the garments of Christian women. Claire Waters, *Angels and Earthly Creatures: Preaching, Performance and Gender in the Later Middle Ages* (Philadelphia: University of Pennsylvania Press, 2004), 87.

5. Beverly Mayne Kienzle describes the twelfth- and thirteenth-century polemics which describe women preachers as "Jezebels," in "The Prostitute Preacher: Patterns of Polemic against Medieval Waldensian Women Preachers," in *Women Preachers and Prophets through Two Millennia of Christianity*, edited by Kienzle and Walker (Berkeley: University of California Press, 1998), 99–113.

6. 1 Cor. 1:17–18, Jean Calvin, *Commentary on the Epistles of Paul the Apostle to the Corinthians* (Grand Rapids: Wm. B. Eerdmans, 1948), 75.

7. St. Augustine, *On Christian Teaching* (Oxford: Oxford University Press, 1997), 134–37.

8. Plato, *Gorgias*, tr. W. C. Helmbold (Indianapolis: Bobbs-Merrill, 1952), 461–81.

9. Sutton, "The Taming," 106. Quoting Dionysius of Halicarnassus, *On the Ancient Orators*, in *The Critical Essays, vol. 1*, trans. S. Usher (Cambridge, MA: Harvard University Press, 1974), 5–15.

10. Calvin, *Commentary on the Epistles of Paul the Apostle to the Corinthians*, 75.

11. Hebrews 4:11–13, Jean Calvin, *Commentary on the Epistle to the Hebrews* (Grand Rapids: W. B. Eerdmans, 1949), 102.

12. Philip Brooks, "Episcopal Convention Sermon," St. Paul's Church, Boston, May 14, 1879. Quoted in Alexander Allen, *The Life and Letters of Phillips Brooks, vol. 2* (London: Macmillan Publishers, 1900), 246.

13. Sarah Coakley, for example, addresses the romantic feminism of Leonardo Boff, arguing that the "feminine 'other'" that he lauds is a "male construct" and a "thinly disguised reorientation of traditional gender stereotypes," in "Mariology and 'Romantic Feminism,'" in *Women's Voices: Essays in Contemporary Feminist Theology*, edited by Teresa Elwes (New York: Marshall Pickering Publishers, 1992), 106–10.

14. Jerusha Matsen Neal, *The Overshadowed Preacher: Mary, the Spirit and the Labor of Proclamation* (Grand Rapids: Wm. B. Eerdmans, 2020). My argument is indebted to Elizabeth Johnson's work in *Truly Our Sister: A Theology of Mary in the Communion of Saints* (New York: Continuum, 2003) who describes her Catholic tradition's outsourcing of the Spirit's work to Mary, Jesus's mother, 89.

15. Krista Ratcliffe, "Eavesdropping as a Rhetorical Tactic: History, Whiteness, and Rhetoric," *JAC* 20, no. 1 (2000): 87–119, quoting Ruth Frankenberg, *White Women, Race Matters: The Social Construction of Whiteness* (Minneapolis: University of Minneapolis Press, 1993), 236–37.

16. Ratcliffe, "Eavesdropping," 101–11.

17. Ibid, 111.

18. Anna Carter Florence speaks of the violence done against biblical texts through reductive explanation in "Put Away Your Sword! Taking the Torture Out of the Sermon," in *What's the Matter with Preaching Today*, edited by Mike Graves (Louisville: WJK Press, 2004). "Explaining" the text propositionally relates to Platonic understandings of "rhetoric is the mere handmaid of right reason," William Wainwright, *Reason, Revelation and Devotion: Inference and Argument in Religion* (New York: Cambridge University Press, 2016), 87.

19. The humanists of the Renaissance wanted rhetoric crowned as "queen of the liberal arts" with a renewed emphasis on rhetoric's transformative power. Wayne Rebhorn, *Renaissance Debates on Rhetoric* (Ithaca: Cornell University Press, 2000), 10. Lucy Atkinson Rose has cautioned that placing the transformation of the congregation into the preacher's job description is "potentially dangerous," placing too much control in the preacher's hands, in *Sharing the Word: Preaching in the Roundtable Pulpit* (Louisville: WJK Press, 1997), 133.

20. Phillips Brooks's desire to be "transparent medium" is linked to his belief in the possibility of "perfectly pure obedient humanity," "Episcopal Convention Sermon." This connection between holiness and "fading away leads to underdeveloped

theologies of personal sanctification and social holiness that imagine themselves "color-blind."

21. Alison Weir describes how, in the Western tradition, women are forced to "*be* mediation, to unify human and divine law, individual and community, the male self with himself and the universal." Weir argues that the flesh and blood female disappears in this "mediation of differences into unity," Alison Weir, *Sacrificial Logics: Feminist Theory and the Critique of Identity* (London: Routledge, 1996), 97. White women's hegemonic descriptions of "women's experience" show the erasure that flows from this mediatrix role. Not only does the particularity of white women disappear. The particularities of women who do not speak from the privilege of whiteness also disappear. Jacquelyn Grant's critique of white feminism continues to have contemporary relevance, *White Women's Christ and Black Women's Jesus: Feminist Christology and Womanist Response* (Atlanta: Scholars Press, 1989).

22. Sally A. Brown discusses the hegemonic danger of postliberal homiletic projects that emphasize the singularity of "story" and "tradition" in passing down communal grammar, "Exploring the Text-Practice Interface: Acquiring the Virtue of Hermeneutical Modesty," *Theology Today* 66, no. 3 (October 1, 2009): 286–87. Gloria Anzaldúa's "How to Tame a Wild Tongue" describes the painful imposition of communal grammar on identity, in *Borderlands/La Frontera: The New Mestiza, 4th ed.* (San Francisco: Aunt Lute Books, 2012).

23. Chanequa Walker-Barnes, *Too Heavy a Yoke: Black Women and the Burden of Strength* (Eugene: Wipf and Stock, 2014). Walker-Barnes description of the cult of true womanhood comes from Barbara Welter, "The Cult of True Womanhood: 1820–1860," *American Quarterly* 18, no. 2, Part 1 (Summer 1966): 151–74.

24. Audre Lorde, "The Master's Tools Will Never Dismantle the Master's House," *Sister Outsider* (Trumansburg: The Crossing Press, 1984), 110–13. Stephanie Jones-Rogers maps the deep roots of white women's complicity with patriarchal racism in the United States in *They Were Her Property: White Women as Slave Owners in the American South* (New Haven: Yale University Press, 2019).

25. Frankenberg, *White Women*, 236–37.

26. Sutton, "The Taming," 121.

27. Gary Macy, *The Hidden History of Women's Ordination: Female Clergy in the Medieval West* (Oxford: Oxford University Press, 2008), 125.

28. Waters, *Angels*, 20.

29. Dwight Conquergood notes that elocutionary training and minstrel shows draw on similar "protocols of taste, civility and gentility," marking racialized "others." "Rethinking Elocution: The Trope of the Talking Book and Other Figures of Speech," *Text and Performance Quarterly* 20, no. 4 (October 2000): 326.

30. Mosese Ma'ilo discusses colonial centralization of power through Bible translation/interpretation efforts, *Bible-ing My Samoan: Native Languages and the Politics of Bible Translation in the 19th Century* (Apia, Samoa: Piula Publications, 2016).

31. Ratcliffe's naming of "many tactics" being used by feminist rhetoric to counter "whiteness" is a good starting place for reflection, 112.

32. Jacqueline Jones Royster, "When the First Voice You Hear Is Not Your Own," *College Composition and Communication* 47, no. 1 (February 1996): 38.

33. Jacqueline Jones Royster, *Traces of a Stream: Literary and Social Change among African-American Women* (Pittsburgh: University of Pittsburgh Press, 2000), 279.

34. Jones Royster's fullest articulation of her method can be found in Jacqueline Jones Royster and Gesa Kirsch, *Feminist Rhetorical Practices: New Horizons for Rhetoric, Composition, and Literacy Studies* (Carbondale: Southern Illinois University Press, 2012).

35. Royster and Kirsch, *Feminist Rhetorical Practices*, 84–85.

36. Donyelle McCray, "Quilting the Sermon: Homiletical Insights from Harriet Powers," *Religions* 9, no. 2 (2018): 46.

37. Donyelle McCray, "Mothering Souls: A Vocation of Intercession," *Anglican Theological Review* 98, no. 2 (Spring 2016): 285–301.

38. Donyelle McCray, *The Censored Pulpit: Julian of Norwich as Preacher* (Lanham: Fortress Academic, 2019).

39. Donyelle McCray, "When Illness Calls: Insights from Julian of Norwich's Call to Frailty," paper presented at the *2010 Academy of Homiletics*, Atlanta, GA.

40. bell hooks, *Teaching to Transgress: Education as a Practice of Freedom* (New York: Routledge, 1994), 31.

41. Shirley Wilson Logan, "'When and Where I Enter': Race, Gender and Composition Studies," in *Feminism and Composition Studies: In Other Words*, edited by Jarratt and Worsham (New York: MLA Publishing, 1998), 55.

42. Logan, "'When and Where,'" 55.

43. Toni Morrison, *The Nobel Lecture in Literature, 1993* (New York: Alfred A. Knopf, 1994), 20–21.

44. Morrison, *The Nobel*, 26.

45. Lis Valle, "Toward Postcolonial Liturgical Preaching: Drawing on the Pre-Columbian Caribbean Religion of the Taínos," *Homiletic* 40, no. 1 (2015), http://vurj.vanderbilt.edu/index.php/homiletic/article/view/4119 (accessed September 20, 2019).

46. Walter Brueggemann, *Texts under Negotiation: The Bible and the Postmodern Imagination* (Minneapolis: Augsburg Fortress Press, 1993), 18. Valle draws on Michael Jagessar and Stephen Burns's use of Brueggemann in "Fragments of a Postcolonial Perspective on Christian Worship," *Worship* 80, no. 5 (September 1, 2006): 430.

47. Ellen Gil-Gomez, "The Practice of Piece-Making: Subject Positions in the Classroom," in *Feminism and Composition Studies: In Other Words*, edited by Jarratt and Worsham (New York: MLA Publishing, 1998), Gomez defines piece-making as "nurturing my fragments and accepting the conflicts they raise inside me," 204.

48. Gil-Gomez, "The Practice," 203.

49. Ibid, 202.

50. Ibid, 204.

51. Lisa Thompson, *Ingenuity: Preaching as an Outsider* (Nashville: Abingdon Press, 2018), 3.

52. Thompson, *Ingenuity*, 3.

53. Ibid, 4.

54. Akanisi Tarabe, "White Clothing and the Fabrication of Identity," *Na Uli: The Davuilevu Journal of Theology and Practice,* issue 1 (August 2015): 28.

55. Much gratitude to Rev. Molly Brummett Wudel for her willingness to share these reflections, written in response to an African American woman's invitation for white women to share their journey of healing from "whiteness" "Yes to all of this," Facebook, June 19, 2019, https://www.facebook.com/molly.brummett.1/posts/10100234148682372 (accessed September 20, 2019).

56. Gil-Gomez, "The Practice," 204.

BIBLIOGRAPHY

Allen, Alexander. *The Life and Letters of Phillips Brooks*, vol.2. London: Macmillan Publishers, 1900.

Anzaldúa, Gloria. *Borderlands/La Frontera: The New Mestiza*, 4th ed. San Francisco: Aunt Lute Books, 2012.

Augustine. *On Christian Teaching*. Oxford: Oxford University Press, 1997.

Brown, Sally A. "Exploring the Text-Practice Interface: Acquiring the Virtue of Hermeneutical Modesty." *Theology Today* 66, no. 3 (October 1, 2009): 279–94.

Brueggemann, Walter. *Texts Under Negotiation: The Bible and the Postmodern Imagination*. Minneapolis: Augsburg Fortress Press, 1993.

Brummett Wudel, Molly. "Yes to all of this." *Facebook*, June 19, 2019. https://www.facebook.com/molly.brummett.1/posts/10100234148682372 (accessed on September 13, 2021).

Calvin, Jean. *Commentary on the Epistles of Paul the Apostle to the Corinthians*. Grand Rapids: Wm. B. Eerdmans, 1948.

———. *Commentary on the Epistle to the Hebrews*. Grand Rapids: W. B. Eerdmans, 1949.

Coakley, Sarah. "Mariology and 'Romantic Feminism.'" In *Women's Voices: Essays in Contemporary Feminist Theology*, edited by Teresa Elwes, 106–10. New York: Marshall Pickering Publishers, 1992.

Conquergood, Dwight. "Rethinking Elocution: The Trope of the Talking Book and Other Figures of Speech." *Text and Performance Quarterly* 20, no. 4 (October 2000): 325–41.

Florence, Anna Carter. "Put Away Your Sword! Taking the Torture out of the Sermon." In *What's the Matter with Preaching Today*, edited by Mike Graves, 93–108. Louisville: WJK Press, 2004.

Frankenberg, Ruth. *White Women, Race Matters: The Social Construction of Whiteness*. Minneapolis: University of Minneapolis Press, 1993.

Gil-Gomez, Ellen. "The Practice of Piece-Making: Subject Positions in the Classroom." In *Feminism and Composition Studies: In Other Words*, edited by Susan Jarratt and Lynn Worsham, 198–205. New York: MLA Publishing, 1998.

Grant, Jacquelyn. *White Women's Christ and Black Women's Jesus: Feminist Christology and Womanist Response*. Atlanta: Scholars Press, 1989.

hooks, bell. *Teaching to Transgress: Education as a Practice of Freedom.* New York: Routledge, 1994.
Johnson, Elizabeth. *Truly Our Sister: A Theology of Mary in the Communion of Saints.* New York: Continuum, 2003.
Jones-Rogers, Stephanie. *They Were Her Property: White Women as Slave Owners in the American South.* New Haven, CT: Yale University Press, 2019.
Jones Royster, Jacqueline. *Traces of a Stream: Literary and Social Change among African-American Women.* Pittsburgh: University of Pittsburgh Press, 2000.
———. "When the First Voice You Hear Is Not Your Own." *College Composition and Communication* 47, no. 1 (Feb. 1996): 29–40.
——— and Gesa Kirsch. *Feminist Rhetorical Practices: New Horizons for Rhetoric, Composition, and Literacy.* Carbondale: Southern Illinois University Press, 2012.
Kienzle, Beverly Mayne. "The Prostitute Preacher: Patterns of Polemic against Medieval Waldensian Women Preachers." In *Women Preachers and Prophets through Two Millennia of Christianity*, edited by Kienzle and Walker, 99–113. Berkeley: University of California Press, 1998.
Logan, Shirley Wilson. "'When and Where I Enter': Race, Gender and Composition Studies." *Feminism and Composition Studies: In Other Words,* edited by Jarratt and Worsham, 45–57. New York: MLA Publishing, 1998.
Lorde, Audre. *Sister Outsider.* Trumansburg, NY: The Crossing Press, 1984.
Macy, Gary. *The Hidden History of Women's Ordination: Female Clergy in the Medieval West.* Oxford: Oxford University Press, 2008.
Ma'ilo, Mosese. *Bible-ing My Samoan: Native Languages and the Politics of Bible Translation in the 19th Century.* Apia, Samoa: Piula Publications, 2016.
McCray, Donyelle. *The Censored Pulpit: Julian of Norwich as Preacher.* Lanham: Fortress Academic, 2019.
———. "Mothering Souls: A Vocation of Intercession." *Anglican Theological Review* 98, no. 2 (Spring 2016): 285–301.
———. "Quilting the Sermon: Homiletical Insights from Harriet Powers." *Religions* 9, no. 2 (2018): 46–52.
———. "When Illness Calls: Insights from Julian of Norwich's Call to Frailty." Paper presented at the 2010 Academy of Homiletics, Atlanta, GA.
Morrison, Toni. *The Nobel Lecture in Literature, 1993.* New York: Alfred A. Knopf, 1994.
Neal, Jerusha Matsen. *The Overshadowed Preacher: Mary, the Spirit and the Labor of Proclamation.* Grand Rapids: Wm. B. Eerdmans, 2020.
Pinkola Estés, Clarissa. *Women Who Run With the Wolves: Myths and Stories of the Wild Woman Archetype.* New York: Ballantine Books, 1992.
Plato. *Gorgias,* Translated by W. C. Helmbold. Indianapolis: Bobbs-Merrill, 1952.
Ratcliffe, Krista. "Eavesdropping as a Rhetorical Tactic: History, Whiteness, and Rhetoric." *JAC* 20, no. 1 (2000): 87–119.
Rebhorn, Wayne. *Renaissance Debates on Rhetoric.* Ithaca: Cornell University Press, 2000.
Rose, Lucy Atkinson. *Sharing the Word: Preaching in the Roundtable Pulpit.* Louisville: WJK Press, 1997.

Sutton, Jane. "The Taming of the Polos/Polis: Rhetoric as an Achievement Without Women." In *Contemporary Rhetorical Theory: A Reader,* edited by John Louis Lucaites, Celeste Michelle Condit and Sally Caudill, 101–26. New York: The Guilford Press, 1998.

Tarabe, Akanisi. "White Clothing and the Fabrication of Identity." *Na Uli: The Davuilevu Journal of Theology and Practice* 1 (August 2015): 24–29.

Thompson, Lisa. *Ingenuity: Preaching as an Outsider.* Nashville: Abingdon Press, 2018.

Valle, Lis. "Toward Postcolonial Liturgical Preaching: Drawing on the Pre-Columbian Caribbean Religion of the Taínos." *Homiletic* 40, no. 1 (2015), http://vurj.vanderbilt.edu/index.php/homiletic/article/view/4119 (accessed on September 20, 2019).

Wainwright, William. *Reason, Revelation and Devotion: Inference and Argument in Religion.* New York: Cambridge University Press, 2016.

Walker-Barnes, Chanequa. *Too Heavy a Yoke: Black Women and the Burden of Strength.* Eugene: Wipf and Stock, 2014.

Waters, Claire. *Angels and Earthly Creatures: Preaching, Performance and Gender in the Later Middle Ages.* Philadelphia: University of Pennsylvania Press, 2004.

Weir, Alison. *Sacrificial Logics: Feminist Theory and the Critique of Identity.* London: Routledge, 1996.

Welter, Barbara. "The Cult of True Womanhood: 1820–1860." *American Quarterly* 18, no. 2, Part 1 (Summer 1966): 151–74.

Chapter 12

Betraying White Preaching

Homiletical Domination, Racial Treason, and the Pursuit of Abolition

Andrew Wymer

The theme of this anthology is "unmasking white preaching."[1] This title evokes Frantz Fanon's *Black Skin, White Masks* and the works of numerous other scholars utilizing the imagery of masks to critically engage race.[2] To the degree that we intentionally follow the non-dominant imagery of this theme to its sources outside of white-dominant discourse, our theme has the potential to draw us outside of white-dominant discourse in ways that decenter white preaching, white preachers, white homiletics, and whiteness more broadly.

However, this theme is not without potential limitations that might subsequently re-center white preaching, white preachers, and white homiletics, even if negatively. The first limitation is that without the addition of further grammatical modifiers our theme may contribute to a perception that we are entering undiscovered or unexplored territory and initiating the unmasking of white preaching.[3] We must acknowledge that our efforts should be categorized as *further* or *continued* unmasking of white preaching joining in a long-standing and significant tradition of unmasking of white preaching in some racially minoritized homiletical discourse. The second limitation is that the theme does not provide an explicit reference to a trajectory whereby, after carefully examining white preaching, we can continue in the long-standing homiletical legacy of some racially minoritized scholars who decentered, deconstructed, and destabilized white preaching.

Drawing upon these observations, this chapter seeks to accomplish two tasks. The first task is to briefly survey homiletical discourse on the nature of black preaching as one example of the long-standing unmasking of white preaching done by some racially minoritized homiletical scholars, drawing from this discourse observations about the identification of white preaching as a distinct racial and homiletical category.[4] In this first section, I will argue that the heart of white preaching is a position of racialized social, political, and economic domination. The second task is to then grapple with a pathway that might lead us—particularly those of us who benefit from whiteness—beyond "reform" of white preaching toward the abolition of white preaching. In this second section, I will briefly survey the concept of "race traitor" in neo-abolitionist discourse and subsequent critiques of it in critical race discourse in the late twentieth century. Through these critiques, I will utilize Richard Delgado's notion of white "responsibility" and Derrick Bell's understanding of "racial realism" to imagine what it might mean to pursue abolition of the brutal systems of whiteness and white preaching amid the contemporary landscape of white domination in the context of the United States.

"UNMASKING" WHITE PREACHING

The burden of grappling with white preaching as a racial and homiletical category has primarily and historically fallen to persons from racialized groups targeted by whiteness. As a result, critical interpretations of homiletical whiteness have been present for some time in racially minoritized homiletical discourse engaging the intersection of race and preaching. While some racially minoritized scholars have long been tugging at the masks of white preachers and white homileticians, forcing, at the very least, partial exposures of their "faces," too often those efforts have been disregarded. Preachers, who are deemed white or benefit from whiteness, have too often been so mired in our sociocultural formation into racial dominance and "privilege," the violently gained economic, social, and political material plunder of whiteness, that we have either ignored or disregarded these critiques.[5]

In Sara Ahmed's article, "Declarations of Whiteness: The Non-Performativity of Anti-Racism," she argues that in order for persons deemed white to move beyond simply performing anti-racism our work must acknowledge that expertise in the subject of race and responding to race lies outside of ourselves.[6] Ahmed can speak into our conversations, reminding us that all persons—including preachers—who benefit from being deemed white must first recognize that expertise in and solutions to white preaching lie outside of ourselves and outside of white homiletical theory or practice. By implication, we must listen to and learn from racially minoritized critiques of whiteness in a way that both engages the complex evil of whiteness and ultimately leaves us profoundly aware that any answers came or will come from outside of ourselves.

Racially minoritized homiletical discourse engaging the intersection of race and preaching has long explicitly and implicitly argued that race distinctively and profoundly shapes participation in the preaching moment within the context of the United States.[7] This is clearly evidenced in a sustained manner in some black homiletical discourse. While I hedge against limiting engagement of race to a black/white binary or to a U.S.-dominant conversation, black homiletical discourse in the United States engaging the intersection of race and preaching represents a significant, sustained body of homiletical literature upon which to draw for the very limited scope of this chapter.

Surveying major contributions from this body of literature reveals key observations: (1) Preaching in the United States is distinctively and profoundly shaped by race, itself an imposition of whiteness. (2) The distinct and profound impact of race on preaching has necessitated recognition of distinct schools of preaching along racial lines (e.g., black preaching, white preaching, etc.) each complete with its own homiletical characteristics. (3) Awareness of and sensitivity to the profound and distinct impact of race on preaching is necessary if preaching is to impact the unfolding drama of race in the United States in a revolutionary manner.[8]

A long-standing, influential theme in black homiletical discourse engaging the intersection of race and preaching is that of identifying the racial and homiletical distinctiveness of black preaching in order to reclaim or preserve its powerful potential to contribute to the survival and thriving of black persons and communities in a white-dominant society.[9] A mid-twentieth-century example of black homiletical scholarship explicitly connecting race and preaching is William Pipes's *Say Amen, Brother!: Old-Time Negro Preaching: A Study in American Frustration* (1951).[10] Pipes identifies the two primary sources of "old-time" black preaching as "the mixing of early American and traditional African religious practices" and "the need for an escape mechanism by a people held in bondage."[11] Cornel West observes that Pipes viewed "black sermonic practices as integral to black culture, social, and political quests for empowerment and emancipation."[12] In Pipes's analysis, he examines the distinct characteristics of old-time black preaching as flowing out of these two primary sources of traditional religious practices and the violent domination of whiteness, the latter of which he explicitly links to "white preachers" and their roles in its maintenance and defense.[13]

This pattern of searching for the distinctive sources and resulting distinctive characteristics of black preaching and the explicit naming of white preaching as harmfully connected to white violence is repeated in Henry Mitchell's much later work, *Black Preaching: The Recovery of a Powerful Art* (1990), which was a compilation of earlier sources published in the 1970s.[14] Like Pipes, Mitchell highlights how black culture and black hermeneutics were fundamentally shaped both by African traditional culture and by the brutality of the Middle Passage and chattel slavery, the latter which were justified by European and Euro-American colonial agents and institutions through the violent imposition and maintenance of racial hierarchies. He then assesses the unique characteristics of black preaching that have emerged from those sources.

The concerns of these earlier works are reflected in *The Heart of Black Preaching* (2000) by Cleophus LaRue. However, LaRue makes a more focused argument that the "heart," or shared characteristics, of black preaching that renders it distinctive is its biblical hermeneutic shaped by black "sociocultural experience."[15] Sharing concerns similar to Pipes and Mitchell for the continued positive impact of black preaching in black life, LaRue argues that clarity about the "fundamentals of African American preaching" is vital, because "our inability to name the basics of black preaching makes it difficult, if not impossible, to teach systematically the dynamics of this style to those who stand within as well as outside the tradition."[16] He is concerned that students and practitioners not only learn the "style" of black preaching but that they might learn the "substance" of the underlying commitment that shapes black preaching from the inside out, rendering it a source of power.[17]

These themes are also present in womanist homiletical scholarship; however, womanist scholars have contributed to discourse engaging race and homiletics by expanding critique beyond a singular focus on race to engage issues of gender, class, and sexuality. One example is Teresa Fry Brown, who, in *Weary Throats and New Songs* (2003), searches for the "distinctive nature" of black women's preaching.[18] She argues the sources of the distinctiveness of black women preaching are (1) the "resistance (weary throats) [sic]," experienced at the intersection of race, class, and gender and (2) the "support" and emergence of revolutionary "new songs" led and experienced by black women in "religious and social communities."[19]

From these works and others outside the scope of this chapter, it should be painfully clear that white preaching exists, and its existence has been being unmasked to some degree for a significant period of time.[20] Those of us who are deemed white or who benefit from whiteness must learn to deeply listen to those persons and schools of thought that have developed expertise in unmasking white preaching. As part of this listening, it is important to continue our own grappling with white preaching as a racial and homiletical category.

Utilizing the imagery of LaRue, the heart of white preaching, which renders it distinct from the preaching that emerges from other racialized social locations deemed non-white by the dominant, white social structure in the United States, is a position of racialized economic, social, and political domination—and necessarily racialized violence. This shared characteristic of racialized domination is one in which white preachers, white congregations, and corresponding white ecclesial structures, whether consciously or subconsciously, impose the structural and material domination of whiteness through the component actions of preaching onto texts, participants, and society in a manner that reflects and perpetuates broader systems of racial domination.

This naming of the violent heart of white preaching is supported implicitly and explicitly in arguments by a number of racially minoritized scholars engaging whiteness from a critical perspective. As an example, in his work, "Sanctification, Liberation, and Black Worship," James Cone names the backdrop of black worship and preaching as the death-dealing "white society," and he describes white worship and "white spirituality that is culturally determined by American values and thus indifferent to oppressed black people's struggle for racial justice."[21] James Harris echoes this critique in *The Word Made Plain: The Power and Promise of Preaching*, in which he decries the complicity of the white church in the maintenance of white supremacy.[22] He writes:

> The God of the white church has historically been grounded in the status quo, the constitution, and a white-supremacy ideology. This "triune god [*sic*]" enables the white church to be an agent of the government, a harbinger of civil religion, an arm of the republic or the democratic state, and a propagator of the state's agenda and ideology.[23]

White church and white preaching have been and continue to be dramatic forces in the maintenance of racial hegemony.

White preaching has too long had the intrinsic and strategic material function of reasserting "white privilege," the violent socioeconomics of whiteness in which structures of whiteness brutally exploit and even exterminate those persons and people groups deemed non-white and redirect economic, political, and social benefits to those whom society deems white. Over the past few centuries, white homiletics in the United States have benefitted from and reinforced the validity and morality of the largesse of fortunes accumulated on bloodied and stolen ground and wrung from slave labor that has been lavished on white churches, predominantly white seminaries, and predominantly white denominations.

The dominating heart white preaching and the material spoils of whiteness from which it benefits have resulted in it centering itself as the pinnacle of Christian preaching to the point that it has escaped recognition on the part of those deemed white as a racial and homiletical category. Emerging out of the heart of violence, white homiletical styles, biblical interpretative stances, ritual movements or language, constructive language about God, engagements of society and culture, or any other unique homiletical components were imposed as homiletical standards while escaping recognition and subsequent critique as racially contextual. In centering itself, white preaching has rendered other schools of preaching as "abnormal" or "other."[24]

ABOLITION AND RACIAL TREASON

In light of the dominance of white preaching, a pressing question for all practitioners and scholars of white preaching who are deemed white by society or who benefit from brutal systems of whiteness is how we can join in the charting of a trajectory along which we pursue the abolition of white preaching as well as all systems of white domination.

In Richard Delgado's "Rodrigo's Eleventh Chronicle: Empathy and False Empathy," two characters, Rodrigo, a law student, and his professor, converse. Rodrigo expresses disappointment at the failure of white, "liberal" empathy to contribute to the struggle against racism, and he argues for the plausibility of two strategies in place of empathy, both of which he thinks have potential to advance the interests of racial minorities.[25] The first strategy for which he argues is Noel Ignatiev and John Garvey's articulation of "race traitor," in which white persons betray whiteness by outspokenly rejecting white privilege and aggressively challenging racism to the point that they both begin to lose some of their material white privilege and the system of white hegemony begins to break down.[26] As his second strategy, Rodrigo argues that white "liberals" must take their "campaigns" against racism out of their "elite" conversations and into conversations with lower-class white persons.[27] As Rodrigo and his professor reflect on the challenge of critically white elites[28] engaging lower-class white persons, Rodrigo observes that "they ['radical' white elites] took the easy way out. . . . They abandoned their own people. Empathy—the shallow chic kind—is always more attractive than *responsibility*, which is hard work."[29]

The term "race traitor" has been deployed in a variety of ways in the United States. In present, popular usage, self-identifying white supremacist groups utilize the term to denounce white persons whom they perceive as supportive or accepting of persons deemed to be racial minorities. Contemporary online forums such as 4chan, 8chan, Daily Stormer, and Stormfront contain numerous examples of this term being deployed in this popular sense as well as variations including, but not limited to, "gender traitor." However, I am engaging the term in specific reference to the emergence of late twentieth-century discourse on the "abolition of whiteness" (which Delgado is referencing as well) and a neo-abolitionist movement that took at least partial expression in the launch of the journal, *Race Traitor*, by Noel Ignatiev and John Garvey.[30]

The mantra of *Race Traitor* is that "treason to whiteness is loyalty to humanity."[31] They define a "race traitor" as "someone who is nominally classified as white, but who defies the rules of whiteness so flagrantly as to jeopardize his or her ability to draw upon the privileges of white skin."[32] Their understanding of the possibility of racial treason and the subsequent disruption of whiteness are based on a political, rather than a biological or phenotypical, interpretation of whiteness as a social system that validates the economic "privileging" of persons and subsequently imposes racial hierarchies according to the privileged or non-privileged status of a particular group of persons.

Racial treason signifies a tactic whereby a small minority of persons deemed white pursue abolition through disrupting the unifying political force of what they believe to be is a silent majority of potentially well-intentioned white persons. They do so by transgressing the rules of whiteness in visible and aggressive ways that disrupt the unification upon which racism and racial hierarchies rely. Acts of flagrant defiance can be varied in their degrees of force up to including violent physical engagements, and these treasonous acts can also result in the violence of whiteness being turned against the traitors themselves as they break the rules of whiteness. As these race traitors cause a breakdown in the white order, Ignatiev and Garvey hope that this will lead to engagement of the silent majority of possibly well-intentioned whites in a way that will lead to the permanent abolition of white supremacy and lead to revolutionary social shifts.[33]

Ignatiev and Garvey argue that this is different than anti-racism. They argue that the term "racism" is nebulous and that anti-racism implicitly accepts racial distinctions as natural while rejecting inequalities based on racial distinctions. They write, "people were not favored socially because they were white; rather, they were defined as 'white' because they were favored."[34] With this understanding of social, economic, and political discrimination as the heart of race and something which racial hierarchies are intended to defend, they argue that social discrimination cannot begin to be addressed until the white race is destroyed as a unifying political and economic force in which persons deemed white hold their position in the racial hierarchy over and against any other human identification or interests. While I will critique this argument later, Ignatiev and Garvey place "faith" in their understanding that "majority of so-called whites in this country are neither deeply nor consciously committed to white supremacy; like most human beings in most times and places, they would do the right thing if it were convenient."[35]

As was recounted earlier, in "Rodrigo's Eleventh Chronicle," Delgado appears to both affirm the concept of race traitor as an appropriate white response, but by juxtaposing it with a critique of the elite liberals whose work never translates to the local level. Delgado may be implicitly critiquing "race traitor" language by insisting that it must be intentionally brought down to the grassroots level in order to organize non-elite whites. In their "rediscovery" of "race traitor," John Preston and Charlotte Chadderton echo Delgado's critique. They argue for what Delgado might call an even more "responsible" concept of "race traitor" that intentionally (1) moves beyond elite conversations to organizing or participating in organized movements, (2) is connected with non-white efforts and not "autonomous," and (3) is always only ever conditional and must be daily renewed.[36]

In *Race, Whiteness, and Education*, Zeus Leonardo critically engages white abolition perspectives, and he particularly critiques what he sees as Ignatiev's failure to deal with the material expressions of whiteness as they are expressed economically, socially, and politically. While I would argue along with Preston and Chadderton that the collective work of the race traitor movement does grapple with the material implications of whiteness, Leonardo's critique of Ignatiev is important to consider. Though he faults neo-abolition with this previous critique, he observes "abolitionism's relentless attack on whiteness and the white frame of mind begins race analysis on the right foot."[37] Leonardo sums up his argument on racial treason and parallels Ahmed's earlier mentioned critique of the performativity of anti-racism, writing, "renouncing one's whiteness is a speech act of revolutionary proportions. It is not guided merely with the pronouncement 'I am not white,' but by the commitment 'I will not act white.'"[38] Leonardo presses racial treason and the broader field of abolition approaches to whiteness to reckon not just with the idea of whiteness but also the material realities of racism.

The political landscape of the past five years in the United States, especially during the Trump regime, reveals a fundamental miscalculation of Ignatiev and Garvey that must be addressed if the concept is to have value for efforts at white solidarity today. They posit that there is a silent majority of "good" whites, who, if provoked with a necessary degree of external stimuli, will enter into an effort to abolish whiteness. The role of racial treason is to disrupt the system of whiteness to the tipping point where this silent majority rises to the occasion of eradicating whiteness as a political force in the world. This calculation must, at the very least, be complicated in the presidential election of 2016 in which a significant majority of white persons in the United States voted to elect a candidate who throughout the election and the subsequent administration repeatedly utilized racialized dog whistles and overtly racist language in an attempt to reasserting white nationalism and white supremacy.[39] There was no "silent majority" of white persons, and it is quite possible that there may never be a "silent majority" of white persons ready to rise up to begin to abolish whiteness. However, there is value in pursuit of abolition and in the notion of racial treason.

Derrick Bell's concept of "racial realism" in *Faces at the Bottom of the Well: The Permanence of Racism* is helpful to this discourse, because it has the possibility of destabilizing naïve white approaches to the pursuit of abolition or racial treason grounded in fantastic, privileged notions of the imminent abolition of white privilege and white power—which upon their inevitable failure would likely reinforce whiteness.[40] Bell argues that (1) racism is permanent; (2) the economic implications of racism are essential to interpreting racism; (3) "salvation" is "through struggle" as opposed to victory; and (4) we must be "realistic" or honest about racism, striving for both "truth and justice."[41] Bell's argument is built on a frank analysis of the whipsawing history of racial progress and regression in the United States, and I believe that his racial realism can re-center our approach to abolition and racial treason by reminding persons deemed white that our primary motive for racial treason should be resistance through which we might be able to grasp at becoming more fully human and entering into solidarity with our racially minoritized human siblings. Ignatiev and Garvey clearly agree with Bell's second point, approaching race from perspectives sensitive to economics and class; however, Bell's first, third, and fourth points fundamentally help us to reimagine racial treason.

If indeed racism, that is the power of whiteness to shape local and global society and economics, is (1) permanent, or at the very least semi-permanent, and (2) our responses to it must be focused on faithful, sustained pursuit of abolition about which we are always realistic, then pursuit of abolition becomes a matter of long-term subversions less focused on one-time dramatic displays of disruption intended to bring about an imminent revolution and more focused on acts of betraying whiteness spread out over the long-term pursuit of abolition. Racial treason can become less triumphalist, itself a troubling characteristic in the context of whiteness and religion, and more focused on active, consistent subversions that are ultimately sourced in non-dominant discourse that conditionally draw abolitionists and race traitors outside of white power structures in ways that allow us to conditionally glimpse a fuller, more responsible human experience in solidarity with racially minoritized siblings.

The pursuit of abolition and the concept of racial treason are also important for ongoing discourse in homiletics in order to push us beyond "reform" or potentially bad faith declarations of concern or what Delgado calls "false empathy" that salve white consciences while perpetuating systems of whiteness.[42] As those of us homileticians who benefit from whiteness consider future responses to white preaching, may we do so in ways that are significant enough to risk declarations of our betrayal of whiteness and white preaching, that is, our commitment to not only not act white but also to act intentionally and consistently to abolish whiteness.

"HOW TO BE A RACE TRAITOR" HOMILETICALLY REVISITED

In "How to Be a Race Traitor: Six Ways to Fight Being White," Ignatiev offers up six concrete examples of how to betray whiteness, and these can be interpreted as just a few of many possible ways to enter into racial treason. Here, I reinterpret these for the context of white preaching, white responsibility, and racial realism. (1) Inside and outside of the pulpit humanly "identify with the racially oppressed." (2) Whenever possible "violate the rules of whiteness" and white preaching "in ways that can have" an ecclesial and "social impact." (3) In the pulpit explicitly critique and trouble your whiteness, and in cases in which racist activity occurs in your congregation or community, publicly and materially reject—if only conditionally, partially, and temporarily—the benefits of white privilege. (4) Explicitly oppose any "mechanism that favors whites" in your church, community, or institution, and consistently engage in activism resisting racism in any of its tangible material expressions (including but not limited to immigration law, mass incarceration and the criminal (in)justice system, environmental racism, housing exclusion, homelessness, wage theft, discriminatory hiring practices, workers' rights, and predatory banking). (5) Do not simply be non-racist or even anti-racist. Be an abolitionist and race traitor "with teeth."[43] "Seek to disrupt" the "normal functioning" of whiteness in your church and community. (6) Remember that racism intersects with issues of class, gender, and sexuality. Work to build a community in which issues of class, gender, sexuality, and ecology are held in hand with race. (7) "Target" your efforts at both "hardcore" white supremacists who might endanger the lives of persons deemed non-white, and also target the "mainstream institutions" and agents through which racism is "reproduced." (8) Be open to "any [homiletical or other] means of attaining the goal of betraying the white race; indeed, the willingness to go beyond socially acceptable limits of protest is a dividing line between 'good whites' and traitors to the white race."[44]

CONCLUSION

I am deeply appreciative of our theme of "[further] unmasking white preaching," and I hope we do not stop here. Having borne witness to the violence of white preaching, we cannot "unsee" it, and, for those preachers and homileticians who are claimed by or who benefit from whiteness, we must betray it and pursue its abolition. In our preaching, our scholarship, and our teaching, we must account for the sustained and ongoing history of racial violence in the theory and practice of European and Euro-American preaching and the ways in which white homiletics—intersecting with patriarchy and classism—has left and continues to leave blood on our hands.[45]

NOTES

1. This was also the theme of the 2019 annual meeting of the Academy of Homiletics held in New Brunswick, New Jersey, from December 5 to December 7, 2019.

2. Frantz Fanon, *Black Skin, White Masks* (New York: Grove Press, 1967).

3. I am intentionally utilizing colonial language here.

4. In order to hedge against any claims that I am essentializing race, "white preaching" is first and foremost utilized here as a political reference to preaching that occurs in social locations that politically benefit from or are perceived to benefit from the imposition of a hierarchy of power according to the fluid racial constructs of whiteness. I do not primarily utilize "white preaching" as a biological reference to the preacher's or the listening community's skin color, though the two usually are correlated.

5. I utilize "violently gained" here to push past a concept of white privilege as "unearned" material benefit and to name how white privilege is an expression of ongoing systemic violence.

6. Sara Ahmed, "Declarations of Whiteness: The Non-Performativity of Anti-Racism," *Meridians* 7, no. 1 (2006): 104–26.

7. I recognize the global implications of whiteness; however, the scope of this chapter and my own familiarity have compelled me to limit the scope of this study.

8. I utilize the term "revolutionary" in its contemporary sense as referencing the emergence of something new rather than its classical sense of referencing the return to something that once existed.

9. This tendency is not without critique. In *Rethinking Celebration*, Cleo LaRue argues that black homiletical discourse needs to move beyond "an endless engagement of contrasts and comparisons with white homiletics," because it "precludes the breaking of new ground in our own black tradition." Cleophus LaRue, *Rethinking Celebration: From Rhetoric to Praise in African American Preaching* (Louisville: Westminster John Knox, 2016).

10. William Pipes, *Say Amen, Brother!: Old-Time Negro Preaching: A Study in American Frustration* (Detroit: Wayne State University Press, 1992).

11. Pipes, *Say Amen, Brother!*, 71.

12. Ibid, xii.

13. Ibid, 86.

14. This work was published in 1990, but it combined two books, *Black Preaching* and *The Recovery of Preaching*, respectively, written in 1970 and 1977. See Henry Mitchell, *Black Preaching: The Recovery of a Powerful Art* (Nashville: Abingdon Press, 1990).

15. Cleophus LaRue, *The Heart of Black Preaching* (Louisville: Westminster John Knox, 1999), 1.

16. LaRue, *The Heart*, 6.
17. Ibid, 7.
18. Teresa Fry Brown, *Weary Throats and New Songs* (Nashville: Abingdon Press, 2003).
19. Brown, *Weary Throats,* 18. Fry Brown's work suggests the limitations of the singular focus of this chapter.
20. As was mentioned previously and bears repeating, it is crucial to note that racially minoritized critiques of whiteness in homiletics are not limited to black scholars. Justo and Catherine González are an example of Latinx voices that explicitly, critically interpret whiteness as it relates to preaching in the United States. The González's utilization of the—perhaps not coincidentally masked—"Lone Ranger" and "Tonto" to critique white, male preaching is sustained throughout *The Liberating Pulpit* (1994). See Justo and Catherine González, *The Liberating Pulpit* (Eugene: Wipf and Stock Publishers, 2003).
21. James Cone, "Sanctification, Liberation, and Black Worship," *Theology Today* 35, no. 2 (1978), 149.
22. James Harris, *The Word Made Plain: The Power and Promise of Preaching* (Minneapolis: Fortress Press, 2004).
23. Harris, *The Word*, 13.
24. In comparison with the sustained work of racially minoritized scholarship at the intersection of race and preaching as part of an ongoing struggle for empowerment and emancipation, the violent heart of white preaching can be maintained with little *overt* effort at all. Since the confines of this chapter limit an exploration of the uniquely white rhetorical characteristics of preaching, I argue that these include active racialized silence; strategic ignorance or disregard for racially minoritized life; misdirection and deception about underlying racialized economic, political, and social agendas; and racially coded language perpetuating racialized domination.
25. Richard Delgado, "Rodrigo's Eleventh Chronicle: Empathy and False Empathy," in *Critical White Studies: Looking Behind the Mirror*, edited by Richard Delgado and Jean Stefancic (Philadelphia: Temple University Press, 1997), 615.
26. Noel Ignatiev and John Garvey, eds., *Race Traitor* (London: Routledge Press, 1996).
27. Delgado, "Rodrigo's Eleventh," 617.
28. Here by "critically white" elites, I am attempting to denote folk who have to some degree critically engaged their whiteness in relationship to non-dominant perspectives.
29. Delgado, "Rodrigo's Eleventh," 617.
30. Ignatiev and Garvey, eds., *Race Traitor* (London: Routledge Press, 1996).
31. Ibid.
32. Noel Ignatiev, "Treason to Whiteness is Loyalty to Humanity," in *Critical White Studies: Looking behind the Mirror*, edited by Richard Delgado and Jean Stefancic (Philadelphia: Temple University Press, 1997), 607.
33. The concept of race traitor as associated with the new abolitionist movement has met with critique from various perspectives, and I recommend reading "Rediscovering 'Race Traitor': Towards a Critical Race Theory Informed Public

Pedagogy" by John Preston and Charlotte Chadderton for comprehensive survey and critical engagement of those critiques. John Preston and Charlotte Chadderton, "Rediscovering 'Race Traitor': Towards a Critical Race Theory Informed Public Pedagogy," *Race, Ethnicity, and Education* 15, no. 2 (January, 2012): 85–100.

34. Ignatiev, "Treason to Whiteness," 608.

35. Ibid, 609.

36. Preston and Chadderton, "Rediscovering 'Race Traitor.'"

37. Zeus Leonardo, *Race, Whiteness, and Education* (New York: Routledge, 2009), 73.

38. Leonardo, *Race, Whiteness, and Education*, 72.

Here I note that "not acting white" is conditional and temporary, and those white persons who "do not act white" are still caught up in the violence of whiteness.

39. Ian Lopez defines dog whistles as "coded racial appeals that carefully manipulate hostility toward non-whites." See Ian Lopez, *Dog Whistle Politics* (New York: Oxford University Press, 2015).

40. Derrick Bell, *Faces at the Bottom of the Well: The Permanence of Racism* (New York: Basic Books, 1992).

41. Bell, *Faces*, 99.

42. Lewis Gordon, *Bad Faith and Antiblack Racism* (New York: Humanity Books, 1999).

43. I heard this phrase from Rev. Seth Kaper-Dale in conversation about sanctuary for immigrants. He emphasizes that immigrants need "sanctuary with teeth."

44. Ignatiev, "How to Be . . . ," 613.

45. Even if this violence is expressed in silence or claims to "impartiality" or "neutrality."

BIBLIOGRAPHY

Ahmed, Sara. "Declarations of Whiteness: The Non-Performativity of Anti-Racism." *Meridians* 7, no. 1 (2006): 104–26.

Bell, Derrick. *Faces at the Bottom of the Well: The Permanence of Racism*. New York: Basic Books, 1992.

Brown, Teresa Fry. *Weary Throats and New Songs*. Nashville: Abingdon Press, 2009.

Cone, James. "Sanctification, Liberation, and Black Worship." *Theology Today* 35, no. 2 (1978): 139–152.

Delgado, Richard. "Rodrigo's Eleventh Chronicle: Empathy and False Empathy." In *Critical White Studies: Looking Behind the Mirror*, edited by Richard Delgado and Jean Stefancic, 614–618. Philadelphia: Temple University Press, 1997.

Fanon, Frantz. *Black Skin, White Masks*. New York: Grove Press, 1967.

González, Justo and Catherine. *The Liberating Pulpit*. Eugene: Wipf and Stock Publishers, 2003.

Harris, James. *The Word Made Plain: The Power and Promise of Preaching*. Minneapolis: Fortress Press, 2004.

Ignatiev, Noel and John Garvey, eds. "How to be a Race Traitor: Six Ways to Fight Being White." In *Critical White Studies: Looking Behind the Mirror*, edited by Richard Delgado and Jean Stefancic, 613. Philadelphia: Temple University Press, 1997.

———. *Race Traitor*. London: Routledge Press, 1996.

———. "Treason to Whiteness is Loyalty to Humanity." In *Critical White Studies: Looking Behind the Mirror*, edited by Richard Delgado and Jean Stefancic, 607–612. Philadelphia: Temple University Press, 1997.

LaRue, Cleophus. *The Heart of Black Preaching*. Louisville: Westminster John Knox, 1999.

———. *Rethinking Celebration: From Rhetoric to Praise in African American Preaching*. Louisville: Westminster John Knox, 2016.

Leonardo, Zeus. *Race, Whiteness, and Education*. New York: Routledge, 2009.

Lopez, Ian. *Dog Whistle Politics*. New York: Oxford University Press, 2015.

Mitchell, Henry. *Black Preaching: The Recovery of a Powerful Art*. Nashville: Abingdon Press, 1991.

Perkinson, James. *White Theology*. New York: Palgrave Macmillan, 2004.

Pipes, William. *Say Amen, Brother!: Old-Time Negro Preaching, A Study in American Frustration*. Detroit: Wayne State University Press, 1992.

Preston, John and Chadderton, Charlotte. "Rediscovering 'Race Traitor': Towards a Critical Race Theory informed public pedagogy." *Race, Ethnicity, and Education* January, 2012.

Chapter 13

Who Are You?

White Identity Formation and Re-formation in Homiletics

Suzanne Wenonah Duchesne

This chapter proposes that non-Indigenous preachers, particularly white, Amer-european preachers from the United States, who are willing to be led through an ongoing practice of critical reflexivity concerning their identity, can open possibilities for the pulpit to become a place where the mask of white supremacy may be peeled away and a decolonizing anti-racist ethic can emerge in their sermons.[1] This chapter describes a decolonizing journey upon which guides and preachers from the Cherokee, Choctaw, MVSKOKE, and Kiowa Nations led this author, a white, Amer-european, christian, settler/immigrant cis-woman preacher.[2] This journey in turn began an ongoing work of conscientization which continues even within this chapter.[3]

Part of the process of preparing this chapter involved constant vigilance against appropriation. This means I do not do this work alone. I checked and double-checked with my guides Suanne Ware-Diaz and Anne Marshall as well as one of the clergywomen I met, Rev. Judy Aaron Deere, to avoid appropriation.[4] They held me accountable throughout the process, and every part of this chapter has been checked with them before, during, and after the writing process.

The narrative format, use of personal pronouns, and substance of the chapter attempt to model a method interwoven with storytelling, protocols, and critical reflexivity that the clergywomen of the Cherokee, Choctaw, MVSKOKE, and Kiowa Nations enacted with me in July 2015 when I visited the Oklahoma Indian Missionary Conference (OIMC) of the United Methodist Church located within the U.S.-occupied territory named Oklahoma as part of a research grant for my dissertation.[5] Since the clergywomen of the OIMC interacted with me through narrative, identity, and relationships, I am hoping to model how these relationships brought about changes in my narrative. I will share the ways in which their guidance opened my eyes to my own need (as one who thought she was an open-minded anti-racist) to now identify as a white settler and to interrogate my own identity. This in turn expanded my views and the way I preached. Through our ongoing relationships, I find myself less apt to romanticize, homogenize, victimize, or identify people as "Other," and more inclined to see people as human beings. I am becoming more adept at recognizing when I am reading texts through an occupier's lens and allowing that knowledge to shift my focus and reconsider meaning while searching for signs of agency and resilience.

Their method shared aspects of what Margaret Kovach, Plains Cree and Saulteaux ancestry and a registered member of Pasqua First Nation located in southern Saskatchewan, outlines in her monograph *Indigenous Methodologies*. Kovach states that though her methods are based on the Nêhiýaw or Plains Cree tradition, they share methodological aspects with other nations such as respect, reciprocity, relationships, protocol, story, and experience based on place and kinship systems.[6] Though the clergywomen may not have been consciously teaching me what could be named by ethnographers, as a particular Indigenous methodology there were aspects of the methods described by Kovach that became evident in our interactions. As I reflected afterward, Kovach's work provided an academic framework for my experience and helped me make sense of my encounters with the clergywomen from the Cherokee, Choctaw, MVSKOKE, and Kiowa cultures.

Before I go any further it is important to say that Margaret Kovach's work is meant to engage both Indigenous and non-Indigenous scholars.[7] She describes how non-Indigenous persons can engage in Indigenous methodologies by beginning with decolonizing one's mind and heart.[8] She says, "Non-Indigenous academics who have successful relationships with Indigenous communities understand this. This means exploring one's own beliefs and values about knowledge and how it shapes practices. It is about examining whiteness. It is about examining power. It is ongoing."[9] She also says, "non-Indigenous scholars who wish to engage with Indigenous knowledges need to connect with Indigenous scholars, people, and communities."[10]

One of the central aspects described by Kovach is the importance of relationships and self-reflexivity of power structures and social location within those relationships.[11] Furthermore, this self-reflection when presented academically is presented in narrative form, which is both grounded in and accountable to the community. Similar to my accountability for this chapter, all ethnographic work requires an ethic derived from respect for the human beings contributing to a project as well as an acknowledgment of centuries of appropriation of Indigenous knowledge by researchers.[12]

Kovach presents the importance of interweaving story in her methodology based on her tradition. She also explains the importance of a prologue for this kind of narrative work, which she says was taught to her by Maori scholar Graham Smith. Beginning with her prologue she describes her autobiographical journey that led to her scholarship.[13] The high value placed on story is evident in her explanation that the prologue "is a precursory signal to the careful reader that woven throughout the varied forms of our writing—analytical, reflective, expository—there will be story, for our story is who we are."[14]

The stories are told not only for the sake of introduction, but as you will see in this chapter, they can become a guide to interrogating identity and understanding identity formation. Oral autobiography was also part of my experience with the clergywomen of the OIMC. Two things Kovach makes clear as a part of enacting an Indigenous ethnographic methodology such as she advocates from her Nêhiýaw, or Plains Cree understanding, is that there is a process of storytelling and analysis of story that begins with a person's narrative and then calls for a critical analysis of that narrative and the identity within the narrative.[15] In this way stories point to the ways in which personal narrative can become a site for critical analysis about the influences of the dominant culture on identity. Likewise, this chapter will describe how critical analysis of experiences and insights from conversations and relationships can lead to a process of critical analysis of identity.

PROLOGUE

I arrived in Oklahoma on a hot July afternoon in 2015, ready to engage in research about ways in which intersections of nationality, language, gender, and racialized identities might influence an anti-racist homiletic by disrupting the black/white binary often used to articulate racial categories.[16] As an anti-racism trainer and graduate student, I studied the development of racialization, systems of white privilege, white supremacy, and white racism, as well as tendencies toward colorblindness and expressions of white fragility.[17] Through this initial study, my work with the United Methodist Church's Committee on Native American Ministry (CoNAM), and personal relationships with members of the Kiowa and MVSKOKE nations, I began to consider complicated aspects of identity.[18]

As I continued to ponder further, I reached out to Anne Marshall who I had gotten to know through Suanne Ware-Diaz. After a few phone conversations about identity and preaching, the possibility of traveling to interview some preachers from the OIMC began to take shape. Anne's value of hospitality came to the fore as she worked diligently to help set up the interviews and make sure I arrived safely. She prepared for me to meet with leaders from the Cherokee, Choctaw, MVSKOKE (Creek), and Kiowa Nations.

As Anne guided me through the process, the actions and stories of the OIMC clergywomen exemplified a complexity of identity that went far beyond a racial category. I thought I was traveling to the OIMC to conduct dissertation research. Instead, the clergywomen from the OIMC shared stories with me and enacted aspects of an ethnographic Indigenous methodology similar to those described by Kovach that turned the interview tables around. It was at this point that I quickly learned, non-Indigenous people require Indigenous guides to help them to navigate the various protocols and to teach them the cultural norms. After I returned home Suanne Ware-Diaz explained it to me in more detail. She told me that the relationship between non-Indigenous persons and guides is not a relationship of equals, and the role of guide is taken seriously.[19] A guide risks their reputation if a non-Indigenous person is disrespectful or fails to honor the community. Therefore, non-Indigenous people must be vetted, and trust must continuously be built as they enter such a relationship. I did not realize it at the time, but my prior interactions with Anne and my friendship with Suanne Ware-Diaz paved the way for these meetings. The women invited me into relationships due to the investment of Anne and Suanne's time and my willingness to learn.

The need for a guide became immediately apparent as Anne introduced me to each woman, and I discovered that I was woefully unprepared.[20] I had my Internal Review Board (IRB) paperwork and my questions ready.[21] As I set up to record the interviews, I would engage in a brief greeting that outlined my research and thank them for their willingness to meet with me. More often than not, before I asked a question, I found myself on the receiving end of a series of questions instead.

The inquiries began with "Who are you?" "Who are your people?" "Where are you from?" "Who sent you here?" I stumbled over my words. I mentioned my dissertation and my scholarship. It soon became evident that I was having trouble answering some of the questions, and I spent a great deal of time talking in circles, explaining myself.

Anne's guidance was crucial for my subsequent preparation. She pointed out that I needed to create a preamble before I began the interviews. Following this guidance, I corrected my introduction to include my involvement with the United Methodist Church CoNAM. Even so, each interview brought new questions, and my preamble grew. As I met with each clergywoman, they patiently listened, offered words of encouragement, and kept asking questions. After I answered their questions, we would return to the paperwork for signatures, and then we would begin the conversation about their preaching. What stood out most to me was that each interview began with questions about my "people" and my geographical "place."

EFFECTS OF UNEXAMINED DOMINANT COLONIAL NARRATIVE

My experience in the interviews illustrates one of the first protocols I encountered. Several of the women I met were Elders in their Nation. Coming from a white, Amer-european, christian, settler/immigrant worldview, and a Western pedagogical background, I struggled with my anxiety to maintain the agenda as stated in the IRB guidelines and follow what I perceived to be proper procedure. Margaret Kovach explains how my preconceived ideas about the interviews came from a Western view of ethnographic research which involves interviewers forming specific questions before the interview, which they pedantically record.[22] She describes how storytelling is a decolonizing act that involves relationship building, rapport, and trust and that an interviewer from her tradition expects to be accountable to an Elder when asked about their research.[23] Thus, there will be a reciprocal conversation such as I experienced.

The length of this chapter precludes me from going into the dominant white supremacist colonial narrative in depth, but let it suffice to say that this narrative has had far-reaching effects on a myriad of power relations from social constructs to state policies. It has been fashioned by the Doctrine of Discovery and gave birth to the concept of Manifest Destiny, both of which inform white, Amer-european, settler/immigrant norms that are detrimental to everyone, including white settlers.[24] Upon further reflection and discussion with Anne, it became clear that dominant cultural understandings of power and privilege were evident in my discomfort with the women taking a leadership role in the interview process. This is only one small example of how the dominant cultural understanding of research and power relations manifests itself. After the first interview with an Elder, Anne introduced me to the protocols for interviewing and explained in detail what I needed to correct before my next meeting.

EFFECTS OF UNEXAMINED PERSONAL NARRATIVE

My experience in the interviews also illustrates the relational protocols concerning introductions and a preamble. When I failed to introduce myself thoroughly, the women began to ask me detailed questions dependent on a comprehensive understanding of personal identity. They modeled for me what it means to truly know thyself. Their self-knowledge manifested itself in their speech from the beginning as they shared their names and it continued throughout the stories they told. For instance, they accompanied signing the IRB paperwork with a story about their names. Their names often indicated tribal bloodlines or persons of eminence within the family and the Nation. Their stories expressed their nationality, further identified their status within the community, and defined their roles within the culture.

Their attention to identity also extended beyond themselves to those around them. Without Anne's guidance, I would not have begun to attend to my own identity. Additionally, in her interview, Rev. Judy Aaron Deere reflected on the struggles of her congregation and the need for curriculum reflective of their identity, saying, "when you're focused on all these programs and try to be a part of the denomination, we forget to do the things that really matter. We are doing a vacation bible school now and it's not even Native."[25] Later in the interview, she shared how she had begun to learn the songs of her congregation. She was sensitive to her multicultural congregation consisting of members from eight to ten different nations. She lamented she could not sing all the languages represented, but she was proud to learn to sing in Cherokee.[26]

The degree to which Deere and the other women attended to identity contrasted with my own. When asked about myself, I feebly tried to offer a story about my name. From what research I had done, I knew that beginning with my great-grandmother, they passed the name down through the women of my family. I was raised with some vague stories about an Indigenous ancestry through my great-grandmother and her brother. Friends told me it is a Lakota name, meaning first-born girl, which is usually changed once she reaches adulthood. This is all I knew because I failed to investigate the stories any further.

Part of my stammering stemmed from some advice Suanne Ware-Diaz offered to me concerning my identity. She explained that speaking about any possible connection to Indigenous descent would undercut any trust I might build, because it is a claim to ancestry I cannot legitimately make since I was raised in white, Amer-european, christian, settler/immigrant culture.[27] In reflection, I realized I chose to disregard the advice of my guide in order to relieve feelings of inadequacy when asked directly about my people. I could not answer fully, because I had not done the work of critical reflexive attention to my identity. Instead of remaining silent, answering honestly, "I did not know," or becoming curious, I chose to offer a story without foundation or research.

The struggle to name my identity and feelings of inadequacy shows how elusive it can be for white, Amer-european, christian settler/immigrants to name their people or origins when they have not taken the time to attend to their identity. Linda Martín Alcoff discusses the various problems associated with defining white identity. She makes the point that white culture in some cases is characterized as "an identity of unfair privilege based on white supremacy; unlike ethnic identities it has no other substantive cultural content."[28] In addition, philosopher Cornel West explains that the racial construct of whiteness creates a "normative gaze" which is "an ideal from which to order and compare observations."[29] According to ethicist Jennifer Harvey, whites who identify with the dominant culture no longer recognize it as a culture, it is just "normal."[30] So how then do white, Amer-european, christian settler/immigrants answer the question, "Who are you?"

IDENTITY FORMATION AND RE-FORMATION

When faced with a question of identity, white, Amer-european, christian settler/immigrants who experience feelings of shame about their white identity or jealousy about those who are aware of their cultural heritage will sometimes deny their whiteness and seek to claim a positive identity by reinventing themselves. Educators Eve Tuck and K. Wayne Yang describe identity reinventions as "moves to innocence . . . that attempt to relieve the settler of feelings of guilt or responsibility without giving up land or power or privilege."[31] Similar to my claims of an ancestor somewhere in my past, settlers will claim Native American heritage while still self-identifying as white, living in Amer-european culture, embracing euro-christian, settler/immigrant norms, and having no ties to Indigenous Nations.[32]

Vine Deloria Jr. muses about the reasons for white appropriation of Indigenous identity, asking, "Is it because they are afraid of being classed as foreigners? Do they need some blood tie with the frontier and its dangers in order to experience what it means to be an American? Or is it an attempt to avoid facing the guilt they bear for the treatment of the Indians?"[33] Any one of Deloria's reasons may be true, and all three indicate what white, Amer-european, christian settler/immigrants have to lose by failing to attend to identity. Nevertheless, the pressure to maintain white supremacy is intense. Robin J. DiAngelo describes how white fragility "born of superiority and entitlement . . . is a powerful means of white racial control and the protection of white advantage."[34] However, the resulting emotional extremes of anger and violence, silence, and withdrawal are all signs of the disturbing ways the colonial narrative acts upon the human spirit. Thus, white, Amer-european, christian settler/immigrants need to remember that regardless of how long ago their ancestors traveled to North American shores, anyone who identifies with the dominant culture has assimilated into the white supremacist culture and become part of the colonial narrative.

Once white, Amer-european, christian settler/immigrants critically reflect upon and realize the effects of assimilation, they may begin to experience the grief accompanying such a realization. However, grieving can become a source of identity re-formation also. To relieve the pressure, some will identify themselves as victims.³⁵ While grieving identity loss is to be expected, claiming victimhood is not. Jennifer Harvey says it clearly, "White culture in the USA is the outcome of different european identities having agreed to assimilate to whiteness in order to reap the benefits of the death-dealing dehumanizing system of white supremacy."³⁶

TOOLS FOR UNMASKING WHITENESS THROUGH ATTENDANCE TO IDENTITY

I offer that for non-Indigenous preachers, particularly white, Amer-european, christian settler/immigrants, to reclaim their humanity, unmask whiteness, and decolonize their preaching, they will want to abandon the assimilation agreement and begin to explore as best they can their ancestral songs, history, and place. When they bring a teachable spirit to the work and begin to examine their identity using a critical reflexive model with a guide such as I encountered in Oklahoma, an opportunity opens up for the preacher to embark on a lifelong journey of unmasking as they begin to confront their own identity assumptions.

The following three lines of inquiry have been learned from my experiences in Oklahoma with the clergywomen from the Cherokee, Choctaw, MVSKOKE, and Kiowa Nations. These suggestions are not necessarily listed in a recommended order, nor are they exhaustive. Rather they are offered as options that can be undertaken simultaneously or consecutively according to the preacher's ability, available resources, and the information available to them.

Critical Analysis of Country of Residence

The first key area of inquiry includes critical analysis of the cultural narratives and values expressed by the country where the preacher resides. A detailed study of the history of colonization and the prevailing narratives expressing national values is a good place to begin. Historical records and narratives are important, but just as important will be additional research of histories written by those on the margins. The preacher can also spend time exploring the geography and topography of the land and the messages that can be derived from the value placed on the land. Another layer of critical assessment can be derived through relationships. The importance of relationships to process the information cannot be emphasized enough. Research and discussion can further expand the preacher's ability to engage critical reflexive analysis about the recounting of national histories and about the ways in which these narratives have informed their values and worldview.

As the preacher becomes more aware of the narratives that inform their worldview, it is easier to identify similar narratives of conquest in a biblical text, an illustration, or a theological perspective. The informed preacher can choose to disrupt white supremacist and colonizing theologies and ideologies, thereby providing an opportunity for the congregation to experience an alternative worldview through the preacher's voice and embodied presence.

Critical Analysis of Personal Narrative

The second area the preacher can embark upon involves an investigation of their personal narrative. This investigation requires not only research but also a critical analysis to peel away the colonizing narratives that intertwine with identity. Discovering family history can be challenging depending on the degree to which the family has assimilated into the dominant culture or the means of their arrival. Deconstructing one's personal narrative and researching family histories often requires access to reports and government files and can have a financial cost that may be prohibitive. Therefore, some of these suggestions may or may not be helpful in some cases.

To begin, a preacher can interrogate family narratives. The preacher can interview family members if they are available. As the preacher compiles the stories, they can critically analyze them for areas requiring more exploration and areas that may call for engagement with a decolonizing lens. Paying attention to the stories themselves, how they are transmitted, and the words and images used can provide clues about what is perhaps happening between the lines. In addition, Elaine Enns and Ched Myer's latest book, *Healing Haunted Histories*, can help with a deconstruction process that investigates both the narrative that has been passed down and the narrative that has been silenced.[37]

A preacher can also conduct genealogical research. Information can be found by searching newspaper clippings for obituaries and birth announcements at the local library or online, archives are available through the free library system, and some have genealogists on staff to help. At the same time, the preacher will want to keep in mind the words of educator Elaine Enns who warns researchers that a focus on family stories alone runs the risk of centering whiteness.[38] Preachers do not want to do this work in order to concretize whiteness but rather to discover the complexities of identity.

Sometimes these family histories are deeply hidden, and family stories only go so far. Due to my family stories, one of the first recommendations an Elder made to me was to take a DNA test. However, there are some cautions associated with this line of inquiry. Besides the financial cost, there are concerns about privacy and misuse of information. Indigenous Peoples hesitate to be tested for good reason, which makes it difficult to identify specific ancestry. There is a history of medical abuse, torture, and seizure of human remains for research and museum catalogs by the U.S. government agencies, universities, and other entities. There is also the potential for testing to become another source of colonization by threatening to overwrite the oral history of migration and the creation stories of peoples with scientific hypotheses researchers often claim as scientific fact.[39] Moreover, the historical use of blood quantum levels to measure the degrees to which one is Indigenous has endangered tribal sovereignty since its first use in 1705 in the Virginia Colony.[40]

DNA analysis is also problematic for the preacher, because, even though the test can point them toward their countries of origin, it requires further research to answer those questions of "who are your people?" and "where are your people from?" To understand these questions further research of the geographical places identified in a DNA analysis will be needed to gain a more complete picture. In the case of Indigenous identity, it is important to remember that this is legally regulated by the U.S. government and tribal governments. If indeed a DNA sample or family history indicates Indigenous ancestry is present, it will take some investigating to discover national affiliation, followed by relationship building, and cultural reclamation under the laws of the particular Nation. In case I have not made it clear thus far, Native American Identity is a community endeavor. I would also offer that this same relational ethic is helpful to keep in mind regardless of the ancestral country of origin.

Once a country of origin is known, preachers can research the country and culture through books, travelogues, and local newspapers found online or at the library. Since language conveys culture, it may be feasible to learn the language. Relationships can also provide unique experiences if they are attainable through pen pals or travel. Additionally, the land can also offer insights. Family histories tied to the land can yield stories of immigration or forced relocation. This knowledge allows preachers to engage more fully with the colonial aspects of their country of origin and white supremacist attitudes within the family narratives. At the same time, the preacher can delve into the aspects of culture and family stories that the dominant colonial narrative has obscured.

Research of families, genealogies, and DNA can take years to compile, and the information may confirm or contradict each other but in any event the complexity of identity formation will be exposed even in the erasures. Historian and activist, Aurora Levins Morales, puts it this way:

The decision to examine exactly who our ancestors, all of them, have been—with each other and with everyone else . . . is an accounting of the debts and assets we have inherited, and acknowledging the precise nature of that inheritance is an act of spiritual and political integrity.[41]

As the preacher becomes more critically aware of the narratives that have formed their family and their worldview, they can better understand the various lenses through which they preach. Their awareness about their own complexity can expand their horizons of interpretation and identification of the complexities of their congregational context.

Critical Analysis of Worldview

The third area for preachers to consider concerns intentionally building relationships with people who have different worldviews from the one the preacher holds. The preacher could begin with written narratives from noted authors and expand to personal relationships. By taking the time to listen deeply, especially if preachers want to engage with an Indigenous community, new insights can present themselves.[42] As the preacher experiences deepening relationships with persons holding different worldviews and cultural experiences, the potential exists for them to envision people and places differently. Their increased awareness of difference can bring their social location into sharper focus as well as their assumptions about other cultures. Narratives that perhaps led them to romanticize, exoticize, or stereotype people can come into question.

Another option is to engage in actions of social justice which allow the preacher to work toward change and develop relationships with people in the midst of building alliances. Throughout the journey, a critical reflexive praxis will provide insights into emotions that arise. In addition, a commitment to community will provide feedback and opportunities for growth.

CONCLUSION

As a preacher whose worldview has been influenced by christian, settler/immigrant culture and a person who is also identifiable as a white, Amereuropean cis-woman, I occupy a position of privilege within the dominant white culture in the United States. The guidance of Suanne Ware-Diaz, Anne Marshall, and Rev. Judy Aaron Deere and my meetings with peoples from Nations with different views and experiences led to a decolonizing journey and continues to conscientize me about the ways in which identity, worldview, and language are tied together. This chapter is one effort to invite non-Indigenous preachers, particularly those belonging to the dominant white, Amer-european, christian settler/immigrant culture in the United States, to consider how the colonizing narratives they live under impact their identity and, in turn, their interpretations, their words, and their sermons.

As I conclude, I am reminded of one expression of identity that stood out among all the others as I met with the clergywomen of the OIMC. In response to my question about identity, Rev. Judy Aaron Deere replied, "Whether I am an Indian or I am not an Indian or what kind of Indian—I am a human being first. I just happen to be a woman. I just happen to be Indian. But I am still just like you."[43] Her stress on her humanity is echoed by many Indigenous Peoples I have worked with through the years. It is not surprising considering the continuing impact of colonization and the Doctrine of Discovery, which is still used today to dehumanize Indigenous Peoples and continues to permeate Western societies, churches, and pulpits.

Rev. Deere's statement exemplifies why the work of unmasking whiteness and exposing colonial narratives is sacred work. By moving this process of humanization forward, it invites all people to live more fully into their humanity. I truly believe that when non-Indigenous preachers work toward a decolonizing homiletic, it becomes evident in the way they think, live their lives, and ultimately the way they preach. But I also know that this is not an easy road to travel and if you enter upon it, you will find, as I have, that we will continue to make mistakes. For every layer of the mask of white supremacy that gets peeled away, another lies beneath. In addition, the white supremacist systems are unrelenting so that the pressure to replace the mask is constant. And yet I also trust that preachers' voices have the potential to become transformed which in turn may perhaps lead to congregational transformation from colonial narratives that infiltrate their worldview and can inspire them to do some unmasking for themselves.[44]

NOTES

1. In this case, non-Indigenous refers to those who do not belong to an Indigenous Nation within the United States. The term Indigenous Peoples will be used in accordance with the UN Declaration on Indigenous Rights. For more on this discussion, see Martin Brokenleg, "A Native American Perspective: That the People May Live," in *Preaching Justice: Ethnic and Cultural Perspectives*, edited by Christine Marie Smith, 26–27 (Eugene, OR: Wipf & Stock, 2008) and University of Minnesota Human Rights Library, "Study Guide: The Rights of Indigenous Peoples," http://hrlibrary.umn.edu/edumat/studyguides/indigenous.html (accessed on September 15, 2021).

I use the term white as described by ethicist Jennifer Harvey, "people who are 'white' are not white in some essential way. Rather, [whites] are racially formed and shaped by way of—and as [they] respond to—the same systems that enable white supremacy" while also recognizing that it is a construct that is signified on our bodies as Linda Martín Alcoff stresses. See Jennifer Harvey, *Dear White Christians* (Grand Rapids, MI: Wm. B. Eerdmans Publishing Company, 2014), 11 and Linda Martín Alcoff, *Visible Identities: Race, Gender, and the Self* (New York: Oxford University Press, 2006), 5.

The term Amer-european comes from Jace Weaver, professor of Religion and Law, who offers a compelling alternative to the term Euro-American stating that he opts "for the use of the term of John Joseph Mathews (Osage), Amer-european, as more adequately reflecting the relationship of the progeny of colonizers to the American land." Jace Weaver, ed., *Native American Religious Identity: Unforgotten Gods* (Maryknoll, NY: Orbis Books, 1998), xi.

2. The term "guide" comes from a conversation with Suanne Ware-Diaz of the Kiowa Nation, who has been a guide and a prayer partner with me for over two decades. Suanne served as one of the highest-ranking Native Americans in the United Methodist Church as the associate general secretary at the General Commission on Religion and Race Native American Portfolio. She shared the importance of recognizing that the communication between white, Amer-european settler/immigrants and Indigenous Peoples requires an Indigenous guide to develop the trust required for a relationship. Suanne Ware-Diaz, Conversation with author, December 17, 2018.

Due to the U.S. government policy of dependent sovereignty, the women I met with hold dual citizenship within the United States and the Cherokee, Choctaw, MVSKOKE (Creek), or Kiowa Nations. The matter of dual citizenship is complicated. In 1831, Justice John Marshall rendered the decision in *Cherokee Nation v. Georgia*, which denied the Cherokee court jurisdiction to assert its rights as a Sovereign foreign entity because the Supreme Court decided that "Indian tribes were domestic dependent nations," thereby creating dependent nations within the United States. Members of federally recognized tribes within the United States received U.S. citizenship with the passage of the Indian Citizenship Act in 1924. For this and other primary documents outlining United States Supreme Court decisions, see Virgil J. Vogel, *This Country Was Ours: A Documentary History of the American Indian* (New York: Harper & Row, 1972), 114 and 196.

The lower-case title christian is intentional. Theologian George Tinker stresses the role of european christianity in the colonization of the Americas using terms such as Western euro-christian to describe the colonizer. For more of Tinker's work explaining the euro-christian worldview, see Tink Tinker, "Rites of Discovery: St. Junipero, Lewis and Clark," *Intotemak* 49 (Fall/Winter 2016): 97–100.

The term "settler/immigrant" is indicative of those who now reside in the United States, emigrated from somewhere else even if it was generations ago, live on land that has been illegally acquired, and ascribe to the dominant culture's capitalistic, white-supremacist norms which led to this illegal confiscation. For the purposes of this chapter, this terminology does not refer to those who were brought here by force, though it is important to note that the system of white supremacy affects all who occupy Indigenous lands. This distinction is another layer of colonization which has been explored in Jodi A. Byrd, *The Transit of Empire: Indigenous Critiques of Colonialism* (Minneapolis, MN: University of Minnesota Press, 2011), Kindle Edition.

3. The word conscientization indicates not only an increasing awareness by preachers who embark on a decolonizing journey but an intentional dedication to continually reflect and act by these same preachers, in this case non-Native preachers, through a commitment to an accountable community. Some intentional actions to foster this commitment to reflection and action will be offered at the end of this chapter. Though this word and concept comes to us from the work of Paulo Freire. I would offer that this chapter also derives its understanding of conscientization from the work of christian ethicist and Mujerista Theologian, Ada Maria Isasi-Diaz, who describes conscientization as the process by which a person's experiences lead them to recognize the difference between the nature of things and cultural differences, to unmask unjust myths, and to explore alternative moral decisions in the midst of the struggle toward liberation. Similarly, I would offer that non-Indigenous persons who want to expose and begin to peel away the mask of white supremacy will need to enter into the struggle of liberation with Indigenous Peoples through relationships which involve ongoing pedagogy from Indigenous guides as described in this chapter. For more, see Paulo Freire, "Education, Liberation and the Church," *Religious Education* 79, no. 4 (1984): 524–45 and Ada Maria Isasi-Diaz, *En la Lucha/In the Struggle: Elaborating a Mujerista Theology* (Minneapolis, MN: Fortress Press, 2004), 160–62.

4. Anne Marshall of the MVSKOKE Nation is a Rural Chaplain in the United Methodist Church. She has been elected to the Muscogee Creek Nation National Council representing the Tukvpvtce District for the 2020–2024 term. She serves as the treasurer for the NE Region of OIMC, and she is the United Methodist General Conference Delegate representing the OIMC. Her important work on the Act of Repentance occurred when she was the associate general secretary of the General Commission on Christian Unity and Interreligious Concerns, the chair of the United Methodist Inter-Ethnic Strategy Development Group, and chair of the Native American International Caucus.

Rev. Judy Aaron Deere (MVSKOKE/Creek) is an ordained elder in the OIMC. I use the title Reverend for Judy in this chapter as a mark of her identity. Education was used as a means of cultural erasure and as such it is not always trusted by Indigenous Peoples. The fact that she went through the colonizing process of education and ordination is a credit to her persistence to answer her call and to maintain her MVSKOKE identity as she navigated all those colonizing systems.

5. This chapter is based on a portion of my dissertation, *Beloved Speech: Language and Legacies of Methodist Women Leaders of the Oklahoma Indian Missionary Conference with Antiracist/Decolonizing Strategies for Preaching*, which presents a three-fold homiletic of which critical reflexive attention to identity is one of the cornerstones.

6. Margaret Kovach, *Indigenous Methodologies: Characteristics, Conversations, and Contexts* (Toronto, ON: University of Toronto Press, 2010), 44.

7. Kovach presents Indigenous methodologies for use within the academy by both Indigenous scholars and non-Indigenous scholars serving in Indigenous contexts or seeking to honor Indigenous Knowledge Systems. For more, see Margaret Kovach, *Indigenous Methodologies: Characteristics, Conversations, and Contexts*, 11.

8. Ibid, 169.

9. Ibid.

10. Ibid, 172.

11. The importance of relationships can be found throughout the monograph; however, Kovach describes a distinctly Indigenous understanding of a relational worldview regarding all of creation which was present in the Cherokee, Choctaw, MVSKOKE, and Kiowa worldview taught to me as well. Kovach, 34.

12. This knowledge is found in stories, rituals, and even in the language of the people. For more information concerning appropriation and theft of Indigenous culture and knowledge, see Richard A. Grounds, "Yuchi Travels," in *Native Voices: American Indian Identity and Resistance*, edited by, Richard A. Grounds, George E. Tinker, and David E. Wilkins (Lawrence, KS: University Press of Kansas, 2003), 304–17.

13. Kovach, *Indigenous Methodologies*, 3–8.

14. Ibid, 3.

15. Ibid, 112.

16. For more on an anti-racist homiletic, see Suzanne Wenonah Duchesne, "Antiracist Preaching: Homiletical Strategies for Undermining Racism in Worship," *Liturgy* 29, no. 3 (July 1, 2014): 13.

17. For more information concerning racialization, see Nell Irvin Painter, *The History of White People* (New York: W. W. Norton & Company, 2011). For more about white fragility, see Robin J. DiAngelo, *White Fragility: Why It's So Hard for White People to Talk about Racism* (Boston, MA: Beacon Press, 2018). For more on colorblindness, see Bonilla Silva concerning discursive rhetoric, especially chapters 3 and 4, pp. 70–71, 98–99. Eduardo Bonilla-Silva, *Racism without Racists* (Lanham, MD: Rowman & Littlefield Publishers, Inc., 2006). For more on white privilege, see Peggy McIntosh, "White Privilege: Unpacking the Invisible Knapsack," *Multiculturalism* (October 1992).

18. This complicated identity is evident in the names given to groups of people by the dominant culture. In this chapter, the term Native American, though often used within the United Methodist Church, will appear sparingly. For more discussion about the use of this categorization and its colonial implications, see Jennifer Harvey, *Dear White Christians* (Grand Rapids, MI: Wm. B. Eerdmans Publishing Company, 2014), 11 and Charles C. Mann, *1491 New Revelations of the Americas before Columbus* (New York: Vintage, 2006), 393.

19. Suanne Ware-Diaz, Conversation with author, December 17, 2018.

20. Anne Marshall, Conversations with author, July 18–22, 2015.

21. I was working under the approval of the IRB of Drew University. This group reviews the methods of researchers who interview human beings in order to protect the participants' rights and welfare.

22. Kovach, *Indigenous Methodologies*, 98.

23. Ibid, 109–10.

24. In 1493, the Papal Bull, Inter Caetera, was issued by Pope Alexander VI. Built upon earlier papal bulls and combined with subsequent decrees, it formed what is now known as the Doctrine of Discovery. The Doctrine of Discovery called for the forced evangelization of Indigenous Peoples and declared Indigenous lands to be empty, thereby allowing seizure of their lands by the church in the name of God. In 1845, John L. O'Sullivan authored an article proclaiming the inevitability of settler expansion across the North American continent. Undergirded by the Discovery Doctrine, the biblical narrative of the Promised Land, and the Monroe Doctrine, Manifest Destiny provided a righteous framework for acquiring more land and accumulating more wealth. Indigenous Peoples were characterized as a "barrier" or "obstacle" to American "progress" and needed to be eliminated. For more detailed information and analysis of the Doctrine of Discovery and its effects, see David Phillips Hansen, *Native Americans, the Mainline Church, and the Quest for Interracial Justice* (St. Louis, MO: Chalice Press, 2017), Robert J. Miller, "Christianity, American Indians, and the Doctrine of Discovery," in *Remembering Jamestown*, edited by Amos Yong and Barbara Brown Zikmund (Eugene, OR: Wipf and Stock, 2010), Lewis Hanke, "Pope Paul III and the American Indians," *Harvard Theological Review* 30, no. 2 (April 1, 1937): 65–102, Steven T. Newcomb, *Pagans in the Promised Land: Decoding the Doctrine of Christian Discovery* (Golden, CO: Fulcrum Publishing, 2008).

25. Rev. Judy Aaron Deere, Interview by author, July 19, 2015, Tulsa Indian United Methodist Church, Tulsa, OK.

26. Rev. Judy Aaron Deere, Interview with author, July 19, 2015.

27. Suanne Ware-Diaz, Conversation with author, 2014.

28. Linda Martín Alcoff, *Visible Identities: Race, Gender, and the Self* (Oxford: Oxford University Press, 2005), 212.

29. Cornel West, *Prophesy Deliverance!: An Afro-American Revolutionary Christianity* (Louisville, KY: John Knox Press, 2002), 53.

30. Jennifer Harvey, "Personal Agency Needed for Antiracist Work," Wabash Center Webinars, November 18, 2020, https://youtu.be/fC_3g79n408 (accessed November 18, 2020).

31. Eve Tuck and K. Wayne Yang, "Decolonization Is Not a Metaphor," *Decolonization: Indigeneity, Education & Society* 1, no. 1 (2012): 10.

32. I use the term Native American specifically here because often this term is used by white settlers who self-identify as Indigenous without doing the work of self-discovery.

33. Vine Deloria Jr., *Custer Died for Your Sins: An Indian Manifesto* (Norman, OK: University of Oklahoma Press, 1988), 4.

34. Robin DiAngelo and Michael Eric Dyson, *White Fragility: Why It's So Hard for White People to Talk about Racism* (Boston, MA: Beacon Press, 2018), 2.

35. Jennifer Harvey, "Personal Agency Needed for Antiracist Work," at Wabash Webinar, November 18, 2020.

36. Harvey, "Personal Agency Needed for Antiracist Work," November 18, 2020.

37. Elaine Enns and Ched Myers, *Healing Haunted Histories: A Settler Discipleship of Decolonization* (Eugene, OR: Cascade Books, 2021), 48.

38. Enns and Myers, *Healing Haunted*, 48.

39. Rose Eveleth's interview with Kim Tallbear, a member of the Sisseton-Wahpeton Oyate tribe and a researcher at the University of Texas at Austin, reveals that from [Tallbear's] perspective, "researchers offering to tell tribes where they're from doesn't look any different than the Christians who came in to tell them what their religion should be." For more information, see Eveleth, Rose. "Genetic Testing and Tribal Identity." *The Atlantic*, January 26, 2015. https://www.theatlantic.com/technology/archive/2015/01/the-cultural-limitations-of-genetic-testing/384740/ (accessed on September 12, 2021).

40. Spruhan describes the history of Blood quantum measurement to determine "Indian" identity, which began to be used systemically in the U.S. courts with the Allotment Act of 1887 in order to divide communal lands and sell off the excess to settlers. By 1935, it was codified in the Indian Reorganization Act. Paul Spruhan, "A Legal History of Blood Quantum in Federal Indian Law to 1935," *South Dakota Law Review* 51, no. 1 (2006): 5, 46–51.

41. Aurora Levins Morales, *Medicine Stories: History, Culture, and the Politics of Integrity* (Cambridge, MA: South End Press, 1998), 75.

42. See Suzanne Wenonah Duchesne, "A Voice Cries Out: The Role of Listening for Revealing Cultural Narratives and Unmasking Whiteness in the Pulpit," Paper Presented at the *Academy of Homiletics*, New Brunswick, NJ, December 2019.

43. Rev. Judy Aaron Deere, Interview with author, July 19, 2015.

44. Charles L. Campbell describes an eschatological vision of preaching and says that though the practice of preaching is limited, it is effective because preaching can bring social practices to the forefront of the congregation's concerns and cultivate new practices. Charles L. Campbell, *The Word before the Powers: An Ethic of Preaching* (Louisville, KY: Westminster John Knox Press, 2002), 86, 141.

BIBLIOGRAPHY

Alcoff, Linda Martín. *Visible Identities: Race, Gender, and the Self*. Oxford: Oxford University Press, 2005.

Bonilla-Silva, Eduardo. *Racism without Racists: Color-Blind Racism and the Persistence of Racial Inequality in America*. Lanham, MD: Rowman & Littlefield Publishers, 2009.

Brokenleg, Martin. "A Native American Perspective: That the People May Live." In *Preaching Justice: Ethnic and Cultural Perspectives*, edited by Christine Marie Smith, 26–42. Eugene, OR: Wipf & Stock, 2008.

Byrd, Jodi A. *The Transit of Empire: Indigenous Critiques of Colonialism*. Minneapolis, MN: University of Minnesota Press, 2011.

Campbell, Charles L. *The Word Before the Powers: An Ethic of Preaching*. Louisville, KY: Westminster John Knox Press, 2002.

Campbell, Elizabeth and Luke Eric Lassiter. *Doing Ethnography Today: Theories, Methods, Exercises*. Malden, MA: Wiley-Blackwell, 2015.

Deere, Judy Aaron. Interview with author, July 19, 2015, Tulsa Indian United Methodist Church, Tulsa, OK.

Deloria, Vine, Jr. *Custer Died for Your Sins: An Indian Manifesto*. Norman: University of Oklahoma Press, 1988.

DiAngelo, Robin. *White Fragility: Why It's So Hard for White People to Talk About Racism*. Boston: Beacon Press, 2018.

Duchesne, Suzanne Wenonah. "Antiracist Preaching: Homiletical Strategies for Undermining Racism in Worship." *Liturgy* 29, no. 3 (July 1, 2014): 11–20.

———. *Beloved Speech: Language and Legacies of Methodist Women Leaders of the Oklahoma Indian Missionary Conference with Antiracist/Decolonizing Strategies for Preaching*. 2019.

———. "A Voice Cries Out: The Role of Listening for Revealing Cultural Narratives and Unmasking Whiteness in the Pulpit." Paper Presented at the Academy of Homiletics, New Brunswick, NJ, December 2019.

Enns, Elaine and Ched Myers. *Healing Haunted Histories: A Settler Discipleship of Decolonization*. Eugene, OR: Cascade Books, 2021.

Eveleth, Rose. "Genetic Testing and Tribal Identity." *The Atlantic*, January 26, 2015, https://www.theatlantic.com/technology/archive/2015/01/the-cultural-limitations-of-genetic-testing/384740/ (accessed on September 12, 2021).

Freire, Paulo. "Education, Liberation and the Church." *Religious Education* 79, no. 4 (1984): 524–45.

Grounds, Richard A., George E. Tinker, and David E. Wilkins. *Native Voices: American Indian Identity and Resistance*. Lawrence: University Press of Kansas, 2003.

Hanke, Lewis. "Pope Paul III and the American Indians." *Harvard Theological Review* 30, no. 2 (April 1, 1937): 65–102.

Hansen, David Phillips. *Native Americans, the Mainline Church, and the Quest for Interracial Justice*. St. Louis: Chalice Press, 2017.

Harvey, Jennifer. *Dear White Christians*. Grand Rapids, MI: Wm. B. Eerdmans Publishing Company, 2014.

———. "Personal Agency Needed for Anti-Racist Work." at Wabash Webinar, November 18, 2020.

Isasi-Diaz, Ada Maria. *En la Lucha/In the Struggle: Elaborating a Mujerista Theology*. Minneapolis: Fortress Press, 2004.

Kovach, Margaret. *Indigenous Methodologies: Characteristics, Conversations, and Contexts*. Toronto: University of Toronto Press, 2010.

Mann, Charles C. *1491: New Revelations of the Americas Before Columbus*. New York: Vintage, 2006.

Marshall, Anne, conversations with author, July 18–22, 2015.

McIntosh, Peggy. "White Privilege: Unpacking the Invisible Knapsack." *Multiculturalism* (October 1992): 30–36.

Miller, Robert J. "Christianity, American Indians, and the Doctrine of Discovery." In *Remembering Jamestown*, edited by Amos Yong and Barbara Brown Zikmund, 51–66. Eugene OR: Wipf and Stock, 2010.

Morales, Aurora Levins. *Medicine Stories: History, Culture, and the Politics of Integrity*. Cambridge, MA: South End Press, 1998.

Newcomb, Steven T. *Pagans in the Promised Land: Decoding the Doctrine of Christian Discovery*. Golden, CO: Fulcrum Publishing, 2008.

Painter, Nell Irvin. *The History of White People*. New York: W. W. Norton & Company, 2011.

Spruhan, Paul. "A Legal History of Blood Quantum in Federal Indian Law to 1935." *South Dakota Law Review* 51, no. 1 (2006): 46–51.

Tinker, Tink. "Rites of Discovery: St. Junipero, Lewis and Clark." *Intotemak* 49 (Fall/Winter 2016): 97–100.

Tuck, Eve and K. Wayne Yang. "Decolonization Is Not a Metaphor." *Decolonization: Indigeneity, Education & Society* 1, no.1 (2012): 1–40.

University of Minnesota Human Rights Library. "Study Guide: The Rights of Indigenous Peoples." http://hrlibrary.umn.edu/edumat/studyguides/indigenous.html (accessed on September 15, 2021).

Vogel, Virgil J. *This Country Was Ours; A Documentary History of the American Indian*. New York: HarperCollins, 1972.

Ware-Diaz, Suanne, conversations with author, 2014 and 2018.

Weaver, Jace, ed. *Native American Religious Identity: Unforgotten Gods*. Maryknoll, NY: Orbis Books, 1998.

West, Cornel. *Prophesy Deliverance! An Afro-American Revolutionary Christianity*. Louisville, KY: John Knox Press, 2002.

Yong, Amos and Barbara Brown Zikmund, eds. *Remembering Jamestown: Hard Questions about Christian Mission*. Eugene, OR: Pickwick Publications, 2010.

Chapter 14

Non-Preaching?

Unmasking (White) Preaching through Negation

Lis Valle-Ruiz

INTRODUCTION

"I speak, therefore I preach.
I speak, therefore I preach.
I speak, therefore I preach."[1]
Bah!
I bet we can preach without words.
Right, your life as living testimony, preaches, I know.
But that's not what I am talking about.
What I mean is that the body is capable of producing logic discourse.
I'm going to turn things around.
I want to decolonize myself
but I need help
so I don't fail.
I give you: burlesque-esque dancer,
the High Priestess Unrobed!
Bold, Disruptive, Sensuous, Mischievous![2]
The one and only, Sofía Divinatrix!
She flips *logos* to show *sarx*,
the logic of words for the logic of the flesh.
She wears a mask to unmask Empire,
not out there in the world,
but here, in the misnamed Kingdom of God.
She gets rid of words to show fleshly flow.
She strips as Isaiah did

to show sign and wonder
of removing the white covering,
the empire, the colonizer,
and embracing being daughter
of Taínos, the original inhabitants of Borikén,
and of West Africans, and European migrants.
She has turned things around.
She has transgressed every homiletical rule she knew.
She has embraced the hermeneutic of suspicion
and fleshly discourse she celebrates with great joy!³

Pura rebeldía. This is why fictional character Sofía Divinatrix refuses to speak when preaching, pure rebellion. This is why I decided to begin this "scholarly essay" with a poem, pure rebellion. Rebellion is the reason why I used the performing art of burlesque to preach "An Exorcism of White Supremacy" (hereinafter, "An Exorcism"). While the use of performance for preaching has been a religious practice for centuries in the Caribbean, including my homeland, Puerto Rico, and some parts of what today we know as Mexico, I took the practice further and used burlesque to preach in order to rebel against white understandings of preaching that were asphyxiating me. The result was burlesque-esque, a deployment of burlesque for proclamation that results in performance art that is not quite a burlesque. I did it to let my colonized body breathe, be, become, and live. I negated the presuppositions of white preaching: speech, pulpit, and worship service; and in so doing I brought to life my best self, the traditions I received from Puerto Rican and Amerindian ancestors, and my prayer/testimony for/of divine liberation from white supremacy.⁴

Some homileticians have argued that unmasking, naming, and defining white preaching results in centering white preaching when we should be decentering it.⁵ The reality is that white preaching has not been systematically conceptualized even though African American homileticians have persistently written in contradistinction to "it," as Andrew Wymer has pointed out. "It," I argued in "Performing Cultural Memory Through Preaching," is [white] preaching, an understanding of preaching that ignores or downplays whiteness as an invisible force that covers everything confusing a white perspective with THE actual thing.⁶ "It" forces the rest of us to define ourselves as whatever we do different to "it," as Gerald Liu has argued. In this chapter, I share "An Exorcism," a burlesque-esque piece by burlesque dancer Sofía Divinatrix as an example of unmasking white preaching through negation. In this way, the elusive "it" that dominates the imagination of homileticians and preachers in the United States and becomes the rod to measure all preaching practices becomes a specific and contained practice, that of white preaching.

This chapter defines white preaching as what "it" does different to Sofía Divinatrix when she rebels, when she lives into her own traditions and brings them to life, when she lives into her own sense of being and expands the practices of her ancestors. Sofía preaches with her body enacting a secular art form, in a room as part of a circus' midway.⁷ Sofía thinks and lives as if she can preach anywhere at any time through any means of communication. White preaching is the opposite: it is tied to words, oratory, pulpit, and worship services. Sofía's burlesque-esque unmasks these aspects of white preaching and refuses to play by the rules of white preaching, when she breaks every possible homiletical rule she knows in order to live. Refusing to reiterate white preaching, Sofía Divinatrix's way of preaching negates the need for words, pulpit, and liturgical context to expand her own received tradition of preaching through bodily movement, from any given space, at any given moment and without words.

More importantly, in "An Exorcism" Sofía Divinatrix enacts her own liberation from the constraints of the whiteness that have dominated her body. When Sofía breaks the rules of white preaching, she turns things around and constrains the whiteness that was constraining her. She ties whiteness in a bundle so that it takes less space and stops being the invisible force that covers and measures it all. When white preaching takes less space, Sofía then has her own space to live and to give birth to new preaching forms that spring forth from her ancestors' ways of preaching.

SOFÍA DIVINATRIX PRESENTS "AN EXORCISM OF WHITE SUPREMACY"

> *But no one can enter a strong man's house and plunder his property without first tying up the strong man; then indeed the house can be plundered.* (Mark 3:27)

Sofía Divinatrix, the High Priestess Unrobed, is my stage name as a burlesque dancer who combines the logic of burlesque with the ancient prophetic practice of symbolic action to produce burlesque-esque. Sofía is one of many fictional characters that I have created to preach.⁸ Sofía Divinatrix was invited to perform as part of the midway of a circus in the summer of 2018.⁹ This invitation gave her the perfect opportunity to join the company of the holy fools (disruptive figures that incite liminality for the sake of the gospel) tradition in an indecent way.¹⁰ Holy Fools, Inc., under the name *Carnival de Resistance*, invited her to share a burlesque piece in their summer season, which was held in Philadelphia.¹¹ At the time, I was preoccupied with my own internalization of white supremacy, particularly in the act of preaching.

Though I had a lifelong practice of preaching through theater, preaching through burlesque was something else. It was the exteriorization of baring the soul.[12] It was baring the body to show what was happening inside the soul. It was also symbolic action to operate a desired exorcism of white supremacy from my own preaching self, both from my body and from my preaching.[13]

Imagine that you were there. You enter a small room and toward your right there is a person lying on a table, seemingly a woman. She is curled up in fetal position with her face toward the wall. You see her back. She is wearing a white winter coat and white lace top thigh high women stockings.[14] She is not wearing shoes and her feet are chained at the ankles. A small crowd gathers in front of the table, they are expecting a performance by Sofía Divinatrix.[15]

Recorded music plays featuring an acoustic guitar. After an instrumental introduction, a male voice sings, "El río de Corozal . . ." A Spanish guitar, as we call it in Puerto Rico, provides the musical accompaniment to the Spanish words of the song.[16] The woman wakes up and soon enough realizes that she is handcuffed. Now she is lying on her back with her knees pointing to the ceiling and she lies back frustrated. She seems to remember something and looks at the audience with a mischievous look that seeks complicity. She turns away from the audience and from beside her, she pulls a very big set of scissors that was out of the view before.[17] She uses them to cut the chains binding her feet.

Slowly and sensually she takes off her stockings one at a time. Removing her stockings reveals that she has the key to her handcuffs. She sits on the border of the table now facing the audience and shows the key to them.[18] She slides down from the table toward the audience. She caresses the floor drawing with the big toe of her foot a meandering line. She does the same with her other foot, getting closer to the audience. She is wearing a half-face mask covered in golden glitter. Her hair is black and straight down to her shoulders. She extends her arms toward a person in the audience, both palms facing up and the key exposed.[19] The person takes the key and Sofía Divinatrix offers the lock of the handcuffs for the person to open them. The person unlocks the handcuffs. Without saying a word, she requests the key, finishes taking out the handcuffs, and places the handcuffs and the key on the table.

Now with the back to the audience she is standing with her weight on both feet, with her legs somewhat spread apart. She shakes her hips to the rhythm of the music that now has picked up a faster pace and features both a man and a woman singing. Sofía unties the belt of the coat and plays with it making it move in a circle shape, first one side, then the other. Her whole body now vibrates while she opens wide the coat still with her back to the audience. Every now and then she looks at them over her shoulder. She slips the coat a little bit showing a shoulder, then she puts the coat back to cover it, and she repeats this until finally she lets the coat drop suddenly to the floor.[20] Under the white coat, Sofía was wearing a bodysuit the color of her skin. A taíno sun covers one breast and a sunflower covers the other one. She is wearing a wide belt made out of many straps and a loincloth featuring brown hand silhouettes.

Sofía now moves quickly to the chair by the table, sits and starts putting on her shoes. They are high heel sandals with thin crisscrossing straps. They are brown and glittery. After tying the first one, she stands sideways with respect to the audience and brings her bare foot up to the chair. She puts on the other sandal and she goes to the coat lying on the floor.[21]

Sofía picks up the coat from the floor, folds it a few times creating a little package with it. She uses the coat's belt to bind the white coat and throws the package forcefully to the floor.[22] She takes a whip that she had tied to her wide brown belt made out of many straps. She whips the bound white coat, again and again growing in anger and pain making it more difficult to breathe with each strike.[23] She suddenly stops, looks at the whip in horror, lets the whip fall off her hand, and watches it fall to the floor as she takes a step back.[24] She looks up and away in front of her, where there is a cross.[25]

She picks up the bound white coat and runs to the cross. She places the bound white coat at the feet of the cross and she kneels.[26] She bows her head and brings her hands together seemingly praying. She notices a small chest to the side of the cross and she opens it. From inside the chest she brings out a set of hands aligned and coming out of a band, all of the same size but different colors: ivory, golden yellow, and dark brown.[27] She lifts them up high in the air and the audience can see them while she is still kneeling with her back to the audience. She slowly lowers the hand until the band reaches the back of her neck. She ties the band around her neck and now the hands are covering the back of her head.

From inside the chest she brings out a long piece of fabric and she puts it over her shoulders hanging from her neck and down from her chest, like liturgical stoles do. She brings out of the chest a bunch of long pieces of fabric. She approaches the audience, puts a stole on a person, gives that person a bunch of long pieces of fabric, and signals with her hands toward the other members of the audience. She goes to another member of the audience and does the same, and then to a third one. Soon enough the members of the audience are vesting one another with the long pieces of fabric. While they finish doing that, she goes back to the table and grabs the very big scissors and ties her whip back to her belt.

By now the music has really picked up a fast pace and loud volume. The male and female voices are now singing in unison, "¡Alabanza! ¡Alabanza!" (Praise! Praise!) over and over. Facing the audience, Sofía is standing with her weight on both feet, with her legs somewhat spread apart and the scissors up in the air. She closes and opens the scissors a few times looking at them.

She closes the scissors and holds them up in the air pointing up while her whole body vibrates, until the music ends. She swings the scissors around, rests them on her shoulder and poses, her knees pointing to the side, one hand holding the scissors, the other hand on her waist. Sofía is looking at the audience.

BURLESQUE-ESQUE NEGATES WHITE PREACHING

The reader of this chapter might be preoccupied with understanding the meaning of the previously described performance. Such preoccupation constitutes a Western approach to ritual as I learned from George Tinker. "That was beautiful. . . . What does it mean?" One of the students said and asked during the walk back, after Tinker had shared with them a ritual.[28] The short answer to that question is that "An Exorcism" showed through symbolic action, rather than by public speech, a utopian vision of a possible future: white supremacy bound and away, under the power of the Christian cross. Hands remain in three different colors as equals: ivory, golden yellow, and dark brown, representing the white-european, indigenous taíno, and black-african[29] ancestry that make up Puerto Ricans.

The meaning of the piece and the authorial intention are not the main concern of this chapter. Rather, this chapter explores how the piece exposes by contrast the phallogocentric (privileging masculinity and words) presuppositions of too many homiletical theories in protestant progressive homiletics in the United States. The next section shows why this chapter needs to break the rules of the academy just like Sofía Divinatrix lives into her own tradition and expands it, thus breaking the rules of white preaching.

SOFÍA DIVINATRIX AS PROPHET AND HOLY FOOL

Playing by the rules of the academy, it is possible to place Sofía Divinatrix as a Prophet and Holy Fool. The problem with this course of action is that it measures burlesque-esque against the scholarship of white, male, and Western tradition, and colonizes Sofía's preaching practice. Another problem of following the rules of the academy is that locating Sofía within the prophetic preaching and holy fools traditions gives the impression that burlesque-esque is born out of the expansion of the aforementioned tradition and hides that it is mostly an expansion of my own Puerto Rican tradition of performance as preaching that taps into even older, pre-Christian traditions. Because it is true that burlesque-esque as a preaching practice hold points of connection with all these traditions, I will still argue that "An Exorcism" is a sermon that belongs to traditions that are as old or older than Christian preaching, the traditions of prophetic preaching and holy fools.

"An Exorcism" is prophetic preaching because the piece denounces evil and proclaims divine justice and liberation. The piece presents the injury inflicted upon people enslaved in the Caribbean long ago but also presents the current injury of whiteness that binds and constricts. Injuries and injustices such as those are examples of what prophetic preaching denounces. As homiletician Marvin McMickle explains, prophets are called to "sound the alarm about the injuries that are being inflicted upon people as well as about the injustices that are taking place."[30] Sofía sounds the alarm through enactment of the injuries.

The piece not only denounces white supremacy covering brown female bodies, but it also proclaims divine justice and liberation. Without words, the piece proclaims the justice that comes not from whipping white supremacy, but from bringing it and placing it at the feet of the cross.[31] Such actions nurture what Walter Brueggemann calls "an alternative consciousness" that "serves to *criticize* in dismantling the dominant consciousness."[32] The piece, as prophetic preaching does, offers another reality. It shows "another time and situation toward which the community of faith may move."[33] The piece, just as prophetic preaching does, offers hope and the promise of liberation, and it enacts "the new reality God will bring to pass in the future."[34]

In addition to constituting prophetic preaching, "An Exorcism" is part of the old and Christian tradition of holy fools. Homileticians Charles L. Campbell and Johan H. Cilliers describe the holy fools as "persons who, for the sake of the gospel, engage in bizarre, obscene, even insane, activities, appearing to be lunatics, idiots, or buffoons."[35] For many preachers and homileticians, the practice of burlesque may be obscene and its use for proclamation of the gospel may seem bizarre and insane. Maybe that is what people thought of Jeremiah when he walked around wearing a yoke, or of Isaiah when he walked around barefoot and naked, both claiming that God told them to do so.[36] Modern psychology may consider them mentally ill, a more politically correct phrase for "lunatic." Here, I break my own rule of downplaying the meaning of "An Exorcism" to show that Sofía's burlesque-esque piece was proclaiming the gospel as it was interpreting scripture. While the specific text may have been lost in translation for the audience, the theological content was clear when Sofía changes strategies, from whipping the bundled coat, representative of white supremacy, to putting it at the feet of the cross and then praying.[37] This act communicated a letting go, a surrender of the problem to the cross as a higher power. While I am sure that my interpretation and application goes beyond what Campbell and Cilliers envisioned when they wrote their book, burlesque-esque does fit their criteria, while also pushing the invisible boundaries of their work and honoring the expressive capacity of the body, even when in sensuous indecent communication. "An Exorcism" constitutes symbolic action proclaiming the good news of liberation from the evil of white supremacy under the power of an empty cross through an absurd and irreverent choice for the medium to communicate the message. Consequently, Sofía is a person who engages in an obscene activity, for the sake of the gospel, appearing to be a lunatic. Sofía is a Holy Fool.

In her attempt to exorcise white supremacy from her body and her preaching through symbolic action, Sofía shows the ability to name the demons of white supremacy within and without, and to envision and enact a new personhood. Sofía envisions, enacts, and offers a new preaching style that is, in the words of Ched Myers, "free of the structures and patterns of domination."[38] As a Latina preacher and burlesque dancer, Sofía was stuck with phallogocentric models for preaching offered as the only model available. Yet, Sofía chose to call forth, conjure, and bring to completion (perform) the more ancient tradition of prophetic symbolic action.

Contradicting what is largely taken for granted in preaching, Sofía exposes ubiquitous white preaching as foolish self-deception. Leaving behind the deceptive narrative that presents white preaching as the only or most valuable way of preaching, Sofía Divinatrix turns to other traditions. She combines symbolic action and burlesque dance to prophetically denounce and proclaim. Preaching through "burlesque-esque" constitutes prophetic preaching that joins the Christian tradition of the holy fools in contradistinction to the normative tradition of public oratory. In doing so, Sofía performs a critical theological function: she unmasks the deadly ways of white preaching by breaking its norms and embodying the proclamation traditions and epistemologies of the Caribbean that white preaching tries to erase.

SOFÍA DIVINATRIX AS PUERTO RICAN ACTRESS PREACHER

Breaking the rules of the academy, it is possible to place Sofía as a Puerto Rican, street preacher, and actress preacher who is expanding my Puerto Rican tradition of performance as preaching that taps into even older, pre-Christian and pre-Columbian traditions. Without books to cite, without ethnographic research (which I hope to conduct in the future), citing only my memories, own experience, and embodied knowledge, I will argue that "An Exorcism" is a sermon that belongs to traditions that are as old or older than Christian preaching, the traditions of sacred bodily expression and of using theater for preaching.

While it is true that there are points of connection between what I later labeled burlesque-esque and white interpretations of the tradition of the holy fools, of the tradition of some Hebrew prophets, and the political implications of Jesus's alleged street theater, it is also true that the ties to other logics are stronger. My brain braided all these strings rooted in a centuries-long tradition of bodily movement and discourse for sacred purposes, in a lifelong experience of theater for preaching and of street preaching, and a lifelong commitment to use performing arts for the proclamation of the gospel and not for entertainment. Elsewhere, I demonstrated that inhabitants of what today we call Mexico enacted religious rituals using what some Spaniards interpreted as theatrics and entertainment. I also demonstrated that taínos did not have a single speaker but the whole community learned by heart their sacred stories and re-narrated them again and again through song and dance in religious rituals called areítos.[39] Growing up in a Presbyterian church where the pastor, José Roberto Colón-Rodríguez, often wrote plays that substituted for pulpit speech, where the pastor invited singers to minister through songs instead of speech, or dancers or poets or mimes, and even advocated for the amendment of the Book of Worship of our denomination to accept these other modalities as proclamation as valid as pulpit speech, I received an embodied tradition of preaching through theater and other art forms. My body knew this tradition even if I had not read the aforementioned histories before. In these experiences were born the presuppositions that I brought into the academy: a person can preach anywhere, anytime, through any means of communication, with or without a worship service to frame the sermon.

Where I expand the Caribbean, Amerindian, and Puerto Rican traditions that I received is in bringing in burlesque, an art form that I did not learn in my own context, Christianity in Puerto Rico, and that most probably is not deemed suitable for religious proclamation for being too sensual and understood as too sexual. Here, I break another rule of good scholarship. I set aside the scholar in me and let the recovering evangelical in me come out to testify that the Divine gifted me burlesque so I could love my body again. Such gift came to me through Sara Green, a classmate at Vanderbilt Divinity School, who herself showed me through example to redirect burlesque to the art of liberation guided by sacred motives, imbuing burlesque with theology to generate an "alter-call."[40] Serendipitously, the burlesque class that I took with Sara as her student coincided with a queer theology class in which I was the teaching assistant, and with an Academy of Homiletics in which Gerald Liu stated that we define our practices against white preaching and Robert Stephen Reid presented a paper on the topic of baring the soul in the pulpit.[41] In a moment, my brain puts it all together and decides, "Burlesque can preach! Burlesque is an embodied way to bare the soul!" At the time, all these "coincidences" compelled me to combine street preaching, symbolic prophetic action, and burlesque dance to share my testimony with my queer students through communication systems that they know well: abject bodies, bodily discourses, and performance.

Having said all that to carve a space for a preaching tradition that, to the best of my knowledge, has yet to be archived with words, I insist that this chapter is not mainly proposing the use of burlesque-esque for preaching even though I had spent time unpacking a daring rebellious choice for doing just that. My proposal is hidden under the surface. My invitation is to refocus. Under the performing art of burlesque-esque it is possible to perceive a preacher who uses her acquired skills, whether through experience or education. Under the specific piece "An Exorcism" it is possible to perceive a preferential option for marginalized communities ostracized as sexual minorities. Under the choice for preaching without speech, pulpit, and worship service it is possible to perceive many traditions all coming back to life together, interwoven, and inseparable although from different times and places. These traditions include pre-Columbian ways of being, worshiping, and communicating as much as the Christian religion that European migrants imported. In sum, even though burlesque-esque for preaching might not be for you to do, what all preachers can most certainly do is to step into their tradition's definition of preaching, deploy their best skills at the service of the preaching task, and honor their own community's ways of preaching and communicating for the sake of testifying about their own experience with the Divine.

SOCIAL NORMS ESTABLISHED BY A WESTERN AND EURO-DESCENDANT GAZE UPON CHRISTIAN PREACHING

Most introductory texts to Christian preaching to date address biblical interpretation and sermon composition.[42] Many of these texts address the importance of exegeting the community of listeners and catering sermons to their culture and needs. All these books share presuppositions, non-stated assumptions, or axioms. The praxis of burlesque, however, has not been considered by white homiletics and it is based on a different set of presuppositions.

"An Exorcism" as a burlesque-esque piece challenges the hidden axioms and exposes the social norms established by a Western and Euro-descendant gaze upon Christian preaching. The modern normative concept of preaching and its hidden assumptions are today shared by many homileticians and preachers, whether Euro-descendants or black, Indigenous, and People of Color. It is not the color of the homiletician or the color of the preacher that results in white preaching. Rather, white preaching is the practice of Christian preaching when it follows social norms established by a Western Euro-descendant perspective. Said gaze privileges oratory and classic rhetoric, which still are standard practices today in many cultures and societies, and establishes it as the only valid means for preaching, as THE norm to be followed by all preachers. Along with oratory and classic rhetoric, words, pulpit, and worship service have become the normative assumptions of most definitions of preaching. Even though I agree with many contemporary definitions of preaching, I do not share such normative assumptions.

White preaching seems to presuppose that preaching requires speech, a pulpit, a worship service, and a decent performance. These are the rules of white preaching that burlesque-esque breaks which expose the cultural presuppositions of white preaching. Burlesque presupposes bodily movement and exposure. Burlesque-esque presupposes a combination of the "sacred" and the "profane" bringing together sensual movement, exposure of the body, Christian witness, and prophetic symbolic action.

"An Exorcism" challenges the requirement for speech and presents a counterproposal to phallogocentrism: silence and bodily expression. Recurring to silence and bodily expression suppresses words to reveal that the body expresses content in a particular structure. There is an exercise in preparation to teach people with disabilities in which the students in training to be teachers put themselves in different situations of disability. These future teachers plug their ears to learn through their bodies what may it be for them to live with a hearing impairment, or cover their eyes to experience what may it be for them to live with a visual impairment. Through such an exercise, the future teachers discover that by suppressing one sense the other senses heighten. Similarly, students of theater learning bodily expression may engage in a series of acting exercises without using words. Suppression of one means of communication heightens another way of communication. As a professional actress and theater teacher, Sofía Divinatrix knows this. In her use of burlesque and symbolic action for proclamation, she suppresses words and heightens bodily communication. This causes the audience to switch the way they pay attention to the piece. They cannot rely on the words and thus the audience becomes aware of the content and structure of the bodily communication.

CONCLUSION

From the perspective of white homiletics, Sofía Divinatrix was not preaching when she performed "An Exorcism of White Supremacy" in a room under a church sanctuary, outside of a liturgical context, without uttering words, when she bodily expressed her theology and biblical interpretation while resembling a burlesque dance. Nonetheless, from the perspective of a Caribbean burlesque dancer familiar with the symbolic action practices of the Hebrew Bible prophets and the street preaching practices of evangelists, preaching through "burlesque-esque" constitutes prophetic preaching that joins the Christian tradition of the holy fools in contradistinction to the normative tradition of public oratory. Sofía was using her own languages to proclaim the good news of divine liberation from white supremacy and from white preaching. She was sharing her testimony and inviting others to go out sharing power to build different ways of interrelating in the world. Sofía Divinatrix was indeed preaching. She just said "no" to dominant homiletic rules. In so doing, Sofía unmasks and refuses reiterating white preaching. Instead, she invites preachers to use less words and more body, to step out of the pulpit and out of the worship service and into where people are.

NOTES

1. These words were part of the play "Words and Flesh Entangled," by Lis Valle and originally performed in All Faith Chapel, Vanderbilt University, Nashville, Tennessee on May 4, 2018.

2. These four words form the acronym BDSM, which stands for Bondage and Discipline, Domination and Submission, Sadism and Masochism.

3. The poetic piece that opens the introduction to this essay is a translation from a poetic piece written in Spanish by Lis Valle to introduce the video version of "Un Exorcismo de Supremacía Blanca." The original Spanish version of the poetic piece as well as the video version of "Un Exorcismo de Supremacía Blanca" were shared at the book presentation "A voltear la tortilla: Método de la predicación anticolonialista" that Seminario Evangélico de Puerto Rico held online on February 26, 2021. See https://fb.watch/6_PMan0U8o/ (accessed July 26, 2021). The book was written by Eliseo Pérez Álvarez published after the first performance of "An Exorcism of White Supremacy" and yet, it is consonant to the philosophy behind "An Exorcism." See, in general, Eliseo Pérez Álvarez, *A voltear la tortilla: método de la predicación anticolonialista* (Montevideo, Uruguay: Fundación Amerindia, 2020). A shorter version of this book appears in English under the title "Voltear la tortilla: Preaching and Theological Method" in *The Future Shape of Christian Proclamation: What the Global South Can Teach Us about Preaching*, edited by LaRue, Cleophus James, and Luiz C. Nascimento (Eugene, OR: Cascade Books, 2020).

4. The use of "ancesters" instead of "ancestors" produces a gender-neutral noun that disrupts gender binaries.

5. Personal conversation between Lis Valle-Ruiz and Andrew Wymer sometime in the Fall of 2020. See also "Truth-Telling and Gift-Sharing: Re-Centering Conversation in the Academy of Homiletics" in *A Series of AoH Conversations to Decenter Whiteness*, videoconference, August 5, 2020.

6. Lis Valle-Ruiz, "Performing Cultural Memory Through Preaching," *Liturgy: Journal of the Liturgical Conference*, 35:3, 3–9. DOI: 10.1080/0458063X.2020.1796434 (accessed May 14, 2021).

7. A midway is the space that surrounds the circus featuring games and entertainment.

8. I have experience an education in the art of creating characters and in the practice of preaching through characters. I have been doing theater in church my whole life. Theater was also my major in my undergrad program. In Puerto Rico, however, I am not unique. Many preachers from different denominations have characters that preach or minister.

9. This was not the first time, nor the last that I was invited to preach as one of my characters.

10. The tradition of the holy fools takes up the words in 1 Cor. 4:9–10 (New Revised Standard Version) that in part reads, "We are fools for the sake of Christ."

11. One of the founders of Holy Fools, Inc., Tevyn East, is disciple of Ched Myers and considers the main piece of the circus a midrash. That Ched Myers was inspiration for both our works only became apparent near to show time.

12. The inspiration to do so came from hearing once more about the debate on self-disclosure in which David Buttrick argues against and Fred Craddock argues in favor. Robert Stephen Reid, "Soul Baring in the Pulpit: Lessons in Storytelling from the Moth," paper presented before the *Rhetoric Workgroup at the 2016 Academy of Homiletics Annual Meeting*, November 16–19, 2016, San Antonio, TX.

13. On symbolic action and "An Exorcism of White Supremacy," see the book that inspired both the content and the shape of the sermon under discussion, Ched Myers, *Binding the Strong Man: A Political Reading of Mark's Story of Jesus*, Twentieth Anniversary Edition (Maryknoll, NY: Orbis Books, 2008). On symbolic action for street preaching, see Stanley P. Saunders and Charles L. Campbell, *The Word on the Street: Performing the Scripture in the Urban Context* (Grand Rapids, MI: Wm. B. Eerdmans Publishing Co., 2000), 93–103. The authors trace the tradition of street preaching from Pentecost, through the Reformation, to the United States (Whitefield). On symbolic action for political protest, see Diana Taylor and Roselyn Costantino, editors, *Holy Terrors: Latin American Women Perform* (Durham, NC: Duke University Press, 2003), and Mark Juergensmeyer, "Theater of Terror: Performance Violence" in his monograph, *Terror in the Mind of God: The Global Rise of Religious Violence*, 121–147 (Berkeley, CA: University of California Press, 2000).

14. She is completely covered in white just as life in the United States was made by and for white people. The best way to survive is to perform whiteness.

15. This is the stage name of the performer. As it is customary for burlesque dancers, they have a stage name and a tag line, in this case, Sofía Divinatrix: The High Priestess Unrobed. The name intentionally means Divine Wisdom combined with dominatrix (a woman who assumes the dominating role in sadomasochistic sexual activities). Sofía Divinatrix is unrobed in honor of Baby Suggs, an unrobed preacher fictional character in Toni Morrison's novel *Beloved*, and in identification with all humans who had preached outside of pulpits and temples because the institutional church has not recognized their call to preach.

16. The song is a well-known song of protest in Puerto Rico. The title is in indigeneous taíno language, though the lyrics are in Spanish. The song tells the story of colonization and the abuses inflicted by Europeans on the bodies of indigenous and black persons. Most likely than not, the audience would not understand Spanish. The

preacher chose to use her own verbal and body languages, privileging authenticity and truth over clarity for the audience. It is also an intentional strategy to render words useless and reveal that the human body in front of a group of people offers both content and form, just as verbal discourses do.

17. This is an example of the theatricality that distinguishes burlesque dancing from strip tease. It also shows that (1) she did not know that she was being handcuffed and (2) that she has tools to liberate herself.

18. The movement constitutes a prelude to the invitation to help her.

19. She finally invites someone to help her. While she has the key, she cannot do it herself.

20. After removing the chains and handcuffs that bound her, now she is able to remove the white coat, symbol of the whiteness that covers everything.

21. It is after removing the whiteness that covers it all that she is able to stand in her own feet and back into her brownness.

22. This is where the "strong man" of prevailing whiteness is bound. It is bound with its own belt. The bound white coat symbolizes white supremacy in bondage. By whipping the bound white coat which represents whiteness and by binding whiteness with its own belt while the song tells the story of European conquistadores whipping and branding the bodies of African people enslaved, the dancer attempts to use the master's tools to bind and discipline the master. For a discussion on how it is not possible to succeed, see Audre Lorde, "The Master's Tools Will Never Dismantle the Master's House" in her collected volume *Sister Outsider: Essays and Speeches*, 110–113 (Trumansburg, NY: Crossing Press, 1984).

23. This action completes the reversals. The white supremacy that covered all, that bound dark brown and golden bodies, and that whipped them to the point of open wounds and even death is now bound and whipped with its own tools. Reversal may feel like liberation and justice for the previously oppressed and recently liberated. Reversal is a frequent theme in Christian biblical texts. Homiletician Mary Donovan Turner has argued that Miriam's victory song constitutes a prophetic performance, a ritual that reverses the fortunes of the poor and the oppressed as is God's intention. Mary Donovan Turner, "Reversal of Fortune: The Performance of a Prophet" in *Performance in Preaching: Bringing the Sermon to Life*, edited by Jana Childer and Clayton J. Schmit (Grand Rapids, MI: Baker Academic, 2008), 87–98. However, reversal may also operate as vengeance or retaliation as in the law of talion. Against such approach, scripture tells that Jesus of Nazareth offered a nonviolent alternative, including offering the other cheek, give the cloak in addition to the coat, and go another mile (Matt. 5:38–42). Similarly, a quotation frequently attributed to M. K. Gandhi states, "an eye for an eye leaves the whole world blind." Furthermore, Paulo Freire and Frantz Fanon warn about the possibility that once liberated or in power, the former oppressed may turn into an oppressor. This reversal scene in "An Exorcism" shows both the need for the liberated to punish the oppressor, and how problematic the desire and execution of reversals can be.

24. Sofía realizes that she is now acting like her oppressor. In her desire for justice, she has become the oppressor. The scene is also problematic from the perspective of kink practice. The ethics of kink scenes require prenegotiation and consent. When

those two are present, the top disciplines the bottom for pleasure/pain that is desired. From such perspective, to whip the coat is to serve the coat.

25. In the previous movements, no explanation is provided for her to stop. The fact that Sofía looks at the cross may suggest that she stopped whipping the coat due to her religious values. Nonetheless, her internal motivations cannot be really known by only looking at her actions.

26. This action may be interpreted as a correction to the prior action. Instead of taking justice into her hands, instead of operating the reversal herself, she takes the bound coat and places it under a power higher than herself.

27. Ivory stands for the hands of the Spanish, golden yellow for the Indigenous inhabitants of the Caribbean islands prior to Columbus arrival, and the dark brown stands for the people from West Africa that the Spanish brought to the lands that we now know as the Americas. On the one hand, these colors stand in contrast to the typical red for Amerindians, yellow for Asians, black for persons of African descent, brown for Latin Americans, and white for persons of European descent, the typical five colors that correspond to the division of the world in five regions or continents. On the other hand, as Brazilian photographer Angélica Dass has documented, said colors are untrue labels of race. Rather, human beings show a wide range of skin tones, humanity's true colors. For more about the Humanae Project, go to https://angelicadass.com/photography/humanae/ (accessed September 26, 2021).

28. George Tinker shared this story at the North American Academy of Liturgy Annual Meeting in Denver, Colorado, January 3–5, 2019.

29. I do not capitalize the words white-european to let dominant narratives take less space. While retaining upper case for terms that refer to those with less power such as indigenous taíno, and black-african is a very attractive and tempting option for a reversal, which is what we may need right now, I keep these words in lower case to rehearse another possible future. This possible future acknowledges the unjust systems that we have now and the value of reversal, as well as the risk for the colonized turning into colonizers and behaving in similar oppressive ways once we get to the top, as Franz Fannon and Paulo Freire have warned us in their work. This possible future demonstrates an idyllic state in which no group will be better than others, and all groups decide to exercise power-with rather than power over. Rehearsal is needed for this possible future to become a reality.

30. Marvin Andrew McMickle, *Where Have All the Prophets Gone?: Reclaiming Prophetic Preaching in America*, Kindle Edition (Cleveland, OH: The Pilgrim Press, 2006), 99.

31. Walter Brueggemann, *Prophetic Imagination: Revised Edition*, Kindle Edition (Minneapolis, MN: Fortress Press, 2001), 9.

32. Brueggemann, *Prophetic*, 3.

33. Ibid.

34. Leonora Tubbs Tisdale, *Prophetic Preaching: A Pastoral Approach*, Kindle Edition (Louisville, KY: Westminster John Knox Press), 10.

35. Charles L. Campbell and Johan H. Cilliers, *Preaching Fools: The Gospel as a Rhetoric of Folly*, 94, referencing, Wendy Wright, "Fools for Christ," *Weavings: A Journal of the Christian Spiritual Life*, 9 (1994): 25.

36. Jeremiah 27 and 28 and Isaiah 20:2–4.

37. The biblical text that Sofía interpreted was Mark 3:27. Ched Myers provided the method for biblical interpretation and the inspiration for the piece in his book *Binding the Strong Man*, where he develops a political reading of the gospel of Mark.

38. Ched Myers, *Binding the Strong Man: A Political Reading of Mark's Story of Jesus*, Twentieth Anniversary Edition (Maryknoll, NY: Orbis Books, 2008), 437.

39. Valle-Ruiz, "Performing Cultural Memory Through Preaching."

40. "Alter-call" was the title of a Burlesque show that Sara organized and that featured several burlesque dances by various artists. All the dancers explored religious themes in their pieces. In naming the show, Sara intentionally played with words to re-frame the altar calls typical of the religious tradition in which she grew up. For Sara, burlesque is liturgical.

41. Reid, "Soul Baring in the Pulpit."

42. A small sample of such books include Thomas G. Long, *The Witness of Preaching*, Third Edition (Louisville, KY: Westminster John Knox Press, 2016); John S. McClure, *The Four Codes of Preaching: Rhetorical Strategies* (Minneapolis, MN: Fortress Press, 1991); Lucy Lind Hogan and Robert Reid, *Connecting with the Congregation: Rhetoric and the Art of Preaching* (Nashville, TN: Abingdon Press, 1999); and Pablo A. Jiménez, *Principios de predicación* (Nashville, TN: Abingdon Press, 2003).

BIBLIOGRAPHY

Brueggemann, Walter. *Prophetic Imagination: Revised Edition*. Minneapolis, MN: Fortress Press, 2001. Kindle Edition.

Campbell, Charles L., and Johan Cilliers. *Preaching Fools the Gospel as a Rhetoric of Folly*. Waco, TX: Baylor University Press, 2012.

McMickle, Marvin Andrew. *Where Have All the Prophets Gone?: Reclaiming Prophetic Preaching in America*. Cleveland, OH: Pilgrim Press, 2006.

Myers, Ched. *Binding the Strong Man: A Political Reading of Mark's Story of Jesus*. Maryknoll, NY: Orbis Books, 2008. Twentieth Anniversary Edition.

Tisdale, Leonora Tubbs. *Prophetic Preaching: A Pastoral Approach*. Louisville, KY: Westminster John Knox Press, 2010.

Chapter 15

An Icon of Exclusion

Deconstructing the Pulpit through the Homiletical Practice of Black Women

Chelsea Brooke Yarborough

INTRODUCTION: THE SINGLE STORY OF THE SERMON

In her TED Talk, "The Danger of a Single Story," Chimamanda Adichie asserts, "Show a people as one thing, as only one thing, over and over again, and that is what they become."[1] When the breadth of reality is confined to the limitations of a single story, we lose track of the richness and diversity of the world around us. Often, the "story" of the dominant culture and its practices is used to define what is normative for everyone. Such single stories are rooted in stereotypes that keep people, places, and ideas in boxes that do not serve the fullness of their narratives and that offer only the limited viewpoint of those with the power to define the story. In a society like the United States, which has been tainted by generations of white supremacy and white privilege, whiteness is an ideological framework that has frequently reaffirmed its own single story, which maintains its power and prestige and excludes those who fall outside of that normative reality.

In a similar way, the "single story" of preaching has often centered the pulpit, a spatial demarcation of power and hierarchy. In fact, the pulpit is so entwined with the story of preaching that the use of a pulpit has come to define what preaching is: preaching is that which occurs in a pulpit. This narrow outlook on what preaching can be and where it can take place immediately excludes both those who have been pushed out of formal places of power and those whose sense of call to proclaim does not require a pulpit.

In most Christian communities of preaching, the pulpit is an icon, revered as an aesthetic marker of power and the locale of the voice of God. When the pulpit is restricted to people with certain forms of power—education, maleness, whiteness, heterosexuality, particular forms of ability, or any other quality regarded as powerful and normative—the voices and stories of all others are disconnected from the voice of God and from the proclamation of the good news. When the pulpit is *decentered*, the options for where preaching happens and what preaching can be expand exponentially. The story becomes much wider and moves beyond space and place into the depths of proclaimer—whether or not the proclaimer has received institutional endorsement. By deconstructing the pulpit itself, we inherently deconstruct the definition of preaching as a pulpit practice and open the door to wonder at all the ways in which God might be speaking.

In this chapter, I broaden preaching beyond the single story of the pulpit by centering the experiences and preaching witness of black women. In a context where "woman" has typically signified white women and "black" has signified black men, black women embody a multiplicity of narratives within their identity. Centering black women is a constructive practice of expanding the narrative of preaching while deconstructing the central identity of preaching as attached primarily and often solely to the pulpit. Through studying the homiletical practices of black women, we can reimagine a new starting place for the stories of preaching. When we center black women's preaching, we deconstruct the iconography of the pulpit as an aesthetic expression of sole power and open new platforms and possibilities of proclaiming. Black women's preaching pushes the narrative of preaching into the margins and lifts up stories that have often been left untold. In this constructive/deconstructive process, we find new definitions of preaching and new places where preaching can be found and heard.

THE PROBLEM WITH THE PULPIT

The origins of the pulpit stem from a history of power, making its reverential place in preaching practice inherently problematic. The pulpit as we know it in contemporary times emerged from an intention to separate the clergy from the laypeople. In the late second century and early third century C.E., there were significant changes to the design of church space. The church, which had consisted of groups of Christians meeting in individual homes, began to expand to gatherings in other places that signified "church." One element of these new gathering spaces was the creation of a "bema." This was a platform built specifically for clergy, which provided a clear designation of who was speaking and leading and who was not. While it can be argued that there were practical reasons for the bema's creation (amplification, for example), the clear aim was that the preaching clergy would be able to be seen above all other worshippers. In *Sacred Power, Sacred Space*, Jeanne Halgren Kilde argues:

> The bema and the separation it created between the clergy and the ordinary worshippers indicate that Christianity was becoming increasingly institutionalized. The new clergy, presiding over the symbolic Eucharist services that were becoming the centerpiece of Christian worship, played a very powerful role, in effect mediating between the gathered assembly and the God they worshipped.[2]

The bema continued to grow and develop over time, and became the pulpits we know across many traditions today. In different traditions, the pulpit has varied meanings based upon that tradition and its liturgical understanding; however, consistent across traditions is the separation of clergy from those who are not clergy, and the signifier that this location—the pulpit—is where God's voice is mediated to the people. This is problematic for many reasons, but especially when we consider the way that power operates: not everyone has access or opportunity to occupy this particular space.

For this reason, decentering the pulpit in our understanding of preaching is important. As a symbol, the pulpit itself creates a hierarchical power dynamic that reifies exclusion in our conceptions of sacred speech. When the pulpit is a central framework for defining preaching, those who do not have access to that pulpit are immediately excluded from the practice and from our understanding of it. In addition, those who *intentionally* preach from other platforms and spaces that are not normatively considered the sanctified space of the pulpit are excluded from our understanding of preaching, limiting our ability to see the expansive nature and purpose of preaching. Therefore, the pulpit as a central spatial framework for preaching excludes whole groups of people, like black women, who have historically been excluded from this formal and institutionally affirmed place of proclaiming. Even in places where black women are affirmed as pulpit preachers, preaching as solely a pulpit practice is problematic as it excludes the wide-ranging practices of proclaimers.

Roxanne Mountford in *The Gendered Pulpit* helps us understand the implications of centering the pulpit by unpacking its problematic nature even further. She argues that the pulpit itself carries a history and ethos that is gendered, having excluded women from preaching for extensive periods of time, and in some traditions still excluding them. As such, when women enter into that space, it is an act of claiming a space not created for their presence. Even in spaces that have begun to be more inclusive and where women can enter the pulpit, Mountford argues that the history and intention behind the creation of the pulpit still remain. She writes, "To make such a claim is to argue that rhetorical spaces carry the residue of history within them, but also, perhaps, something else: a physical representation of relationships and ideas."³ Thus, the pulpit reiterates *masculinized* exclusionary limitations, while also being the sole locale for understanding the nature, purpose, and practice of preaching. As Adichie says, "Show a people as one thing, as only one thing, over and over again, and that is what they become."⁴

When that which is revered has been a space of maintaining hierarchical and patriarchal power based on the residue of historical oppression, then it is critical we change our starting place for talking about preaching. The aim is not to eradicate the pulpit—because it is going to remain a significant place where preaching happens—but to move beyond its function as a gatekeeper for what preaching is and can be.

With this in mind, preaching is a pulpit practice, but far from solely a pulpit practice. Black women proclaimers have continually stretched and expanded the definition of preaching through their practice, carving out creative space and utilizing a myriad of platforms to develop expansive understandings of preaching. They have necessarily moved outside of pulpits and beyond the idea that the "big chair" is the place where God must speak, as they have had to find God in themselves and affirm their own calls when the larger church would not. Teresa Fry Brown argues, "Like their foremothers, many contemporary black women have creatively moved beyond the 'Big Chair Syndrome.' Many know that all ground is holy. God is everywhere. The tremendous power of the pulpit in the black church tradition can be liberating or oppressive."⁵ This recognition of an expansive platform for proclamation and a reclamation of one's own voice, in spite of institutionally rooted exclusion, marks a fertile ground for prophetic vision to consider what preaching can be.

Both in and beyond black churches, black women have not often been given places to preach but have taken what was needed for them to live into their calls. Where pulpits were not available, they chose other platforms for speaking, creating new memory in spaces away from the gendered and exclusive pulpit. Some were educators weaving theological assertions to support their practices of creating better space for black students. Others found themselves on the front lines of protests, proclaiming hope by demanding new practices. Even when pulpits were available, some chose spaces more aligned with their call and took their preaching beyond the confines of the pulpit. *For black women proclaimers, the pulpit is already inherently decentered and removed as the primary locus of preaching*. The possibility of preaching platforms is as varied as the black women preaching. Black women proclaimers bring a multifaceted lens to preaching, pushing against the single story and inviting a broader perspective. This does not mean that black women do not preach from pulpits, but their engagement with the space is different.

Black women embody multiple stories and disrupt the single story by virtue of not being the dominant norm in places of power, and more importantly by engaging in practices that push against normative forms of power and privilege within their preaching. Through the preaching of black women, we are invited to consider the ways an intersectional approach to preaching illuminates the diversity of its practice. Intersectional approaches not only ask us to name the layers of ones' identity, but to consider how these different identities speak to power and social constraint within a given context.[6] To start with black women's preaching means to shift the definition of preaching from the universalizing place of the pulpit and to consider more fully the specificity of preaching as it emerges from individual proclaimers rooted in the complexities of their stories.

As such, black women's proclamation demands a closer examination of how we define preaching. If preaching is primarily defined spatially and through power differentials, then the practice of preaching will always mirror the ills of those parameters. However, black women's preaching moves us beyond static definitions and spatial demarcations to the nature and purpose of preaching. In so doing, we do not lose the pulpit as a preaching space, but instead gain multiple other spaces. The "icon" of preaching can be expanded and the practice opened to a wider range of proclaimers.

BLACK WOMEN'S PREACHING: A NEW CENTER, AN EXPANSIVE HOMILETIC

When formerly decentered stories and identities are centered, old confining ideologies are pushed past their previous limits and deconstructed, creating more room for the expansive nature of reality. Preaching is already a practice beyond the confines of the pulpit, and certainly beyond the limitations of a pulpit defined by particular affirmations of privilege and power. When black women's preaching is centered, new images for both preachers and the biblical text emerge, enlivening the possibility of what preaching is and can mean. In addition, traditional concepts for what is considered a sermon are expanded as different historical practices of preaching are uncovered, illuminating new possibilities for the contemporary practice. Finally, new spaces for preaching are discovered as black women intentionally carve space for themselves outside of the confines of institutions and create preaching homes elsewhere.

Black women's preaching expands our preaching practices, because it begins from the experiences of black women, instead of black women's experiences being marginal and/or addendums to the conversation. In *Ingenuity: Preaching as an Outsider*, Lisa Thompson attends to the preaching practices of black women starting from their preaching itself. Instead of justifying their preaching through the homiletical authority of others, she listens to preaching women and develops methods and concepts of preaching practices around what they say. By focusing on the embodied preaching practices of black women, she shows us the necessarily imaginative practices of black women preachers that are missed when black women are not visible. In her conclusion, she writes, "Our imaginings have been overwhelmingly stifled by a default imagery of maleness and what masculinity looks like alongside whiteness; and in turn, anything that moves in contradiction to such imaginings is inherently deficient."[7] Black women's practices have been seen as deficient because they were different and were not in alignment with the type of homogeneity that whiteness as a framework requires. Black women push against the old memories of gatekeeping and, at best, begin to carve new memory into the spatial identity of the pulpit. Though the women in Thompson's study are pulpit preachers, their embodiment within the pulpit is subversive to the hierarchical construction. By stepping in as marginalized preachers, proclaiming through imaginative interplay and positing ideas beyond the whiteness and maleness that had been normalized, black women offer a different and more expansive homiletic.

Black women-centered preaching also expands our notion of the text and of God. This is important because theology and scripture have been used to reinforce the power dynamics of the pulpit and maintain boundaries around who is allowed to preach and who is not. These power dynamics mimic ideas of status and power outside of the worship space, which is why it is critical to decenter the pulpit and to center preachers who use a myriad of platforms but have been excluded from the pulpit—specifically, black women.

Womanist ethicist Katie Cannon suggests ways that black women preachers challenge normative understandings of the text. In *Katie's Canon*, Cannon asserts, "A womanist critique of homiletics challenges conventional biblical interpretations of sin-bringing Eve, wilderness-whimpering Hagar, henpecking Jezebel, whoring Gomer, prostituting Mary Magdalene and conspiring Sapphira."[8] These tropes are rooted in white supremacy, sexism, patriarchy, heterosexism, and other frameworks that limit the women in the text to these stereotypical and negative visuals. Cannon argues for a womanist deconstruction of preaching through a reimagining of the biblical text. By starting here, we are also then pushed to reimagine who God is and how the Godhead is enlivened and seen in and through women as well. When a reader puts black women and their experiences at the center of preaching, the reader interprets marginalized women in the text through a more compassionate and generous lens. Through the intersectional lens that black women embody, a person may read in more textured ways, and notice the women in the text as the complexity of their stories. Instead of the tropes Cannon names, the women reveal their full stories as women marked by the socio-political realities in which they were living, and read through the lens of honor instead of condemnation. Therefore, lifting up black women preachers involves not only expansion in terms of who can preach, but also in the preaching rhetoric and interpretation that offers new ideas and identity to preaching. The preaching of black women helps dethrone the masculinized vision of a white normative God, which is so often reproduced through the icon of pulpit power and exclusion.

New Preaching Platforms

Centering black women's preaching practices pushes us beyond the pulpit even as it includes the pulpit. Black women have preached at protests, in hospitals, at kitchen tables, and many other spaces created by their call, even if these were not affirmed institutionally. More recently, black women have found spaces online, creating communities built on inclusivity and navigating the real lived experiences of black women in ways that the institutional church has often ignored. Again, when the central pulpit is built on exclusion and lack of belonging, those left out create an otherwise ethos that is counterintuitive but is the means by which people have found spaces to preach. Melva Sampson of Pink Robe Chronicles recreated a communal online setting through the collective proclamation of call and response found within the chat, but is doing something otherwise: creating a space of belonging for black women and other black people who have not always been afforded the luxury of belonging in more institutionalized black church spaces. In "Digital Hush Harbors: Black Preaching Women and Black Digital Religious Networks," Sampson names these spaces "digital hush harbors."[9] She offers two other examples, The Gathering and WereSurthrivors, and writes that in such spaces, "Black preaching women deploy livestreams as digital hush harbors in ways that are challenging traditional hierarchies of Black church authority and changing the nature of religious space." These spaces do not require pulpits or governing bodies. The aim is for communal belonging, where everyone has a space in a way that is not often afforded in a more traditional church. This type of black women's preaching pushes the narrative of what preaching is while also taking an additional step to offer ecclesiological nuance about what it means to be in church. Again, by centering black women's proclamation, new possibilities emerge for what it means to preach.

Beyond Orality

Centering black women preachers not only opens new rhetorical spaces as shown in the previous section, but it also forces us to consider other homiletical artifacts that might be seen as preaching and how we might engage them. When preaching moves outside of a defined space, the possibilities for what constitutes preaching expand as well. Donyelle McCray illustrates the powerful preaching of Harriet Powers by looking at the "sermon quilts" that

Powers creates. Powers, who defined her quilts as sermons, also claims for herself that she is a preacher. While it is unclear whether she was also a formal pulpit preacher, her most clear and striking homiletical artifacts are the ornate quilts she created that themselves preach. Describing Powers's sermon *Bible Quilt*, McCray writes:

> Powers exhibited her *Bible Quilt* at the Athens Cotton Fair of 1886. While the quilt has muted tones today, back then it danced with vivid shades of pink, green, and orange. And more, the quilt had distinctive marks of African American craftwork, including contrasting sash trim, the placement of squares at most corners, and deliberate instances of asymmetry. Silhouettes of humans, animals, and celestial bodies were appliquéd in panels to depict distinct biblical stories and give them a universal quality.[10]

These quilted sermons were aesthetic proclamations and an expanded understanding of preaching.

The quilt sermons of Harriet Powers push against the ableism that would require preaching to be rooted in oral skills and also open access for others who are able to craft, create, and offer a sermon in unexpected forms. By looking at Harriet Powers's quilts as sermons, not only do we remove the pulpit as the locus for preaching, the art form expands beyond orality into other art forms. When talking about the uniqueness of Powers's preaching, McCray asserts, "In sharing her insight, she chooses a medium that is typically associated with domestic settings rather than liturgical ones, suggesting she sees a role for proclamation outside the pulpit."[11] What is exciting here is how Powers's practice offers new images of "preacher"—preacher as quilter, creating something both convicting and practical—which pushes our ideas of preaching beyond notions of power over and brings us into community with. Powers's quilts show us that preaching is a practice that requires not central space, but the sense of call to proclaim a word to community—and the creativity to put that call into action.

CONCLUSION: A CONSIDERATION BEYOND THE SINGLE STORY

Centering black women's preaching practice is a means to move beyond the single story of preaching as pulpit practice, which is rooted in the perpetuation of the homogeneity and normativity of those who have been in power. By centering the expansive nature of black women's preaching, the pulpit's place as a permanent and untouchable icon—a space to be revered as the sole locus of preaching—is removed, and new ideas and possibilities for preaching necessarily emerge both historically and in the contemporary moment. Black women's preaching practices disrupt the iconography of power established by the historical aesthetic, and the privileging of the pulpit both in academic research and in practice. By lifting up different homiletical practices and centering those not afforded the luxury of absolute access to the pulpit space, we are challenged to discover new avenues, arenas, and possibilities for preaching. The living word, not subject to confinement by any space, is given new air to breathe, be, and become. This is the aim of preaching, not to continue to reinforce the unjust power dynamics of our societies and systems that serve as catalysts for oppression. Instead, preaching is an inbreaking of something otherwise—something more beloved, more just, more whole, and more possible—into this world.

Deconstructing the iconic nature of the pulpit, along with its fraught history and exclusive implications, requires resisting the "single story." It begins by centering new narratives that offer more textured and robust approaches to preaching. Black women's preaching practices are critically imaginative as they stem from the experiences of the margins and expand beyond formal places of preaching and power. When the pulpit is decentered, white supremacy, sexism, hierarchy, patriarchy, and their inherently exclusionary nature are also decentered. If preaching is a practice geared toward inviting us into deeper wholeness, belovedness, and oneness with God, then it is critical that we move beyond an aesthetic of exclusion and expand our ideas and practices of preaching beyond the pulpit. This is where a liberating homiletic begins: inclusive and expanded beyond the prescribed center and rooted in the practices of those for whom the pulpit was not always accessible, but who nevertheless chose and found ways to preach.

NOTES

1. Chimamanda Adichie, "The Danger of a Single Story." New York, 2009. TED Global video, 18:33, https://www.ted.com/talks/chimamanda_ngozi_adichie_the_danger_of_a_single_story (accessed September 25, 2021).

2. Jeanne Halgren Kilde, *Sacred Power, Sacred Space: An Introduction to Christian Architecture and Worship* (New York: Oxford University Press, 2008), 24.

3. Roxanne Mountford, *The Gendered Pulpit: Preaching in American Protestant Spaces* (Carbondale, IL: Southern Illinois University Press, 2003), 17.

4. Chimamanda Adichie, "The Danger of a Single Story." New York, 2009. TED Global video, 18:33, https://www.ted.com/talks/chimamanda_ngozi_adichie_the_danger_of_a_single_story (accessed September 25, 2021).

5. Teresa L. Fry Brown, *Weary Throats and New Songs: Black Women Proclaiming God's Word* (Nashville, TN: Abingdon Press, 2003), 21.

6. In thinking through this lens of intersectionality, I pull from Patricia Hill Collins and Sirma Bilge. They write, "Intersectionality is a way of understanding and analyzing the complexity in the world, in people and in human experiences. . . . When it comes to social inequality, people's lives and the organization of power in a given society are better understood as being shaped not by a single axis of social division, be it race or gender or class, but by many axes that work together and influence each other." Patricia Hill Collins and Sirma Bilge, *Intersectionality* (Cambridge: Polity Press, 2016), 2.

7. Lisa L. Thompson, *Ingenuity: Preaching as an Outsider* (Nashville, TN: Abingdon Press, 2018), 175.

8. Katie Cannon, *Katie's Canon: Womanism and the Soul of the Black Community* (New York: Continuum, 1995), 114.

9. Melva L. Sampson, "Digital Hush Harbors: Black Preaching Women and Black Digital Religious Networks," *Fire!!!* 6, no. 1 (2020): 45–66, https://www.jstor.org/stable/10.5323/48581553 (accessed April 12, 2021), 52.

10. Donyelle McCray, "Quilting the Sermon: Homiletical Insights from Harriet Powers," *Religions* 9, no. 46 (February 2018): 2, https://doi.org/10.3390/rel9020046 (accessed September 25, 2021).

11. McCray, "Quilting the Sermon," 5.

BIBLIOGRAPHY

Adichie, Chimamanda. "The Danger of a Single Story." Filmed 2009 at TED Global Video, New York. Video, 18:33, https://www.ted.com/talks/chimamanda_ngozi_adichie_the_danger_of_a_single_story (accessed on September 25, 2021).

Cannon, Katie G. *Katie's Canon: Womanism and the Soul of the Black Community.* New York: Continuum, 1995.

Collins, Patricia Hill, and Sirma Bilge. *Intersectionality.* Cambridge: Polity Press, 2016.

Kilde, Jeanne Halgren. *Sacred Power, Sacred Space: An Introduction to Christian Architecture and Worship.* New York: Oxford University Press, 2008.

McCray, Donyelle. "Quilting the Sermon: Homiletical Insights from Harriet Powers." *Religions* 9, no. 46 (February 2018): 1–7, https://doi.org/10.3390/rel9020046 (accessed on September 25, 2021).

Mountford, Roxanne. *The Gendered Pulpit: Preaching in American Protestant Spaces.* Carbondale, IL: Southern Illinois University Press, 2005.

Sampson, Melva L. "Digital Hush Harbors: Black Preaching Women and Black Digital Religious Networks." *Fire!!!*, no. 1 (2020): 45–66, https://www.jstor.org/stable/10.5323/48581553 (accessed on September 25, 2021).

Thompson, Lisa L. *Ingenuity: Preaching as an Outsider.* Nashville, TN: Abingdon Press, 2018.

(In)conclusion
Lis Valle-Ruiz and Andrew Wymer

Frequently at the end of a project, it is common to reflect on whether or not it achieved its objectives or was "successful." Yet, the very term is charged with capitalistic notions of success, Western paradigms of linearity, and is reminiscent of imperial and colonial actions of conquest. If we are being honest with our idealistic expectations when we began this project we have not conquered. We have failed to unmask white preaching completely. In this sense, we find ourselves here at an (in)conclusion which is more of an ellipsis than a period.

We have only begun to remove the mask and can barely appreciate the contours of the face behind the mask. We have also accomplished the continuation of a very long homiletical conversation. Certainly our shared work has continued the task of unmasking white preaching and identifying particular manifestations of racial hegemony, resistance, and possibilities in homiletics; however, this volume simply touches the surface of unmasking the violence of white preaching as well as alternative possibilities. It is our hope that this volume cues us to more fully identify the harm of white preaching, increase our awareness of the possibilities for resistance, and spur our imagination of alternative possibilities in homiletics.

We believe that the evocative frame of HyeRan Kim-Cragg's chapter (chapter 9) presenting "multitasking" preaching as a means of addressing the complexity of unmasking whiteness in preaching and pursuing alternative possibilities can be expanded to encompass the manner in which our guilds, institutions, and individuals might move forward in view of racial hegemony, resistance, and possibilities in homiletics. We strongly believe that we cannot leave white preaching untouched or unexamined, yet we must continue to envision and implement alternative possibilities. This is indeed a complex and difficult "multitask" that encompasses both/and. We can warily attend to the histories, symbols, and myths of whiteness that have shaped our imagination of what preaching can or "should" be, while also moving forward into new possibilities.

At least one thing that we hope is abundantly manifest in the voices in this collection is a stark awareness that the status quo of white-dominant homiletics is untenable. If we are truly committed to unmasking white preaching through attention to racial hegemony, resistance, and possibilities in homiletics, significant change is needed. We cannot and should not be white elites who invite "Others" to the table while keeping the same table, the same seats, the same seating arrangement as it has always been. The task of unmasking white preaching has intense implications for our guilds, our institutions, and ourselves. This task must go deeply into the roots of the problem and generate new structures of producing scholarship, of being colleagues, of teaching our students, and of modeling self-examination and acceptance of outside critique for them and for the multiple communities they represent and to which we belong.

At this point, we offer you a provocation rather than a conclusion. We refuse to synthesize. We refuse to thoroughly assess the "success" of this volume. We share some hopes. We try our best to leave you dissatisfied with a short and perhaps abrupt and incomplete "conclusion." Let this collection be for you inconclusive fragments to ignite your imagination and arouse you to another start, another beginning, the next cycle of this conversation, because there is still too much work to do to unmask white preaching.

Index

AAPI. *See* Asian American and Pacific Islanders
abolition, 14, 25, 62, 130, 171–72, 176–82
Academy of Homiletics, 1–5, 213
accountability, 71, 90, 99, 105, 111, 148–50, 185–86, 189, 198
accountable. *See* accountability
African American, 26, 32, 34–35, 70, 86, 92, 102, 116, 131, 141, 145–47, 160–61, 168, 173–74, 206, 228
Afro-Caribbean, 86
agency, 13, 105, 127, 147–49, 157–58, 163, 186, 200, 202
Ahmed, Sara, 172, 178
Amer-european. *See* European American
Amerikkka, 45–46
ANA. *See* Asian American and Pacific Islanders
Andrews, Dale, 131, 142, 145
anti-black, 47, 111
anti-racist, 3–4, 12–13, 70, 93, 141, 143, 145–48, 150, 180, 185–87
AOH. *See* Academy of Homiletics
appropriation, 115, 147, 185–86, 191
architecture, 46–50, 133
Asian American. *See* Asian Americans and Pacific Islanders

Asian Americans and Pacific Islanders, 55–65, 69, 131, 133

bible reading, 89
biblical interpretation, 38, 40, 59, 62, 73, 128, 130–31
biblical translation, 56, 64, 130, 132, 160
black: lives, 77, 111–12, 118, 174; preaching, 142, 147, 162, 171–76, 225–28; women, 40, 149, 156, 158, 162, 174, 221–30
blackness, 157
Brown, Teresa Fry, 51, 145, 174, 224
Brown v. Board of Education, 31–32
burlesque, 205–7, 210, 212–15

The Canadian Truth and Reconciliation Commission, 99
Caribbean, 20–24, 26, 206
Chinese preaching, 59–60, 62–63
civility, 85–94, 128
Civil Rights Movement, 32–35, 40, 86, 102, 143, 146–47
class, 29, 37, 87, 113, 127, 129, 143, 147, 158, 161, 174, 176, 179–81
clergy, 10, 33, 69–81, 145, 185–88, 222–23
collective memory, 114

233

collusion, 20, 76
colonial, 1–8, 10–11, 13, 45–46, 50, 52, 54, 57, 64, 82–83, 97–99, 101–4, 115, 117, 128–29, 131, 133, 135–36, 142, 160–61, 174, 189, 191, 194, 196, 231
colonialism. *See* colonial
colonized, 129, 161, 206
colonizer, 161, 197, 206
colorblind, 188
conflict, 88–90, 143, 148, 161
Confucian, 59, 63
conservative, 1, 29–33, 35, 38–39, 65, 82, 86, 88–91
cultural memory, 117, 206

decenter, 1–8, 14, 98, 102, 105–6, 132, 145–47, 171, 206, 222–26, 229
decolonial, 2, 6–8, 10, 98, 104, 106–8, 142, 147, 149–50, 185–86, 189, 192–93, 195–96, 205
decolonize. *See* decolonial
deconstruct, 14, 70–71, 74, 80, 103, 171, 193, 221–22, 225, 229
demon, 80, 212
destabilize, 5, 64, 171
dialogue, 8, 73, 85–90, 93, 102–3
dismantling, 4–5, 11, 13, 50–51, 80, 104, 127, 159, 211
domination, 2, 29, 36, 47–48, 50, 114, 171–76, 212
Duke Chapel, 45–54

elocution, 159
embodiment, 63, 142, 146, 157, 160, 162–63, 193, 212–13, 226
empire. *See* imperialism
epistemological ignorance, 13, 111, 113–15, 117–18
European, 1, 4–6, 20–21, 61–63, 98, 101, 130, 132, 155, 174, 180, 192, 206, 210, 214
European American, 185, 189–92, 195–97, 206
evangelical, 1, 11, 26, 30, 32, 38, 58–65, 74, 86, 93, 213

exegesis, 13, 129–31
exorcism, 206–8, 210–12, 214–18

Falwell, Jerry Sr., 30–40
feminine, 157, 163, 165
flesh, 133, 157, 163–64, 205–6
Floyd, George, 71, 85, 92–93, 100, 111
foreign missions, 19–28, 55–56

gender, 46, 50, 60, 65, 70, 72, 74–75, 113, 127–28, 131, 133, 142, 147, 156–58, 161, 174, 176, 180, 187, 223, 224
geography, 6, 61, 101, 106, 143–44, 188, 192, 194
Gilbert, Kenyatta, 6–7, 145–46
God. *See* theology
gospel, 19–21, 25–27, 47, 50–51, 55, 58, 106, 128, 207, 211, 213
Green vs. Connally, 32, 38

han, 46
hierarchy, 20–21, 221, 229; patriarchal, 40; in preaching, 21, 29–30, 223–24, 226–27; racial, 11, 24–25, 29, 33, 39, 100, 174, 177
Hispanic, 8, 36
Holy Spirit, 19, 51, 63, 90, 157, 163
homiletics: field of, 1–14, 29–30, 55–65, 112, 131–32, 142–43, 171, 174–75, 179, 181, 210, 213–17, 226, 231; theological education, 6, 30, 46, 61–62, 70, 78, 81, 143–45, 148, 175
homogeneity, 5, 87, 101, 186, 226, 228

icon, 225, 227–28
iconography, 222, 229
imperialism, 4, 20–22, 24–25, 45, 129–30, 205–6
inclusive, 26, 30, 50, 98, 223, 229
indigenous, 25, 46, 64, 69, 97–99, 102–8, 114, 135, 185–88, 190–92, 194–96, 210, 214
individualism, 36, 50, 158
integration, 31–32, 38, 51, 148
internalization, 58, 207

Index

intersectionality, 147, 149, 156, 163, 174, 181, 187, 225–26

Jennings, Willie, 50, 99, 145
justice, 40, 48, 51, 73, 87–88, 135, 143, 145–48, 179–80, 211; racial, 3, 105, 111–12, 116, 175; social, 63, 91, 144, 195

King, Jr., Martin Luther, 32–33, 89, 145, 147
Korean culture, 133–34
Korean diaspora, 45–46, 56–63
Korean preaching, 56–63

liberal, 86, 88–91, 115–16, 176–77
liberalism, 116
liberation, 59, 63, 81, 175, 198, 206, 211–13, 216
liturgy. *See* worship

maiden, 156, 158, 163
mainline Protestant, 1, 8, 12, 13, 57, 58, 69–75, 85–87, 92–93, 132
majority, 56, 61, 74, 78, 85–86, 88, 92, 118, 141, 177–78
marginalization, 5, 40, 63, 105, 131, 146, 214, 226
militarism, 35, 39–40, 45, 111, 128
minoritized, 1–2, 4–5, 10, 14, 51, 81, 134, 171–73, 175, 179
minority, 32, 34, 59, 177
monument, 11–12, 45–51
Moral Majority, 29–40
mother, 22, 31, 42, 45, 56, 64, 118, 135, 158, 160, 190, 224

narrative, 7, 37, 58, 103, 112–15, 117–19, 185–87, 189, 191–96, 212, 221–22, 227, 229
neo-abolitionist. *See* abolition
normative, 1, 5, 29, 60, 141–42, 191, 212, 214–16, 221–23, 225–27

orality, 227–28
oratory, 207, 212, 214–16

patriarchy, 19, 40, 50, 130, 135, 147, 155–57, 159, 162, 166, 181, 224, 226, 229
pedagogy, 2, 5, 141–50
performativity, 49, 147, 172, 178
polarization, 85–86, 92
postcolonial, 2–4, 6–7, 10, 13, 129, 135, 161
postliberal, 112
power, 2, 13, 15, 29–30, 32, 35, 40, 48–49, 51, 57, 61, 69, 88, 90–93, 100, 103–4, 113, 127–29, 131–34, 141, 144, 147–48, 156–57, 159–60, 163, 173–75, 179, 186, 189, 191, 210–12, 216, 221–29
Powery, Luke, 48, 51
practical theology, 10, 85, 131–32
practice, 1–3, 5–7, 9–10, 23–24, 30, 34, 47, 55, 57, 59, 87, 89, 93, 97, 136, 140, 142–43, 145, 149–50, 157–63, 172–73, 180, 185–86, 206–8, 210–11, 213–16, 221–29
proclamation, 19, 21, 26, 49–51, 55, 87, 104, 145–46, 148, 206, 212–13, 215, 222, 224–25, 227–28
prophetic, 14–15, 51, 69, 73–74, 76, 86, 88, 103, 146, 163, 207, 210–13, 215–16, 224
Puerto Rico, 8, 57, 206, 208, 210, 212–13
pulpit, 5, 13–15, 33, 49–50, 69, 72, 79, 87, 93, 118, 128, 133, 135, 148, 159–60, 180, 185, 196, 206–7, 213–16, 221–29
Purple Church, 78, 85–88, 90, 92–93

race riot, 48, 51, 116, 118
racial: formation, 6, 14, 59, 104, 113, 142, 145, 148, 172, 187, 191, 194, 196; identity, 6, 8, 14, 22, 24, 55–56, 58–60, 64, 76, 86, 92, 98, 100, 113, 117, 127, 142–44, 148, 158, 162–63, 185–96, 222, 225–27
racism. *See* systems
reconciliation, 97–99, 101–6, 145

rhetoric, 26, 90, 92, 128, 141, 143, 156–63
ritual, 5, 162, 210, 213

segregation, 31–33, 38
settler, 1–2, 5–6, 8, 11–12, 97–106
settler colonial. *See* settler
settler fragility. *See* white, fragility
sexuality, 35–36, 142, 147, 157–58, 174, 180, 213–14, 222
slavery, 20–21, 23, 25, 34, 57, 62, 115, 143, 174
solidarity, 9–10, 93–94, 100, 105–6, 178–79; homiletical space, 1, 4, 11, 15, 46–50, 55, 61, 105, 132–34, 161–63, 207, 214, 222–29; pedagogical space, 148–49
speech, 33, 104, 133, 145, 148, 157–58, 160–61, 178, 189, 206, 210, 213–15, 223
Spirit. *See* Holy Spirit
state-sanctioned violence, 1–2, 46
statue. *See* monument
storytelling, 105, 114–15, 185, 187, 189
subversion, 14, 21, 160, 179, 226
symbol, 51, 63, 86, 113–14, 119, 133–34, 207–8, 210, 212–13, 215, 223, 232
systemic racism, 37, 69, 88, 90, 92, 142
systems, 1, 4, 6–9, 25, 57, 69, 88, 99, 101, 104, 149, 172, 175–76, 179, 186–87, 196, 214, 229

Taíno, 161, 206, 209–10, 213
Taylor, Breonna, 71, 93, 111
terrorism, 46, 149
theology of race, 13, 19, 30, 49
Thomas, Frank, 51, 145
tolerance, 93, 98, 102, 105
tradition, 2, 30, 34, 38, 46, 147, 156–58, 160, 162–63, 171, 173–74, 186–87, 189, 206–7, 210–14, 216, 223–25, 227

trauma, 4, 12, 55, 58, 63–64, 156, 161
treason, 171, 176–80

unmasking whiteness, 1, 3–5, 8, 29, 34, 39, 45–46, 58, 70, 127, 131–32, 134, 136, 143–46, 148, 150, 171–76, 180, 192, 196, 205–6, 231

West, Cornel, 173, 191
Western, 3–4, 14, 21, 25, 46, 60, 62, 99, 130, 133–34, 156, 163, 189, 196, 210, 214, 231
white: flight, 143–44; fragility, 12, 14, 71, 76, 97–106, 187, 191; institutions, 11, 13, 21, 29–30, 33, 39–40, 46, 51, 55, 63, 143–44, 146, 156, 174, 180, 222–25, 227, 231–32; normativity, 58, 60–63, 131, 134, 141, 145, 149, 191, 212, 214–16, 221–23, 225–27; preaching, 1–10, 20–21, 23–26, 29–30, 33, 40, 46, 49–51, 55–56, 58, 60, 62, 64, 69, 71, 73–75, 77–79, 98, 102–3, 105, 112–14, 127–28, 134, 142, 146–49, 171–76, 180–81, 206–7, 210, 212, 214–16, 226, 231–32 ; privilege, 12, 21, 29, 38–39, 41, 48, 69, 75–76, 79, 81, 99, 101–2, 114, 132, 135–36, 141, 145, 148, 155–59, 162, 172, 175–77, 179–80, 187, 189–90, 195, 214, 225; supremacy, 4, 9, 19–26, 45–51, 63, 69–70, 74, 76–77, 80–81, 85, 87–88, 91–94, 97–102, 105, 115, 117, 131, 143, 155, 175–78, 180, 185, 187, 189–94, 196, 206–8, 210–12, 215–16, 221, 226, 229
witness, 21, 51, 85–86, 93–94, 108, 147, 180, 215, 222
womanist, 144, 145, 174, 226
worldview. *See* narrative
worship, 21, 24–25, 59, 62, 70, 78–79, 85, 87, 94, 132–33, 141, 161, 175, 206, 207, 213–16, 223, 226

About the Contributors

Christopher M. Baker teaches on Critical Approaches to Race and Theology at Saint Paul School of Theology. In his research and writing, he draws from Critical Race Theory, Philosophy of Race, and Critical Whiteness Studies, as well as film theory and comic book studies, to construct a counternarrative theology that critically engages "race" and "whiteness" as theological and sociopolitical constructs. In addition to his academic work, he has two decades of preaching experience.

Gennifer Benjamin Brooks holds the Styberg chair in Preaching and is the tenured Ernest and Bernice Styberg Professor of Preaching, director of the Styberg Preaching Institute and the Doctor of Ministry Program at Garrett-Evangelical Theological Seminary, and dean of the Association of Chicago Theological Schools Doctor of Ministry in Preaching program. She is an ordained elder and full clergy member of the New York Conference of the United Methodist Church and pastored local churches in rural, suburban, urban, and cross racial settings. She was assistant dean of New Brunswick Theological Seminary for four years. Brooks holds a Bachelor of Business, cum laude, and a Master of Business Administration from Pace University, a Master of Divinity, summa cum laude, and a Doctor of Ministry from New Brunswick Theological Seminary, and a Master of Philosophy and Doctor of Philosophy in Liturgical Studies from Drew University. She is the author of several books and articles, including *Good News Preaching*, *Unexpected Grace* and contributed to several preaching commentaries including *Working Preacher*, *Feasting on the Gospels*, and *Connections*.

Suzanne Wenonah Duchesne is visiting assistant professor of Worship and Preaching at New Brunswick Theological Seminary with a Doctor of

Philosophy in Liturgical Studies from Drew University. She is an ordained elder in the Eastern Pennsylvania Conference and Communications chairperson for the Northeastern Jurisdiction of the Native American Ministries Committee for the United Methodist Church. Her scholarship has been guided by her relationships with members of the Kiowa, Cherokee, MVSKOKE (Creek), Choctaw, Chickasaw, Abenaki, Penobscot, Shinnecock, Southern Ute, Lenni Lenape, and Yuchi Nations. In addition to her scholarship in antiracist and decolonized preaching and worship, she has published articles, curriculum, and resources concerning Missing and Murdered Indigenous/Native Women and Girls, the Doctrine of Discovery, John Wesley's experiences with various nations during his work in Georgia, and the legacy of Methodist involvement with Native American Boarding schools.

HyeRan Kim-Cragg holds the inaugural Timothy Eaton Memorial Church Professorship in preaching at Emmanuel College of Victoria University in the University of Toronto. She is the first racialized faculty member who became full professor at Emmanuel where she serves as graduate degree director. Kim-Cragg is the author of many books including *Postcolonial Preaching: Creating a Ripple Effect* (2021) and *Interdependence: A Postcolonial Feminist Practical Theology* (2018). Her work appears in *Homiletic*, the *International Journal of Homiletics*, *Liturgy*, and *Religious Education*.

Peace Pyunghwa Lee is a spiritual director, preacher, and an educator committed to decolonial and feminist praxis. Formative experiences of growing up in Korea and the Philippines and later immigrating to the United States as a preteen have imbued Peace with a humanizing and inclusive perspective. At the core of her faith is the affirmation of the sacred worth of all persons, as *imago Dei*.

Gerald C. Liu is director of Collegiate Ministries, Initiatives, and Belonging for the Global Board of Higher Education and Ministry of the United Methodist Church. He is also project manager for an online sermon studio pilot from the Perkins Center for Preaching Excellence at Southern Methodist University. At the time of writing, he was assistant professor of Worship and Preaching at Princeton Theological School. An ordained United Methodist Elder of the Mississippi Annual Conference, he carries the honorific of a Minister in Residence at the Church of the Village, a United Methodist Congregation in Manhattan. He is the son of culturally Buddhist immigrants from Taiwan and is the author of *Music and the Generosity of God* (2017) and *A Worship Workbook: A Practical Guide for Extraordinary Liturgy* (2021).

Debra J. Mumford serves as dean of the Seminary and Frank H. Caldwell Professor of Homiletics at Louisville Presbyterian Theological Seminary. She is ordained in the American Baptist Churches USA. She holds a Bachelor of Science in Mechanical Engineering from Howard University, a Master of Divinity from the American Baptist Seminary of the West (now Berkeley School of Theology), a Master of Arts in Biblical Languages and Doctor of Philosophy in Homiletics with an allied field in New Testament from the Graduate Theological Union. She is the author of *Exploring Prosperity Preaching* and *Envisioning the Reign of God*. She has authored many lectionary and commentary articles for *Working Preacher*, *Feasting on the Word*, and *Lectionary Homiletics*.

Jerusha Matsen Neal is assistant professor of Homiletics at Duke Divinity School. Before coming to Duke, she taught for three years at Davuilevu Theological College in the Fiji Islands. Her recent book, *The Overshadowed Preacher: Mary, The Spirit, and the Labor of Proclamation* (2020), describes a theology of the Spirit that confronts preaching's "unholy ghosts."

Andrew Thompson Scales serves as the chaplain and executive co-director of the PC(USA) campus ministry Princeton Presbyterians. Andrew completed a PhD in Homiletics at Princeton Theological Seminary in Spring 2019, and his dissertation focused on the homilies of Archbishop Óscar Romero. He has taught preaching courses at New Brunswick, Lancaster, and Princeton Theological Seminaries.

Rev. Dr. Leah D. Schade is associate professor of Preaching and Worship at Lexington Theological Seminary in Kentucky. An ordained Lutheran minister for twenty years, Leah earned both her MDiv and PhD degrees from the Lutheran Theological Seminary at Philadelphia (now United Lutheran Seminary). She has pastored three Pennsylvania congregations in suburban, urban, and rural contexts and is the author of five books, including *Preaching in the Purple Zone: Ministry in the Red-Blue Divide* (2019). Leah is currently conducting a longitudinal research study about ministry, preaching, and social issues that has surveyed nearly 3,000 clergy and 1,000 laity since 2017.

David Stark is assistant professor of Homiletics at the University of the South, School of Theology. He is an ordained elder in the United Methodist Church, holds a ThD from Duke University, and serves as the English language editor for the *International Journal of Homiletics*.

Sarah Travis teaches worship and preaching at Knox College, Toronto School of Theology, University of Toronto. She is an ordained minister of the Presbyterian Church in Canada, and she is author of *Decolonizing Preaching: The Pulpit as Postcolonial Space*, *Metamorphosis: Preaching after Christendom*, and *Unspeakable: Preaching and Trauma-Informed Theology*.

Rev. Lis Valle-Ruiz is assistant professor of Homiletics and Worship and director of Community Worship Life at McCormick Theological Seminary, Chicago, IL. She earned her PhD in Homiletics and Liturgics from Vanderbilt University, Nashville, TN, where she also studied gender and sexuality. Her research interests lie at the intersection of preaching, worship, and performance studies. Her current research project is on digital mediations of worship and preaching practices. Rev. Valle received a ThM in Homiletics from Princeton Theological Seminary and an MDiv from Louisville Presbyterian Theological Seminary. She also holds a JD and a BA in Education from the University of Puerto Rico. Theater is her lifelong passion.

Richard W. Voelz is associate professor of Preaching and Worship at Union Presbyterian Seminary in Richmond, VA, and an ordained minister in the Christian Church (Disciples of Christ). He has authored three books, including *Preaching to Teach: Inspire People to Think and Act* (2019), *Tending the Tree of Life: Preaching and Worship through Reproductive Loss and Adoption* (2018), and *Youthful Preaching: Strengthening the Relationship between Youth, Adults, and Preaching* (2016). He also serves as associate editor for the "Between Text and Sermon" section of *Interpretation: A Journal of Bible and Theology*.

Andrew Wymer is assistant professor of Liturgical Studies at Garrett-Evangelical Theological Seminary in Evanston, Illinois. He is ordained in the ABCUSA, and he previously taught at New Brunswick Theological Seminary. His research engages liturgical and homiletical theory and practice with attention to race, power, and justice.

Chelsea Brooke Yarborough is assistant professor of Liturgical Studies and Styberg Teaching fellow at Garrett-Evangelical Theological Seminary. She received her PhD from Vanderbilt University in Homiletics and Liturgics. Her research reimagines the nature and purpose of preaching and worship through the rhetoric and ritual practices of both contemporary and historical black women. Chelsea is also an ordained minister, a poet, and an enneagram teacher, aiming to create spaces for healing and wholeness for all whom she engages.